Making It:
The Business of Film and
Television Production in Canada

Making It:
The Business of Film and Television Production in Canada

Barbara Hehner, Editor

A Co-publication of the
Academy of Canadian Cinema & Television
and Doubleday Canada Limited.

Canadian Cataloguing in Publication Data

Main entry under title:

Making it: the business of film and
television production in Canada

Co-published by the Academy of Canadian Cinema & Television.
Bibliography: p.
Includes index.
ISBN 0-385-25118-1

1. Moving-picture industry – Canada.
2. Moving-picture industry – Canada – Finance.
3. Television industry - Canada.
4. Television industry - Canada – Finance.
I. Hehner, Barbara
II. Academy of Canadian Cinema & Television.

PN1993.5.C3M35 1987
384'.83'0971
C87-093050-8

Cover design: Nancy Jackson

Text design: Debbie Williams

Index: Riça Night

Cartoon illustrations: Mark Melanson

Typesetting: Mary Scally & The Coach House Press

Printed and bound in Canada

Preface

Experienced film and television producers in Canada are a rare commodity. Even rarer are those who are willing to reveal the secrets of their success. Rarer still is written material that is relevant to film and television production in Canada. How often do Canadian writers, directors, and talent yearn for a "good producer"? *Making It* is an effort to provide a "how-to" manual for producers without a long list of credits to their name. It is a step-by-step guide through the complex business of taking a great idea to the screen.

The authors included in this book are among the leading Canadian experts in their fields. They were specifically commissioned to write the original material for *Making It*. Their viewpoints are their own, and their successful track records are their credentials.

Two years ago, inspired by Academy member Gerry Flahive, the Academy of Canadian Cinema & Television developed a proposal to provide training information to potential producers. The Department of Employment and Immigration's Industrial Adjustment Service recognized the need to develop qualified and knowledgeable producers in this country, and provided the funding to do so. A Committee was established under the much-debated acronym FATTAC, which stood for Film and Television Training and Advancement Committee – quite a responsibility! Under the Chairmanship of Canadian composer and policy-maker Louis Applebaum, whose wise guidance and overviews were invaluable, the Committee included representatives of the production community: Ron Cohen, Martin Harbury – both of them were called on as authors, readers, planners, and strategists, too – and Michael MacMillan; as well as the Academy's representatives: Penny Hynam, whose experience and managerial abilities were invaluable resources, Maria Topalovich, the Academy's Director of Communications, her assistant Shannon Macgillivray, and myself.

The challenges of this project were considerable, the paper work astounding! Representing the Department of Employment and Immigration, Aline Revoy showed extraordinary patience and flexibility in dealing with the all-too-confusing world of showbiz. Her belief in the project made it possible. Her humour and experience were very much appreciated. And where would we have been without the highly skilled services of our editor, Barbara Hehner, who quickly learned that brilliant filmmakers are not necessarily conscientious writers. What was to be a 6-month writing period became 18 months of entreating authors, changing schedules, writing, and preparing endless editorial notes, questions and revisions. She has had to sacrifice her own writing and family life to make the authors of *Making It* look impressive. The expert and generous legal advice of Douglas Barrett was invaluable to us. To our co-publishers, Doubleday Canada Limited, and especially Denise Schon, our thanks for ensuring that this book will reach its target market. To our designer Debbie Williams our thanks for the great look of the book. Mary Scally spent endless hours inputting the manuscript onto computer disks and through the magic of Coach House Press's typesetting equipment, the text was interpreted and reproduced direct to film pages for printing.

And of course, we thank our authors – some fast and efficient, others slow and wise. But they have all provided us with a rich text of invaluable material. Many, many thanks to you all for your commitment and care.

Andra Sheffer
Executive Director
Academy of Canadian Cinema & Television

Table of Contents

A Note from the Editor

When Andra Sheffer first talked to me about this book in the spring of 1985, I had no idea how much the film business would come to dominate my life. Shortly after I began editorial work on *Making It*, after 15 years in book publishing, I returned to school in the Graduate Film and Video Programme at York University. So, as the manuscript progressed, I was both teacher and student. I offered whatever guidance I could to those who had fearlessly faced disgruntled crew members, demanding stars, nervous investors, and an unpredictable public, but now, in their new role as authors, understandably found a blank sheet of paper intimidating. The authors, in turn, generously shared with me their hard-won expertise in the exhilarating, exhausting, and – yes, sometimes – glamorous world of film and television production.

I echo Andra Sheffer's heartfelt thanks to the Academy staff and dedicated FATTAC committee, who were essential to the production of this book. Special thanks to committee Chairman Lou Applebaum for his unflappable, unfailing support. Andra Sheffer herself is one of the hardest-working people I have ever seen in action – without her energy and determination, this book would not have come to be. In addition, I would like to thank Viveca Gretton for research, Patricia Johnson and Chapelle Jaffe for advice and enlightenment, and all the authors' assistants, receptionists, and secretaries, who courteously took my messages and tactfully prodded their very busy, jet-hopping bosses – I needed and appreciated their efforts.

Barbara Hehner

CHAPTER ONE

So You Want to Be a Producer

by Ronald I. Cohen

*R*ONALD I. COHEN, current Chairman of the Academy, is the producer of the miniseries Race for the
Bomb for CBC, Radio-Canada and TF1, and partner in
the Montreal law firm of Campeau & Cohen. He was the
first Chairman of the Academy and has been actively
involved in the Academy's activities for the past eight
years, including the recent extension of the Academy to
television and the establishment of the Gemini Awards.
His seven feature films, including Ticket to Heaven,
have been nominated for many Genie Awards. He has
also served as the Chairman of the Federal Task Force
on Distribution, Marketing, and Exhibition of Films in
Canada.

Introduction: What Is a Producer, Anyway?

A very famous actor was driving tranquilly through the
American Southwest. A young man, somewhat less
mobile, stood thumb-extended at the side of the highway. The star noticed the young man and stopped to
pick him up. Nodding the hitchhiker's customary
thanks as he slipped into the passenger seat, the
young lad suddenly took note of the driver's
renowned face and gasped stutteringly, "Do-do you
know who-who you are?"

Producers don't have that problem. Like the other
film creators who work "behind the camera," they tend
to be faceless to the public. Their power may be
immense. But even if their names are known, their

visages, like those of corporate presidents, tend to be unfamiliar. More than that, though, what they *do* also is unknown. How often does this dialogue occur between a producer and a new acquaintance at a cocktail party away from the film circuit: "And what do you do for a living? ... You're a film producer? Now that must be exciting! Is that like a director?" It's a fact that almost every other job on a film production is more clearly defined than the producer's. Consider the following examples.

The director is responsible for all creative aspects of the production – in other words, how the tale is told cinematically. This includes, among other things, deciding which actors are best suited to which roles, how they will perform them, how they will be dressed, how their performances will be shot, and so on.

Under the overall guidance of the director, the production designer is responsible for the physical appearance of the production: the locations, sets, dressing, props, and the like. The director of photography (also known as the DOP, cinematographer, DP or lighting cameraman, depending on your origins) is responsible for translating the physical appearance of the production onto film, by choosing lenses, camera movement, and the lighting to be used. The DOP's instructions are executed by the camera operator and his or her crew (as to lenses), the gaffer and his or her crew (as to lights), and the key grip and his or her crew (as to camera movement). The best boy is the first electrician. The stillsman (or set photographer) takes pictures of what is happening. Craft services personnel feed the crew, actors, and invited guests. We could go on and on. Any major production involves the skills of dozens of people. And their job descriptions are both precise and constant.

But what of the producer? What does he or she do? And why would anybody want to be one?

Aren't producers responsible for "getting the money"? Well, yes ... sometimes. Aren't they on the set every day, making sure that everything happens as it was planned, that no one spends too much money, that overtime is under control, and so on? Well, sure ... but it depends. Aren't they the ones who, off the set, ensure that the actors are happy, that seriously disruptive quarrels are kept to a minimum, that the set "hums"? Of course ... in some cases. Oh, sure, they make the deals with the distributors and report to the investors about progress on the revenue front. True ... but not all the time.

And why are there so many *kinds* of producers? There are executive producers, line producers, associate producers, co-producers – as well as just plain producers. Are their jobs any better defined?

In fact, their *jobs* are only marginally better defined. The point really is that there are many producer functions, some of which have been whimsically described above. These and other tasks not yet mentioned are all undertaken by *someone* on the picture. Perhaps it is most illuminating to think of producing in these terms: as a series of functions that will be performed by one or more individuals receiving one, some, or all of the producer credits mentioned in the previous paragraph.

Let us now begin at the beginning of the process, by looking at the tasks that, by and large, fall into the hands of the producers. We will then stop and look at which *kind* of producer usually (but of course not *always* – who said this would be simple?) undertakes which responsibilities.

Before diving into this subject, there is a useful concept for you to bear in mind in understanding the producer's role and the difficulty of defining it. The producer is not unlike the president of a company (who is usually also its Chief Executive Officer). The role of a corporate president is not necessarily easily defined either. The individual with that title is *the boss*, and the role is more or less what the president / boss wants to make of it. It is, for example, possible that the president will be both the Chief Executive Officer *and* the Chief Operating Officer. However, the bigger the corporation, the more unlikely it will be that the president can assume both roles. Similarly, the bigger the film or television production, the less likely it is that a single producer will carry out all the functions.

A related analogy can be drawn about the other roles on a film in relation to that of the producer. The most important creative individuals can be thought of as vice-presidents. For example, the director might be seen as the Senior Vice-President, Creative Affairs. The line producer, where there is one (more about this later), or the production manager might be labelled the Vice-President, Finance. The production designer would be the Vice-President, Artistic Affairs, and the director of photography would be the Vice-President, Photographic Affairs. (The analogy to common corporate titles is, as you can see, stretched, but the basic point is fair.) As you slide down the production hierarchy (and, by analogy, the corporate ladder), you find middle management and non-managerial roles.

One thing to understand right at the outset is that the person exercising the authority at the earliest stages of the process is invariably described (or describes himself or herself) as *the* producer. Whatever the person may later be called on the finished picture (as the result of the manipulation of credits which is part of the horse-trading that goes with "putting the deal together"), at this stage he or she is simply called the producer.

The Story

The producing function really begins with the choosing of the story to be filmed. This will be dealt with in much greater detail in Chapter 2, but, for these introductory purposes, we must be clear that it is the first and pivotal producing decision. This does not mean that the producer thinks up the story in the first place; it does mean that he or she decides to *film* the story.

The story can come from anywhere. Many are the inspired creation of the screenwriter alone. That is the meaning of the "original screenplay" category in the Genie Awards. Where the source for the screenplay is a book (such as *Surfacing, Le Matou,* or *The Apprenticeship of Duddy Kravitz*), a song (such as *Middle Age Crazy*) or a series of newspaper articles (such as those in the *Montreal Star* which served as the basis for *Ticket to Heaven*), to choose a few examples, the screenplay is said to be "adapted from another medium."

Whatever the nature of the screenplay, the idea for it may arrive on the producer's desk in a myriad of ways. A screenwriter or director may approach the producer with a idea, a treatment, or even a completed script. A magazine or newspaper story may suggest a screenplay. So may a current "hot" best-selling book (such as *Gorky Park*), an old classic (such as *Anne of Green Gables*) or a stage-play (such as *Tribute, Same Time Next Year, Annie,* or *A Chorus Line*). The producer may, in any of these cases, or simply based upon his or her own idea, commission a screenplay. In the end, the point is the same – the *producer* must choose the tale to be filmed.

An incidental and (to some) obvious part of the same responsibility is that the producer must arrange for financing the acquisition of the rights to the story upon which the screenplay is to be based, as well as for funding to support the screenwriting and other development expenses.

The writing and / or rewriting of the script must be supervised, inspired, encouraged, and periodically criticized. This will usually be the next of the producer's functions, unless the producer has already, at this early stage, engaged a director. Although the responsibility will still be the producer's, from the point at which a director is engaged, the producer begins to delegate some of the *creative* responsibilities.

The Money

Filmmaking is very much a chicken-and-egg situation. One of those chickens (or is it eggs?) relates to budgeting and financing. At the stage when one believes that a worthwhile picture idea is in hand (usually at script stage, but it can be earlier), the quest for production funding begins. There are, however, no absolute rules. Robert Evans' unorthodox first step in seeking the financing that ultimately brought *The Cotton Club* to the screen was to create the artwork for the film's poster.

It is obviously useful (although not entirely necessary) to know how much funding one requires. That entails *budgeting before seeking dollars.* One does not, however, always want to spend the time and money to produce a budget "on spec". Nor, for various reasons, is one always in a position to wait. That may mean *seeking dollars before budgeting.* Whichever process comes first, both are in the hands of the producer.

While coming chapters will deal in detail with these matters, a few introductory words are appropriate. (Chapter 2 deals with this subject obliquely; Chapter 5 covers preproduction in much greater detail; Chapter 3 covers the specific question of budgeting, and Chapter 4 deals with financing.)

The Budget

Budgeting is a detailed and painstaking process. Nor does it happen only once on a picture. It has been said that *Joshua Then and Now* went through about 15 script drafts and revisions. If that sounds like a lot, you might ask the producer how many *budgets* were done. It's not that I'm privy to inside information in that particular case, it is just that this is the general rule in the budgeting process. Why is budgeting so complicated and why does it take so long, you might well ask.

To the extent that budgets are done before the script is finalized, they are speculative. Since they take into account *every* detail in the screenplay – every actor, prop, extra, special effect, vehicle, costume, and so on – any change in the script that affects any one of those items necessitates a corresponding change in the budget.

Breakdown and Boards

In order to appreciate how meticulous the budgeting process is, you have to examine it step by step. First, the first assistant director (first AD) "breaks the script down" by preparing a detailed analysis of every prop, extra, effect, etc. on his or her breakdown sheet. In talking to the director, the AD also determines whether the shooting will require extra cameras, lenses, or lights beyond the ordinary package, and whether extra equipment such as cranes, camera trucks, or helicopters will be necessary to shoot the scene as the director envisages it. Everything costs.

The first AD also "boards" every scene by writing the number assigned to every actor on a strip of cardboard-like material (the strips used are too thin for whole names) and arranging these strips in an efficient shooting pattern on a large, ever-expanding board, which makes it possible to determine how long each actor will be needed. (The strips are generally arranged according to actor availability, location availability, or day vs. night shooting.) We are once again in the presence of chickens and eggs. We need to know how long each actor will be needed in order to budget (you can generally assume that eight weeks of Margot Kidder will cost more than two), and yet the board can be re-jigged in order to ensure that the expensive actors are not there for undue amounts of time. No producer wants to pay for the long-term sightseeing, tennis, or backgammon recreations of an expensive performer, if it can be avoided.

All of this information organized by the first AD enables the producer or (more likely) his or her production manager to determine the cost of making the epic. That's when the cries of "It's not possible!!" and "Well, he can't have the bleep-bleep helicopter for five days!!" go resounding through the halls. And budgets, like scripts, are then cut, trimmed, and varied. *P.S.* The cost is always too high the first time round. This is one of the reasons why there is always more than one budget draft.

The Financing

To the uninitiated, this seems like the *sine qua non* of the producer's function. While this introductory chapter and the book as a whole will attempt to flesh out your understanding of the role of the producer, it is hard to deny that this is the essence of it. It is a certainty that, if the producer doesn't take care of the financing, no one else will.

Question: Where, then, does the financing come from? And when? Answer: Anywhere. Always too late. (At least, it *feels* that way.) The sources are generally limited. They include private or individual sources (doctors, lawyers, business executives, brokers, etc.); public sources (Telefilm, the various provincial funding agencies, etc.); private and public sources outside Canada (usually accessed in the case of co-productions with one of Canada's film-partner countries); and distributors and end-users (conventional broadcasters, pay-cable systems, home video companies, etc.).

There is an old adage which asserts that everyone has two businesses: his or her own and show business. There is no doubt that there are few more flamboyant and public art-on-your-sleeve businesses. Few principals in any industry strive as much for recognition and favour. And none succeed more. After all, it is the goal of the business to entertain and divert, both in good times and bad. And the people always go, watch, or listen. Those who don't, read about it in their newspapers and magazines or see it, for free, on television.

So people tend to feel that they know something about the film business. It seems to them that they are closer to it than to a hole in the ground in an unpopu-

lated section of natural resourceville, or to a manufacturer of widgets. Thus, in some cases, they feel more confident about their film investments than about others that seem farther from their ken and more mysterious. Taxation incentives have flushed money out of the woods, but there have always been, and will always be, individual "angels" who will be prepared to invest in entertainment products even without especially favourable tax laws.

In the absence of an individual or a small number of individuals willing to put up a large amount of money, the route to film funding is via private placement or public offering. (These are discussed more fully in Chapter 4 and in Chapter 9, where Douglas Barrett comments on the legal aspects of financing arrangements.)

Public Sources of Funding

The public sources of money are, in a sense, more straightforward. Telefilm, the Ontario Film Development Corporation (OFDC), the Alberta Motion Picture Development Corporation (AMPDC), and the Société générale du cinéma du Québec have eligibility rules that are readily obtained, although somewhat less easily followed. Some of the agencies are more inclined that others to become involved in creative evaluations, and the producer generally views this tendency as frustrating and unnecessary. On the other hand, the government agencies are generally very encouraging regarding production that is of cultural or economic benefit (or both) to their constituencies. Once they have made funding commitments, their reliability is virtually bankable.

Distributors and End-Users

Then there are the distributors and end-users. It should be pointed out that some of their commitments may be essential to the triggering of some of the public funding mechanisms. A broadcast licence will, for example, be essential before a producer is eligible to receive money from Telefilm Canada's Broadcast Fund. Further, a pay-television commitment can add to the funding which that fund will be prepared to match.

Correspondingly, a Canadian theatrical distributor's commitment will be essential to the producer's entitlement to participate in Telefilm Canada's new Feature Film Fund. Furthermore, in order to attract private money via public offerings, the producer will generally require the manifestation of some commercial interest on the part of an outside distributor or end-user. This has the effect of assuring, if not guaranteeing, a return of some part of the individual's investment.

The varied distribution deals that can be made are dealt with in depth in Chapters 6 and 7; the point to be made here, however, is that the producer will at this stage be seeking *cash*, not promises, in order to make the movie. This of course means that the deal should either provide cash during the production period (easier said than achieved) or should be so certain and *un*-contingent as to be *bankable* during the production period. A deal that is subject to contingencies or uncertainties will not be one on which a financial institution will want to take a chance. That consideration must be factored into the negotiating process from day one.

There now. Once the producer has acquired the story and the financing, all that's left is fun. Correct?

Hiring Talent More chickens. More eggs. Can you finance a picture without hiring your director and actors? Well, yes, but it certainly is easier, as a general rule, if some or all of these are lined up if not actually "in place". The producer will almost never want to firm up deals for talent until the financing is secure; otherwise, there is a risk of being saddled with "pay-or-play" obligations in the event that the financing falls through or the picture is delayed. (A pay-or-play obligation is a contractual commitment to use – and pay for – the services of an individual, or to pay *even* in the event these services are not required.) This is risky business, more common to studio-financed deals, and rarely if ever seen in the independent sector.

Whenever the deals are made with talent and crew, they will be overseen by the producer. Unless the director has "come with the package," he or she will be the choice of the producer, although possibly also subject to approval by the financier(s), government authorities (such as Telefilm), and / or the distributor (if one is in place).

Thereafter, the principal roles will be cast by the producer and director, working in concert with a casting director. The choice of actors depends on many – sometimes conflicting – factors. The distributor will generally want the biggest, most recognizable names. (All the better, Little Red Riding Hood, to sell your picture!) The director will want the best actors, whether known to the public or not. (All the truer to the telling of the tale, my dear.) Telefilm will probably want *Canadians*, period. And the producer, wanting to balance everyone's desires, while assuredly having a few of his or her own, will be looking to the budget's bottom line. (All the better to please the completion guarantor and make the picture with the available dollars.)

The key crew members (the director of photography, production designer, costume designer, set dresser, composer, and editor) will be selected by the producer and director together; the production manager, accountant, and personnel in the "numbers" area will be the responsibility of the producer; and the first AD and his or her department will fall more into the hands of the director.

Other Creative Considerations

Since Chapter 5 deals in great detail with preproduction, production, and postproduction issues, I will merely observe here that the producing functions will, of course, include the choice of locations. (In the largest sense, this means determining the country where the production will be shot in whole or in part and, in the narrowest sense, means choosing the street or building in which the drama will occur.) The producer also decides the seasons during which to shoot, the duration of principal photography, and so on. The list of issues, large and small, often seems endless.

Other Business Issues

There is a correspondingly long list of financial or business issues to attend to. These include: providing an appropriate corporate structure, arranging the standard insurance package and a completion bond, concluding banking arrangements, calculating and providing for the meeting of the cash flow, filing the necessary applications with the immigration authorities (and possibly seeking guild approvals) if Americans or other foreigners will be working in Canada, making corresponding arrangements with Revenue

Canada for the payment of fees and withholding of taxes, where appropriate, with respect to the foreigners' services, dealing with the relevant unions and guilds, and so on. Much of this requires sophisticated legal help and none of it should be underestimated either as to the time it will require or the complexity it will involve.

Production

Let's suppose that the miracle occurs. Everything does indeed come together. The script reaches final acceptable form. The budget is in a form that satisfies the completion guarantor, the public financing agencies, the Securities Commissions, and the other financiers. The director and stars necessary to receive the approval of the distributor and Telefilm have been chosen. The financing comes together. What next?

The movie or TV program gets made. But what becomes of the producer's role at this stage? In fact, do we still have only *one* producer, or has he or she multiplied? Probably there are now several producers, both because of the deal and because of the work, although not necessarily in that order.

The chances are that the financing was not the simple (and heady) result of straighforward studio financing. More likely, the money will have come from several quarters. Some, like Telefilm or the provincial funding agencies, will probably not impose a producer, executive producer, or associate producer on the original producer, at least not to represent their money. However, they have been known to do so in circumstances where they feel that the producer who has taken the project through the initial development stages does not have the experience necessary to properly spend or protect the money or to derive the maximum benefit for the investor once the asset (i.e. the film) has been created.

On the other hand, financing of a co-production will, by the nature of the venture, result in the presence of a *co*-producer representing the second country's involvement in the enterprise. (There may also be a third country's co-producer, although rarely more.)

A major financing participant, or someone who has arranged a presale or distribution arrangement that has been used to help secure the financing necessary to make the picture happen, will often insist on a shared producer or executive producer credit.

Even where there is no outside imposition of a producer or executive producer, the original producer will likely reach the point where he or she feels the need to share the burden. As Martin Harbury and Bob Wertheimer attest in Chapter 5, there are *many* preproduction and production matters to attend to, and a producer may well engage a line producer who will occupy the functional producing post above the production manager. The line producer will rarely receive that credit on the finished film or program. Instead, it will either be producer, co-producer, or associate producer, depending on the power and sensitivity of the primary producer.

There is not always a separate line producer on a production. The producer may exercise the line producing function alone or may share it with an extremely capable production manager. However, one way or the other, the function will need to be carried out on every production. Depending on how smoothly the production is running, how close to time and budget, and so on, the line producer will be present on the shoot for some period of time every day. The fewer the problems, the less the presence.

Other types of producers and executive producers tend to show up occasionally or not at all during the shoot. Then, sooner or later, mercifully, the production ends. It's clean-up time. Who does what?

In a flash, it seems, most members of this big, intense, generally happy family "wrap" and head off to their well-deserved rest or the next job. The production manager, the accountant, and the line producer, if there was one, complete the last production cost report.

In the meantime, during some or all of the shoot (and certainly by the time it ends), the postproduction process has begun. The editors are taking the footage shot daily and assembling scenes. When their work has been completed (anywhere from days after the conclusion of principal photography, in the case of television, to months after, in the case of a feature film moving slowly), the sound department takes over. They salvage location sound, search for sound effects (those creaking saddles, gunshots, and the sputtering 1930 Model A which match the picture so wonderfully didn't happen on location!), record replacement dialogue (ADR), match footsteps, clothes rustling, and so on in the studio (using a Foley) and marry it all to the picture. Meanwhile, music is being composed and recorded and it all comes together in the "mix". (For more about the postproduction phase, see Chapter 5.)

But if everyone has gone home, who has been watching over this phase? The original producer, and possibly the line producer, depending on what he or she was engaged to do. In addition, there may be a postproduction supervisor. But the buck stops on the desk of the producer. The producer's responsibility doesn't end with the delivery of the answer print or the program, either. Someone has to distribute the product.

Marketing

Since there are two entire chapters on distribution (dealing with both domestic and international distribution) in this book, I will not dwell on this topic long. Suffice it to say that the producer again carries the ball. In the event that the picture has been made with studio (that is, distributor) or network (that is, end-user) financing, the producer will want to be involved in the releasing plans, the creation of the marketing plan for the picture, or the broadcast scheduling of the television program. (There are few volunteers to go up against the Super Bowl!)

There is also the question of receipts. The producer will always want to ensure that he or she is receiving a "fair count". There are questions to ask and occasionally even audits to conduct or lawsuits to launch. Investors and holders of profit points want to know that they are being treated fairly and benefiting from the returns that are due, and these people look to the producer to ensure this.

Where the distribution process is more complicated, and the sources of revenue are more than one or two in number, there will likely be a sales agent for the film or program involved. The producer will still retain his or her supervisory responsibilities; however, much of the work will be in the hands of others, as described in Chapters 6 and 7.

How to Get Started as a Producer

There is certainly less hassle and probably more money in being a major star or director than in being a producer. But if a producer is, nevertheless, what you want to be, where do you begin?

There is no general rule. People have become producers by many routes. Some of Canada's best producers have begun "on the floor." Whether as a production assistant, a location manager, a third AD, an assistant to the production manager, or otherwise, they had the opportunity to learn the workings of the system. Starting at that level, they had the oportunity to learn how the pieces fit together and to *do* the jobs that later, as producers, they had to ask others to do. There is an undeniable value in having lived through the responsibilities yourself.

During the height of the tax shelter financing of films in Canada (the late 1970s and early 1980s) a number of lawyers and accountants who had expertise in negotiating, understanding and raising financing, and tax legislation (but little in filmmaking itself) became producers. Although they did not have the benefit of experience "on the floor," they worked with other line producers or production managers who did. Those who survived necessarily became familiar with the mechanics of the industry and many are among the most successful of Canada's producers today. The same kind of producer development occurs in the United States and elsewhere in the world, although not necessarily fuelled by a tax shelter era. The shift from entertainment law to production, either directly or by way of an interim stop as a studio executive, is not uncommon.

Successful directors, already solidly immersed in their craft, often feel that the only way to ensure the integrity of their creative desires is to be their own producers. That is the source of the not uncommon "produced and directed by" credit. Some directors, like Norman Jewison and Steven Spielberg, having lived through unpleasant experiences while getting early projects launched, have gone on to produce or executive-produce films that they have called upon other directors to create. Powerful actors such as Warren Beatty and Barbra Streisand have also taken the route of nearly total control by producing their own epics.

To sum up: the producer's position, even if not easily defined, is one of innovation, leadership, and control. Those who exercise its authority necessarily live its ups and downs, its risks and rewards. All of the other filmmaking crafts, essential to the success of the process, must endure the waiting for the telephone to ring. While the insecurities of the producer are not fewer, it is generally the producer who gets to make the call.

CHAPTER TWO

The Property

by Peter O'Brian, with additional material from Jack Darcus and Richard Nielsen

*P*ETER O'BRIAN *is arguably Canada's most success-ful and award-winning producer. His credits include* My American Cousin *(6 Genie Awards, and the International Critics Award at the Festival of Festivals),* The Grey Fox *(7 Genie Awards),* One Magic Christmas, Discovery *(Expo 86), and* John and the Missus.

Vancouver-born filmmaker Jack Darcus has developed and written five feature films, as well as producing and directing four of them. He specializes in low-budget productions and his two recent films, Deserters *and* Overnight, *have received numerous Genie nominations.*

Producer and screenwriter Richard Nielsen has extensive, award-winning production experience. As a producer, his television credits include The Newcomers *and* Connections, *as well as the feature film* The Wars. *His writing credits include* Labour of Love, Canada's Sweetheart: The Saga of Hal C. Banks, *and* Little Vampire. *He has received the Wendy Michener Award, the Wilderness Award, and the Anik Award.*

Introduction   Let's start with a definition: in the broadest possible terms, applying to anything from television game shows to theatrical feature films, a property is the *writ-*

ten description of a specific concept. It must be in writing because verbal statements of stories (or game-show premises) cannot be protected by copyright, and it must be specific in that it stresses the unique aspects of the story or concept. A story property, then, requires characters, plot, atmosphere, and any other supporting details to distinguish it from all similar stories, past and present. An entertainment concept such as a game show or a documentary series also requires a detailed description of its unique characteristics.

In this chapter, we will concentrate on story properties. The screen story and its full written form, the screenplay, form the basis of almost every dramatic motion picture ever made. The single most important decision a producer or director makes in the complex process of creating an original motion picture is: what story to tell.

On this one decision rests the potential for success or failure, whether that is defined in terms of art or business. Every other decision, no matter how big or small, is predicated on the story decision. The story is, without doubt, the central issue, the "what" of a motion picture project. Even though many ordinary films have been raised to prominence by the brilliant performance of a certain director or actor, the underlying story will always be found, retroactively, to have possessed enough dramatic appeal to support their success.

Wherever on the planet movie people go to talk about and sell the projects they want to produce, whether they are idealistic filmmakers or market-oriented studio heads, the first and most important question about a movie is "What's it about?" Only when this question is satisfactorily answered does the interest shift to other key questions, about the director, writer, cast, location, budget, financing, distribution, and so on.

To the director / filmmaker, the property represents

the blueprint of a vision and the creative plan for a complicated artistic endeavour. To the businessman, the property represents the ownership of an asset that can be exploited in the market place for profit.

The producer, having contracted the rights to the property, is the person in control, who must understand both the artist and the businessman and interpret the needs of one to the other. To the producer, the property represents the goal to be accomplished, the contract to be fulfilled, and the control to do so on behalf of all concerned. And finally, to the audience, whose attention all movie people so earnestly seek, the property represents the entertainment it hopes to enjoy through motion pictures, arguably the most powerful story-telling medium human beings have yet created.

Sources of Properties

Where do the ideas or stories – which henceforth we will call properties – come from?

In general, properties for dramatic motion pictures come from two sources. Most are based upon previously published or performed material (novels, short stories, stage plays, and musicals). A producer interested in hedging his or her bets will be most attracted to such material, which has already proven it can attract attention. The second source is original screenplays. Since they've had no prior exposure, they are the higher risk items, but they often have the virtues of freshness and originality, expressing the writer's particular viewpoint and background.

In the United States, few original properties are produced. The feature film business relies as much as it can on adaptations, which lessens the risk. In Canada, however, up to the present, most feature films have been based on original material. Canadian publishing and theatrical enterprises have rarely acquired the wide public acceptance needed for a secure launch as a film. Although there are exceptions: for example,

Duddy Kravitz, Who Has Seen the Wind, and *Joshua Then and Now,* many more productions are based on original works, which places Canadian producers in the high-risk end of the business and introduces some complex problems of co-operation and ownership. (Note for producers: there is a wealth of Canadian material that has not yet been adapted and developed for the screen by creative Canadians, including the novels of Robertson Davies and Margaret Laurence, and many others.)

Within the industry, there are three categories of people who think in a purposeful way about acquiring or developing properties: producers, distributors, and writers. (Directors, actors, stage hands, and makeup artists think about properties as well, but when they do so they're stepping out of their own particular disciplines and are becoming, in effect, producers.)

Distributors become originators of properties because they are the first to feel the responses of the market. When they feel a tug at the box office or in the ratings, in response to a particular performer or genre, they want to be able to throw out the same bait with the next cast. In television, this instinct has created an industry so addicted to imitation that it threatens its own existence by excluding almost everything new – thus, in the long run, leaving itself with little to imitate. Distribution, whether or not it actively generates the property, establishes the focus for those who do. That focus can be regarded either as tyrannical or as useful discipline, depending upon one's point of view.

Writers tend to generate properties that are less market-driven than those developed by distributors. Writers' properties are apt to be a reflection of their own sensibilities and are therefore more likely to be new and original. However, writers, having created properties, must go in search of producers who share their vision. Either that, or they must become producers themselves.

Producers, of course, don't simply sit back and wait for proposals to come to them; they carry on the relentless search for suitable material in the following ways:

a. evaluating Canadian and other literature, theatre, poetry, and so on;
b. reviewing, each day, current affairs stories and "human interest" stories reported in newspapers and magazines and on television;
c. canvassing film agencies and institutions:
   i. Telefilm Canada
   ii. Provincial film institutions and development corporations
   iii. Arts Councils
   iv. the Academy of Canadian Cinema & Television library and Script Database Program, with over 100 script outlines submitted annually by Canadian writers. (These projects are available for development and are distributed bi-monthly to all interested producers, at an annual subscription fee of $25.)
d. creating an original idea or story;
e. listening to the ideas of friends and acquaintances.

Producers are essentially property seekers and creators, because everything else they do is dependent on their possession of a property. A producer isn't in business until he or she has one, and development can't begin unless the property possesses the quality to attract both money and talent. Its relative appeal to the possessors of each (that is, money and talent) will usually determine *how* it's developed.

Acquiring a Property

If the idea you have had, as a would-be producer, involves the clearing of rights to a book, a script, or concept developed by someone else, it is essential that you acquire these rights in an unencumbered way.

The reason for this is not just to ensure that no one else can act on the property's behalf, but also to allow it to become, over time, the creative property of all who acquire a say in how the film proceeds. Giving a novelist, for example, full control of a script or final say in how characters are developed pre-empts the creative contribution of all the talent you hope will like the property enough to make it – at least partially – their own.

If the idea is your own original brainwave, you should register it in a way that enables you to prove that it is indeed yours. Don't spend money to do this, however. Simply mail yourself a registered letter with a description of the property in it and don't open the letter when it arrives – in this way the date of its creation will be established. The writer, as copyright holder, can also file a script, treatment, or specific outline with the Writer's Guild Script Registry Service of ACTRA (the Alliance of Canadian Television & Radio Artists). This costs $5 for ACTRA members and $12 for non-members. Recognize, however, that in general you can't copyright an idea, only the specific written expression of an idea.

In Canada, unsolicited scripts are the greatest source of properties. These scripts are mailed from all points in the country to producers, wherever the latter can be found. The deluge of scripts is such that few producers have time to think of original ideas since they, and their staffs, are kept continuously busy reading their mail. Out of this flood of writing have surfaced some of our best (and worst) films, and it is in evaluating this material that the most difficult choices are made and the greatest risks are taken.

To Option or to Buy?

Suppose that you, as a producer, receive an appealing outline or script. You now need to control the rights in order to proceed. Here an ethical question emerges: do you "shop" this attractive idea from the writer in Churchill, Manitoba to see whether there's any interest in it, or do you option it first? At what point are you required to own the rights? The answer is: before you represent yourself as the owner of them. It is incumbent on the producer to option any interesting property or, more rarely, to purchase the rights.

Should you option the property, or buy it? (An option is a down payment, giving the producer control of the property for a fixed period of time.) An option allows both parties – the would-be producer and the original creators of the piece – time in which to develop a property. It allows them to get to know each other and to share the progress of work toward production. A purchase, on the other hand, frees the producer of any such co-operative obligations. It also frees the writer to pursue other aims in life. The choice is a delicate one, requiring sensitivity and foresight on the producer's part. If the property in question is in outline form, or the hiring of other writers is contemplated, then any agreement with the original creator must allow for revision by others.

Following is an excerpt from ACTRA's Writer's Independent Production Agreement (IPA), Article A-10:

> Definition: An option means a written agreement to acquire from a writer specified rights in literary material for a specific fee and within a specified time.
>
> An option contract between a producer and writer shall specify:
>
> a. The option period, including renewals, which shall not exceed three (3) years;
> b. The minimum fee for each year of the option, which shall not be less than ten percent (10%) of the fee payable on the exercise of the option;
> c. The minimum option fee(s) paid (which with respect to any period following the first eighteen (18) months shall not be applied to the fee payable on exercise of the option);

d. The stage of development of the literary material to be acquired on the exercise of the option (e.g. treatment, draft, screenplay, final teleplay, etc.); and

e. If the option contract provides for assignment, that the producer shall give written notice to the writer immediately upon such assignment.

An option contract between a producer and a writer of one month or less shall be completely negotiable between the producer and writer and shall not necessarily be subject to the provisions of this Article.

Legal Aspects of Optioning a Property

Whichever way you wish to proceed, the steps in acquiring a property are the most important transactions you will undertake as a producer. For complicated deals involving questions of copyright, chains of title, and title searches, an experienced entertainment lawyer is essential. (See Chapter 9 for more on this subject.) An experienced lawyer can be helpful in all contractual negotiations, but keep in mind that unless you can afford one it is best to do your own thinking. A good rule of thumb is that any deals you enter into should be clearly understandable in your own words before being rendered into legalese.

As a general proposition, if the idea is yours, you need not fear that a writer, in working for you, will acquire rights in it. The ACTRA and U.S. Screenwriter's Guild agreements contain provisions that protect the writer's intellectual property and these can also be used to protect yours. What is essential is that the rules be written down in the agreement between you, as the originator of the property, and the writer who has been hired. There may also be cases where the kind of participation you require means that you will be surrendering part of your ownership. This, too, needs to be clearly spelled out in advance.

Having chosen to option a property, you have the right to act on its behalf for a fixed period of time. You may then seek investment toward its development. This will usually involve encumbering the title to the property and raises a series of questions to which there are no clear answers. For instance, what happens to the rights to a developed property, encumbered by obligations to Telefilm Canada or other funding agencies, as well as private monies, if the option is not picked up by the producer? Does this leave the producer with debts? Does this leave the writer with "damaged goods"? What happens to the producer if the writer chooses not to renew the option?

Telefilm Canada used to insist that if a script was not produced within a set period of time, actual ownership of both the script and property would revert to them. It is important that agreements between the various participants be written in such a way that you, as producer, will retain ownership of the basic idea, even though those who have participated in its development will retain certain rights to revenues derived from it. There are no rules in practice to cover these situations and each must be solved on a per-project basis. Again, the services of experienced legal counsel can prove invaluable.

Properties –
Risky Business

There is one sense in which the very term "property" is misleading, since it implies, and is meant to imply, that what we have been discussing can be compared with other forms of property, such as a house or stocks or bonds. You might, therefore, expect a lively trade in properties; yet while this is true as it applies to literary properties (novels, plays, and so on) and is even occasionally true of real-life adventures (sold exclusively to the highest bidder), don't expect, if you have developed a property from a private notion, that midway through the process you'll be able to sell it for real money.

The mortality of properties is so high that, no matter how interesting and original a property may appear to be, people will not commit real cash to acquire it. What they will do, if they are sufficiently interested, is become your partner, investing their time, money (in some cases, the taxpayers' money), and reputations. Don't scorn such help through pride and the all-too-human tendency to want to be able to say "it's mine, all mine." The process by which bright ideas make it to the screen involves so much risk, sacrifice, and hard work that it must be considered intrinsically a co-operative venture.

In a recent year, more than 30,000 screenplays were registered in the United States. Only about two hundred made it to the screen. In Canada, the numbers are smaller, but they tell the same story. Most properties are never made. The conventional wisdom of the American film industry (and the pattern is similar in Canada) is that one in ten reasonable potential properties acquired by professional producers are actually put into serious development; of these, one in ten will be produced. Where, then, does the development stage end? Sometimes it goes on for years, or even decades. Even properties in production continue to develop during the filming itself, as the screenplay and other creative components undergo modification and, it is hoped, improvement.

The Writer

Of the three key individuals who create a motion picture property – the producer, the director, and the writer – the writer is next to "carry the ball" after the producer has made the decision to proceed, acquired rights, and allocated funds for development. On the business side of making movies, the writer is traditionally treated with more suspicion and disrespect than any of the other vital creative contributors to a film production. This shabby treatment has been chronicled at length by many screenwriters, including William Goldman in his book, *Adventures in the Screen Trade.* One of his explanations for this cavalier attitude towards writers (which is as good as any other) is "Everyone knows the alphabet, so everyone's a writer."

The fact is that there are very few great screenwriters and, if one can be found, he or she must be highly valued and carefully heeded. Even though it is the director who must actually realize the vision through a technically complex process, overseeing scores of craftspeople, artists, and technicians, the screenwriter should be considered no less a filmmaker than the director.

Selecting the best writer for the property is the next milestone decision to be made after the selection of the property itself. If the individual is not known to the producer at the outset, or is not the initial creator of the property, then the choice must be made by an agonizing process of meetings with candidates and discussions with story editors and other development personnel, until eventually rapport is established and reputation is confirmed. The writer should have a working compatability with the producer and the director, a love and knowledge of the subject in question, and the particular writing skills to bring it off.

A list of screenwriters with feature film and television drama experience is published by ACTRA, the collective bargaining agent for screenwriters in Canada. Detailed background and credit information about screenwriters is available in the Academy of Canadian Cinema & Television's *Who's Who in the Canadian Film and Television Industry*. Before making any commitments, immerse yourself in the ACTRA Writers' Agreement to determine your obligations and rights.

Development of a Property

The producer's development of a property must be based on its marketability. In general, and sadly, the more the property resembles something familiar, the more attractive it will be to most potential investors. Without commitment from a distributor or broadcaster, the producer has a worthless property. Knowing this, the producer may be tempted to second-guess the market place and only put forward material with a familiar premise. Certainly it is wise to remember that the more original the premise of the property, the more adept and energetic the producer must be in seeking out potential markets. This often involves tailoring the packaging and description of the piece in an attractive manner for the few markets that exist. The Canadian market place is very small and involves only a few serious players who can advance a property toward production. The producer is advised to study the realities of this situation very carefully.

Taking the First Steps

In specific terms, what do you do? You go to Telefilm Canada, and in Quebec, Ontario, Manitoba, and Alberta you can also go to their respective provincial film development funds. If you have a television property, you should also take it to one of the three networks or a television station. You should talk to a distributor, too. What you will be doing is testing the property and gathering expert opinions concerning it. Talk to creative talent: directors, actors, and so on. Having done all this, you should know a number of things about your property that you didn't know in the beginning:

a. whether people like it;
b. how much they like it;
c. whether they are prepared to pay or help pay for the next stage in its development;
d. whether they're prepared to commit to its production at its present stage of development; or, if not
e. how much money is needed to get it to the stage where people *are* prepared to commit production funds.

In short, the development "package" can now be formulated, with any necessary revisions to the writing, potential casting, promotional art, and market research. Your conversations with actors, directors, and writers will have indicated to you whether the talent you like likes the property and whether they may be willing to have their names associated with it. A word of caution here. Don't commit yourself to all the talent you consult at this stage, because you may not be able to deliver on your implied promises to them. Your partners not yet in the fold may not agree with your choices.

It's important to decide whether a property should be developed into script form before it's presented to talent, to investors, or to end-users, be they distributors or networks. Since all these people may want to have a say in how a script is written and developed, it can be counterproductive to go ahead to script stage without their input. In other cases, it may be essential to have a polished script. Only you, based on your own instincts and the marketability tests you have been able to devise, can determine whether you will require a script or not.

Developing Television Properties

Our entire discussion up to now has been based on the assumption that the developer of the property is someone who wishes to produce or at least control it through the production stage. That's probably a safe assumption, so far as feature films are concerned. It's much less likely to be the case in television production. The British creators of *Steptoe and Son* received royalties from *Sanford and Son*, its American imitation, but had no creative role in it (and it's doubtful they wanted to have any). Bernard Slade, the Canadian who created the *Partridge Family*, wrote an early episode or two but then retired to collect his cheques as the show's creator. Similarly, television game shows, at a less complicated and demanding level, are properties that have a value whether or not the creator becomes a producer. Indeed, it's safe to say that most people developing television series are hoping that the property, once it is in production, will outgrow their wish to remain closely involved with it. Nevertheless, it is customary for the originator of a property to remain involved in the process at least until production is assured. Properties, as such, lack preset established "prices", an indication that someone has to love a property in a special way for it to become a reality.

When Is a Property Ready for Marketing?

In the A-to-Z process of bringing a motion picture to life, from the first idea to the first theatrical run, the formal development of a property may be said to be complete when it is ready for marketing. When the property has been developed adequately, it must be ready for assessment by distributors, investors, bankers, agents, and anyone else it takes to get the property produced as a motion picture. The following are development components that must be in order to make a property ready for financial marketing:

1. *Rights.* The first requirement by any financial institution or established production or distribution entity is that the producer has all necessary rights and proof of same. Without the rights, there is no discussion; without the rights there is no property. (See Chapter 9 for further discussion of rights.)
2. *Screenplay.* The screenplay must represent the true intent of the producer and must be presented at the highest level of quality possible, from the writing itself to the form of the layout, the typestyle, and even the cover. Everything counts.
3. *Director.* Most production entities prefer to develop a property with a director attached to it. The director brings a point of view to the creative development, so that the property can be better assessed in terms of its potential as a motion picture.
4. *Cast.* The director can also help to cast the major parts, and performers may agree to appear in the film or program, subject to terms and availability. This helps the property to come to life in the imagination of all those who must support it before it can be produced, and it can be of particular value for script rewriting with specific performers in mind.
5. *Schedule.* The schedule demonstrates the amount of work to be done and the time to be spent to shoot the film, and it can also indicate production style, whether lavish or cut-rate. The schedule begins to establish the professional credentials of the production team.
6. *Budget.* The budget is important in revealing the standards, the priorities, the production style, and the marketing intentions of the producer. The art of budget estimating is a mystery indeed. (Chapter

3 tackles this topic in greater detail.)

7. *Financing and Marketing Plans.* Such plans answer the question: can the property in question be financed as a motion picture and does it have a chance of being profitable? (Chapter 4 explores this and other aspects of financing.)

8. *Key Art.* Key art includes such items as script cover design, advertising and promotional material, possible company logos, and a preliminary title design. All of this helps to indicate what kind of property is being proposed and what audience it may appeal to, which in turn will help to determine the marketing plan.

The development plan of a motion picture property should include all of these components, since a project is rarely approved for production without a thorough consideration of all of these items.

The Development Budget	The development components might be budgeted as follows:*

1. Story Rights $3,000
   First year option on a novel whose negotiated purchase price is $50,000
2. Screenplay contracted by installments $29,601
3. ACTRA Fringe Benefits 8% $2,368
4. Legal costs re: Option, Literary $4,000
   Purchase, Writer's Agreement
5. Secretarial, Equipment, Printing, Courier, $5,000
   Mail, Phone, Support Materials
6. Research Allowance $500
7. Travel Allowance $2,000
8. Key Art Allowance $500
9. Accounting $1,000
   TOTAL $47,969

* N.B. In Canada, the director's involvement is not priced in the budget. It is strictly a matter of negotiation and not yet conventional, the way it is in the U.S. motion picture development industry. The story editor is optional. Corporate overhead is also not calculated here.

The above model assumes going from "scratch" to polished screenplay. In some cases, however, particularly where a best-selling literary work is involved, the above budget would be inadequate.

Development monies expended are "above the line" expenses in the overall film budget, and it is common practice for them to be repaid to the investors or lenders on the first day of principal photography. There is no correlation between the size of the development budget and the film's final costs, although some form of proportionate reason tends to prevail.

Financing the Development of the Property

As all sectors of the Canadian film and television industries have come to recognize the critical importance of the development of good properties, government agencies, arts councils, and pay and free television have made strong financial commitments to development programs.

Telefilm Canada

Since April 1, 1985, through the Broadcast Fund, and now more recently through the Feature Film Fund, Telefilm Canada has made funds available for script and project development. Only Canadian producers are eligible to apply to these funds. (In addition, there is a category in the Feature Film Fund to which distributors may apply.) Telefilm provides up to 50 percent of the development budget, to a maximum of $100,000, in the form of a non-interest-bearing advance, repayable on the first day of principal photography. For a project to be eligible, broadcaster or distributor commitment to it is required. Up to 10 percent of the Broadcast Fund's $60 million may be allocated for development.

Provincial Agencies

The provinces of Ontario, Quebec, Alberta, Manitoba, and Nova Scotia have established film offices to create and stimulate employment by attracting investment. These agencies provide development monies to producers resident in their respective provinces.

The Ontario Film Development Corporation will provide development loans to Ontario producers or production companies, or to experienced Ontario screenwriters and filmmakers. The OFDC provides interest-free loans to a maximum of $35,000, repayable on the first day of principal photography. Matching funds are not required, although preference is given to those projects with private sector investment and those that demonstrate support from distributors and broadcasters.

The Société générale du cinéma du Québec provides grants directly to writers only. No matching funds are required. It also provides up to 50 percent, to a maximum of $15,000, for an option or purchase of rights.

The Alberta Motion Picture Development Corporation funds producers only. It acts as a bank, with loans repayable on the first day of principal photography. Eligible producers must have five years of experience and either have been an Alberta resident for one year before application or be able to establish that the project is of significant benefit to the Alberta industry. Development loans may range as high as $200,000, reflecting higher development expenses for producers in the west.

Film Manitoba, funded by the Canada-Manitoba Economic Regional Development Subsidiary Agreement on Communications and Cultural Enterprises, provides equity investment, loans, or interim financing to Manitoba-based production companies of up to 50 percent of the development budget, to a maximum of $25,000. Projects are evaluated by a point system, and funds are repayable on the first day of principal photography.

Fund for Pay Television

Established in 1986 by First Choice Pay Television, this million dollar fund is a source for script development money, primarily for dramatic feature films and made-for-pay programming written by Canadians.

Writers with at least two previously produced dramatic scripts and a letter of interest from a producer, may qualify for up to 50 percent of the approved budget, to a maximum of $6,700, to create script treatments; 50 percent of a writer's fee, to a maximum of $7,700 for first draft scripts, *plus* 50 percent of the approved development budget; and / or 50 percent of a scriptwriter's fee to a maximum of $3,000 for final draft screenplays. Grants are repayable interest-free on the first day of principal photography.

Arts Councils

Both the Canada Council and the Ontario Arts Council have, through their program of grants, contributed to the development of Canadian productions, although usually with a bias toward non-commercial, experimental ventures.

TV Networks and Independent Stations

To qualify for Telefilm's Broadcast Fund, a licence to broadcast must be obtained. Networks and local stations may commit to a percentage of the financing in the form of a broadcast licence, with attendant broadcast rights.

Private Sector Development

Private sector development tends to be ad hoc and project-by-project. Each producer and / or production has its individual modus operandi. Producers usually borrow development funds required to "match" or complete the government agencies' funding. These funds are usually repayable on the first day of principal photography. Not all projects developed will be produced. However, private sector investors may place undue pressure on the producer to bring unworthy projects to the screen. Therefore, each producer must also be prepared to risk development money to be in the game.

With the exception of the Arts Councils (which operate on a jury system) all of the above funding sources evaluate work by means of readers' reports. This is intended to be a "blind" system in which the readers are unaware of the writers' identities, and vice versa. In practice, the intention often fails. The producer should remember that a negative report is not fatal, while a positive one can be very helpful. It's a clumsy system, but likely the only workable one and should be looked upon with grim black humour at all times.

In Closing

A strong, independent motion picture industry depends on the quality of all its components but, in particular, on the quality and numbers of original properties. Only by the appeal and value of our film stories can we develop a reliable mainstream of quality production sufficient to create the world-wide demand we need for profitability and recognition. To illustrate his own emphasis on the property as the key to successful motion picture production, producer Denis Héroux has said that the three most important elements of a film are the story, the story, and the story.

Whatever generous amounts of money have been allocated in the agencies for development of our stories as motion picture properties, more must be placed. Whatever efforts writers, directors, and producers have made to create great new properties, the tempo of the drive must increase, so that the promise of the Canadian cinema, with all its talents, will be fulfilled and will continue to excite filmgoers in Canada, the United States, and the rest of the world.

In fact, the initial quality every property must possess is that at least its creator must be able to love it. Development and production and distribution are simply the broadening of that circle of affection until it includes as large a segment of the human race as possible.

CHAPTER THREE

The Budget

by Douglas Leiterman

*D*OUGLAS LEITERMAN, *who is chairman of Motion Picture Guarantors Inc., has been a writer, cameraman, unit production manager, director, producer, and – on one occasion – an actor. He has run production, financing, and distribution companies. He has produced or directed for CBC, CTV, TVO, CBS, PBS, and Talent Associates. Before he heard about movies, he was a reporter, parliamentary and foreign correspondent for the Southam newspaper chain. He once operated a cable TV company and is remembered by some as the Executive Producer of* This Hour Has Seven Days.

For those who know how to read them, budgetary plots can be as intriguing, and sometimes as dramatic, as the script itself. And though the authors of budgets never see their names in lights and seldom win awards, they have the satisfaction of knowing that without them no picture can be made, and if their advice is not followed, the mighty will tremble and empires may fall. The budget is the business plan of the movie. It is no more – and no less – than the detailed answer to one simple question: "How much will it cost?"

If a budget is skillfully prepared and faithfully followed, it can make a film set run like a well-greased dolly track. If it is sloppy, ill-conceived, or deceitful, it can plague the production, drive away future investors, and worst of all, irretrievably damage the picture. It is my opinion, based on the scanning of around a thousand budgets and a detailed acquaintance with maybe five hundred of them, that budget-making is one of the most esoteric and least-understood arts in the movie business, and that the people who make them should someday have a Genie award all their own.

Who Prepares the Budget?

Who are the practitioners of the black budgetary arts? They are known as PMs (production managers). They are the first hired after the screenplay is written (and sometimes before – see below); they know all the secrets of the production and in what closets the skeletons may rattle; and for their knowledge and discretion they are better paid than just about anyone on the crew except the director. This is hardly surprising, since PMs set the pay scales of everybody else and may even demand that the producer ante up if the picture is in trouble. So vital is their role that when a dispute developed between the (famous) director/producer of a $34 million mini-series and the (unknown outside the industry) PM, and neither would stay unless the other was fired, it was the PM who kept his job and the director/producer who was jettisoned.

Where do production managers come from? Some of the best began as assistant directors; many were production accountants, location managers, or unit managers. Some are ex-producers who didn't have the stomach for money-raising. Few set out to become production managers, but most wouldn't trade the job for any other. They have enormous power and prestige among those who know, and they get to work longer on the production than anyone else in the crew, starting "prep" from 5 to 30 weeks ahead of shooting and sometimes finishing their work after the final print is delivered (though typically winding down a week after shooting).

Whatever their backgrounds, they must possess sufficient depth of experience to weigh the conflicting demands of art and commerce, to arbitrate the battles of department heads, soothe the temperaments of artists and directors, gauge the thickness of the ice with union stewards and insurers, stand up to harassed producers, fend off bank managers, and make peace with completion guarantors. The best of them are shrewd, slow to ruffle, impossible to outmanoeuvre, blessed with cast-iron constitutions and an unfailing sense of the ridiculous. For these admirable qualities they may earn the undying gratitude of the producer, the director, and those in the crew who hope to work again soon – and upwards of $1800 to $2500 a week. One production manager I know put up his own credit cards when the production cheques bounced, and another, now a senior official at Telefilm, cleaned out the ladies' latrine with the help of the executive producer when the star refused to use it because of the smell.

Production managers are in the cat-bird seat when it comes to privilege and power. They hire and fire most of the crew, approve or deny overtime and cash-float vouchers and entertainment disbursements, decide how many assistants a department can have, who gets the best bedrooms on location, who borrows the rented Mercedes on weekends, who drives Liz Taylor or Gordon Pinsent to location, and who gets first crack at props, wardrobe, and damaged equipment when the film is finished.

Many PMs consider it their job to keep track of the personal eccentricities of their charges – who is companioning whom, who is offering what to whom, and so on. This kind of sleuthing gives the PM a little leverage when needed and may help him or her to forestall the frictions that develop when crews are shooting far from home. "They're like a pack of children," says one PM who started his career 30 years ago with David

Lean. "When the sun is shining, they are all jolly and gay, but when the rain begins they run with the pack and, if someone doesn't stop them, you can have a morale problem overnight which can add thousands of dollars to the cost of the film."

I once asked a PM who had a reputation for prescience how he was able to keep such close tabs on the private liaisons of the 70-odd people on his location. "Easy," he replied. "I'm the last one to finish at night, so I just thumb through the message slips before I leave to see who is calling whom." If knowledge is power, the person who runs the budget is the repository of both, and there may be the temptation sometimes to use power unethically. Some have sought sexual favours or kick-backs, but generally in Canada the people who manage the budgets maintain a high moral standard or they don't last.

Who Reads the Budget?

Everybody who can get his or her hands on it reads the budget, because it holds all the financial secrets of the production. The budget is, of course, closely guarded and "need to know" rules are rigorously applied. Normally, only the producer gets to see the "Above-the-Line" section (sometimes called the top of the book) which details the amounts paid to producer, director, writer, and stars; and the "Other" section (the bottom of the book) revealing overheads, finance, legal insurance, publicity, and the like. The director and the department heads (art, camera, sound, continuity, location, stunts, makeup / hair, transport, postproduction) may or may not be shown the budget categories relating directly to their work. On the theory that people who know the estimates tend to use them up, many production managers do not confide all the numbers to their department heads, preferring to juggle the numbers as the needs arise. The producer, and of course the production accountant, know all.

Outside of the production company itself, the budget will be seen by the bankers and financiers (it's their money); the insurance broker (who needs it to calculate premiums and exclusions and to settle claims); the distributor or broadcaster (who wants to make sure of putting up only his or her fair or agreed share); the lawyers (who need it to write the contracts, and sometimes to calculate their fees); and the completion guarantor (whose work is described more fully later in this chapter). Probably only one of the above will get past the topsheet of the budget. However, they will all gain comfort from having the whole fat package in their file and knowing that, even if the script is not hugely literate, the star is ingesting foreign substances, and the director is exercising his *droit de seigneur* with the leading artist (most investors take all this for granted and would be a little disappointed to know that the reality is often much tamer) at least the business plan is reliable and they won't have to dip into the family trust for money to finish the film.

How Much Money Is Enough?

The classic transition of a "passive investor" into a movie expert usually evolves in three stages. First his public comment: "Lousy script. Needs a coupla rewrites." Next his opinion: "S'not commercial. It'll never sell." And finally when he reaches the zenith of self-confidence, he will solemnly intone: "It can't be made for 3.5 mil" (or whatever the budget may be). In this chapter we're not concerned with the script or the market potential, but we can say with some assurance that on the matter of how much it will cost to shoot a script, there are few opinions worth the asking.

"Tell me how much money there is and I'll make the picture for it," says one producer I know, and that's very close to the truth. If there is only $500,000, he'll go non-union, non-ACTRA, non-DGC (Director's Guild of Canada, which includes not only directors but writers, assistant directors, production managers, accountants, production designers and so on), use 16 mm

Arri cameras or Betacam (video), put everybody on "flats" (a fixed weekly rate no matter the hours worked), shoot eight or nine pages of script a day, and wrap it up in 18 days or less.

If there is $5 million available, he'll budget for a name director and give him six weeks, bankable actors, IATSE (International Alliance of Theatrical and Stage Employees), ACFC (Association of Canadian Film Craftspeople), or NABET (National Association of Broadcast Engineers and Technicians) crews, assistants for most departments, and Winnebagos all round.

If it is $10 million (it's still the same script), he'll book the kind of stars who rate a personal assistant and return air tickets for nannies and/or spousal equivalents, 8 to 12 weeks shooting, limos for the director's wife to go shopping, union drivers even for the assistant props, catering by Petit Gourmet, and a Luma crane air-freighted from Hollywood for the Director of Photography (DOP), who may wear white gloves laundered (of course) by the wardrobe department.

As an accountant said to his employer, "Boss, the numbers can mean anything you want them to mean." This is especially true in the movie business. That's why you have the anomaly of one picture that is desperately tight at eight million, and another that comes in on the money for one-tenth of that amount. The curious thing is, it's often quite impossible to predict which of them will be a success. Ted Kotcheff directed *The Apprenticeship of Duddy Kravitz* for less than $1 million in 1974, but it was relatively more successful than *Joshua Then and Now*, which he directed in 1984 for $11 million.

How much is enough, in general terms, no one will ever know. But in order for filmmaking to function as a business, investors need to know what a particular film will cost, where the money will go, and where, at the end of the day, it actually went. With a properly drawn budget as a guide, it is possible to know the answers to those questions in great detail.

Preparing the (Preliminary) Budget

If this chapter is to deal, not with how things ought to be, but how they really are, then let's state plainly at the outset that no Canadian producer I know can hand a script to a production manager and say "Budget it the way it ought to be done and I'll come up with the money." What the producer says to the PM instead is: "I've got 2.8 (or whatever number it may be); I need a third of it for my end (financing, overheads, insurance and completion bond, the producer's fee, and development costs), and you'll have to do the picture for the rest."

Next, the production manager will pepper the producer with the questions that will establish the skeleton on which the PM will build: Who is the director? How many stars? Where and when will it be shot? In a studio or on location? Union or non-union? Film or off-line edit? Period setting or present-time? Any stunts or special effects?

The decision you, as producer, make on who will do the preliminary budget may have far-reaching consequences. The credibility of the first budget will affect your chances of raising money and getting a completion bond, and if it is way off-base at the start you may make commitments for talent or crew that you will not be able to keep.

In the off-season (December to March) you may find a production manager who will do a rough budget for $500 to $1000. When everybody's busy it will cost you double that. You need the best talent you can afford, and ideally you want the production manager who will go on to make the picture with you, since no one likes to correct someone else's mistakes.

Some experienced producers do the preliminary budget themselves, and some enterprising ones even do it on a photocopy, using a similar budget with a few numbers changed. (This practice is not highly recommended, because Telefilm and other funders have people on staff who can spot a phony budget in about ten seconds.)

The truth of the matter is that in the earliest stages, *no one* can do a meaningful budget, because few of the parameters have been established. Yet financiers will often demand a budget before they will read a script, so you might as well have it prepared, date it, note the author, clearly mark it *preliminary*, and perhaps append a footnote confessing its shortcomings.

Fine-Tuning the Budget

This is the stage that separates the pros from the guesstimators. Your main elements (finance, director, some artists, key crew) are now in place and you need serious work on the budget by a professional production manager, ideally the one who will work on the picture with you. Few choices you make will be more important, for this man or woman will become your priest, confessor, ally, and friend. Together you will face, and defeat, the forces of evil that conspire against filmmakers. The skills, fortitude, human values, and ethical standards of each of you will be tested, and you will likely end up either lifelong buddies or the kind of friends who wave across the room at the annual Genies.

You will go through many drafts of your budget in this stage, numbered and dated, each change reflecting new input as your production manager signs deal memos with crews and you negotiate the contracts with distribution, interim financiers, director, bonder, and stars (for more about this, see Chapters 5 and 9). You will try to be open and honest with everyone, because it really does pay off in the long run, but you may also come to realize that not everyone has the same "right to know." There's a lot of horse-trading going on now, and most of it has to be done with the door closed. Your production office begins to resemble the battle headquarters of a small army.

The Budget "Line-by-Line"

The best way for you to understand the budget-making process is to go through the standard DGC budget format "line-by-line." (In some circles it's fashionable to prefer the British, American, or Australian format, but essentially all budgets contain the same information, although perhaps in different order.)

The DGC budget has four sections:

a. Above-the-Line: this covers costs for story and script, development, producer, director, and stars.
b. Below-the-Line Production: covers cast (except stars) and all shooting personnel and facilities;
c. Below-the-Line Postproduction: covers editing, mix, titles, versioning and packaging, etc.;
d. Indirect Costs: including contingency, completion guarantee, legal, insurance, audit, finance, and sometimes overheads.

See the production budget summary at the end of this chapter for an example of how the budgeting was done on a recent Canadian production. In most other countries, the designations are similar to the DGC, except that b, c, and d are often combined as one "below-the-line" category. Since most of the elements are self-explanatory, let's just highlight points that might be overlooked.

Above-the-Line

1. *Story Rights.* What you pay for the right to film a story, an article, or maybe just a song. Get experienced counsel before you buy an option or make an offer. Beginners usually offer too much. (Chapter 2 discusses the property in more detail, and Chapter 9 discusses the legal aspects of buying or optioning a work.)

2. *Scenario.* Remember the fringe benefits (pension fund, insurance, and so forth) if the writer is a member of ACTRA; travel and living expenses connected with script and rewrites, and typing, word-processing, and copying costs. If foreign

actors are engaged and work in Canada under ACTRA permits, they are entitled to Canadian fringes, not the higher U.S. fringes.

3. *Development.* This category comprises everything the producer has spent developing the project up to the point of preproduction. It includes travel, legal costs of negotiating the property, financing, distribution, and key elements. It may well include trips to Los Angeles and / or London, Paris, or Peking, with stays at the best hotels, since otherwise nobody returns your calls. (One producer won a distribution contract on the strength, among other things, of the impression she made by driving to Palm Springs in a rented Rolls. Others have driven a rent-a-wreck and stayed at Howard Johnson's and still closed the deal, but they are

the exceptions!) For a fuller discussion of the development and preproduction phases, see Chapter 5.

4. *Producer.* This category includes executive producers (but not line producers, who are below-the-line), travel and living expenses of all producers and sometimes their secretaries. Telefilm limits producer fees to 5 percent of the budget.

5. *Director.* When you sign the contract with the director, make sure it includes the usual termination clauses, giving the producer or the completion guarantor the right to fire the director if he fails to do his job.

6. *Stars.* This category includes the cost of obtaining permits, travel and living expenses, fringes, and also travel and living expenses for "companions", if any. Make sure there are no stop dates in their contracts; i.e. that they have made no other commitment back-to-back with your production, in case your picture runs over schedule.

Below-the-Line

1. *Cast.* Must be based on the Day-out-of-Days (see Chapter 5) and the Board or Shooting Schedule (see Chapter 5). Unless you are using non-union people, there will be an ACTRA administration fee and fringe benefits, and also a deposit held by ACTRA until all its members have been paid and disputes settled.

2. *Extras, Stunts, and Stand-ins.* The Director should approve the budget breakdown on these people. Don't economize on stunt people or animal trainers – you need the best you can find. On low-budget films, explore various strategies to obtain low-cost extras and stand-ins. Staging a free sporting event is a common practice.

3. *Production Staff.* Getting top people here is money well spent. But guard against loading the budget with more assistants than you really need.

4. *Continuity.* This is the person (sometimes called a

script supervisor, or script girl in the UK) who has the vital job of making sure that the star's elbow, cigarette, etc. is in the same position in Scene 16, shot on day 3, as in Scene 46, shot on day 14. This person also times the scenes, notes all the script and dialogue changes as they happen, and notes the director's choice of takes. The inexperienced need not apply.

5. *Design*. This is the area where most budget overages occur. The problem is that the design department is hired early when there's (relatively speaking) lots of money. Some production designers spend it very freely indeed, right down to monogrammed match covers. The best of them can do marvels with small budgets, but there are others who may go wildly out of control if you fail to demand detailed estimates for each location and see that they stick to them. In one recent Canadian over-budget production, some design categories were exceeded by 1000 percent.

6. *Props / Set Dressing*. You can spend a fortune in this category, but resourceful props people can often find what you need for peanuts. If you buy, lock up the stuff after shooting, as otherwise it tends to have legs. On one major Canadian production, two truckloads of period furniture vanished without a trace.

7. *Wardrobe / Makeup / Hair*. The best horror story I know was on a big-budget historical drama, when a crate of wigs got lost in transit and didn't turn up for two weeks. The cast and crew played pinochle and the insurers paid $750,000 under the "extra expense" coverage for the time lost.

8. *Camera Equipment*. The final look of your picture will greatly depend on whether your art department over-spent by so much before you began shooting that your director of photography (DOP) couldn't have the Panaflex camera, high-speed lenses, crane dollies, and HMIs (high intensity

lights) that were needed to make your picture look like the millions it cost. Both the DOP and the director should sign the equipment list. Stedicam can sometimes substitute for complicated dolly shots.

9. *Food.* Good lunches pay off in productivity. Expect to feed a lot of extra hangers-on and visitors who always turn up at lunch break.

10. *Transportation.* On big pictures there's a driver for everybody. Low-cost producers insist that crew drive themselves instead of being driven, if they remember how. This is easier to do outside the major cities, where the unions are less likely to object.

11. *Film Stock.* Give your director as much as is needed, but if money is tight, be careful about whom you hire to direct. Hold the director to daily averages and printing ratios – see that he or she doesn't burn up too much stock too early, and only prints the "good takes". Video-assist can help a lot here, if you can afford it. It is a small video camera attached to the film camera which allows the director to see exactly what is being shot.

12. *Music.* Make your music deal before you lock the budget. You can spend a lot or a little, and there are companies that will provide music for a low fee in exchange for the right to market it.

Indirect Costs

1. *Contingency.* This is an extra allowance added to the budget to cover unexpected expenses. It has to be at least 10 percent of the budget, including above-the-line and below-the-line, in order to satisfy the completion guarantor. Make sure it's a real contingency to cover the totally unexpected or unpredictable, not to cover budget deficiencies you already knew about but wanted to hide.

2. *Insurance.* Film insurance is complicated, and you need a specialist to guide you safely through the maze, making sure that you are covered but not

smothered. There is an insurance checklist put out by the principal entertainment brokers which is a good guide. Insurance usually costs around 2 percent of the budget.

3. *Completion Guarantee.* Required by banks, interim funders and investors. The completion guarantor contracts to deliver a finished picture at no further cost to investors than the budget. The guarantor's fee is 6 percent of the budget excluding contingency, and he or she usually offers a no claims bonus if the producer is a good risk. In order to fulfill this commitment, the guarantor has virtually unlimited powers, including the right to take over the production, fire the director or other personnel, and the authority to hold the producer to his or her budget and schedule. If required, the completion guarantor must provide the money to complete the film.

4. *Legal.* You need an experienced entertainment lawyer. He or she may give you a package fee and will certainly earn it. Many film lawyers will help find your finance and distribution, know the home numbers of the stars you cannot reach and the weak points of their agents, assist you at Telefilm, speed up the bonding process, and fend off union problems and lawsuits. Some lawyers become so fond of the business that they discard their silk ties and become producers themselves.

What the Budget Detectives Do

Vetting the budget is the business of the budget detectives, an elite group of ex-production managers who know what to look for and have the advantage of second-guessing. They may work for investors or interim funders, but usually they vet for completion guarantors. They come up with queries that are discussed with the production manager and/or producer. If there is a logical explanation why no overtime is needed for the props department, well and good. If not, it goes on the deficiency list, with an estimated further cost attached. Then, one of the following will happen:

a. the budget will be increased;
b. the contingency will be increased;
c. surpluses in other categories will be re-allocated;
d. savings will be made (fewer shooting days, locations, set-ups, people, or supplies);
e. the producer will allocate amounts otherwise due to him, such as his fees or overheads, to make up the shortfall.

There is usually no argument on the budget shortfalls, because PMs are skilled and independent professionals whose considered judgments are not easily influenced by their employers and who seldom differ on costs once the facts are established and the intentions of the director made known. A script may call for an ogre to shrink in size until he fits inside a bottle. If it's for TV, the director may use a blue cyclorama and an electronic insert and it will cost nothing. On film it may require matte shots and opticals and cost a bundle. Or, on the other hand, the director may be able to use models purchased at Woolworths.

If a scene calls for the star to jump out of the cockpit of an airplane, a stuntman may be hired to do just that, with air-to-air shooting from a camera plane alongside, and a parachute opening out of frame. Or it may be done with the plane sitting on the ground, its propellor blowing up a slipstream, at a fraction the time and cost.

Every experienced production manager has favourite cushions – items they're pretty darn sure will cost less than budget. The smartest PMs hold on to their cushions right up to the last, so they can be magnanimous when the director is tearing his or her hair or the DOP is pleading for a crane. One budget manager always allows $3000 US for de Forest, an American research firm that checks the script line-by-line for possible liability. It's a good thing to have, but Canadian insurance brokers don't usually require it (they will take a declaration from your lawyer instead), and this PM finds the sum of money comes in handy to cover overages in phones, photocopying, and messengers. A British production manager who won't let me use his name puts a few thousand in his budgets for "protective clothing." (If any is needed, in fact, the stuntman supplies his own, but you never know, says my friend, there might be another Three Mile Island disaster.) Nuclear contamination, by the way, cannot be insured against.

Some budgets are so unprofessional that it's hopeless to try to vet them. A PM now in government service described one such travesty as a "fine work of fiction" and turned it down. Yet, I've seen millions of dollars raised from unsuspecting investors based on budgets that wouldn't wash in first-year film school. *Caveat emptor.*

Cash-Flowing the Budget

After the budget you need the cash-flow, the road map that shows the date and amount of all cash flowing in and flowing out. In any week where there's not enough cash to cover the outflow, you have a cash-flow deficit and that's where you need interim financing.

Interim financing, including set-up fees, interest and legals may cost anywhere from 25 to 100 percent of the maximum loan, depending on the risk. (If this seems exorbitant, remember that this is where several Canadian banks, and producers, lost millions in 1982 when the film boom collapsed. They loaned money against the sale of units to investors who were suddenly not to be found, having discovered that only about 20 percent of feature films, anywhere, make a profit for their investors.)

Producers who can't – or won't – get interim funding may try to cash-flow their deficits. That's a polite way of saying that they will "borrow" from suppliers and sometimes crew and their Visa card to carry on until the next cash comes in. This is a dangerous game at which many have been burned, leaving a trail of unpaid bills and going on to other fields of endeavour.

A few have managed to survive the drought, however, and the usual tool is the deferment, which at its simplest level means getting people to agree to wait a while before they are paid. If directors, suppliers and artists are hungry, or anxious to see a film get made, they may be willing to defer all or part of their salaries. (See Chapter 4 on Financing.) The producer, of course, is the first to get deferred, and usually the last to be paid. One film lawyer I know won't let his producers defer: "You put in two years of your life, you're entitled to buy groceries," he says. Others feel that a producer deferment is a good guarantee that the producer believes in the product, since he or she won't get paid unless it makes money.

Deferments come in bizarre forms and marvellously improbable recoupment positions. They may also be called participations or equity. (See Chapters 4 and 9 for a fuller discussion.)

Managing the Budget: The Cost Report

The tool for managing the budget and staying on target is the cost report, put out and signed by the production manager and the production accountant weekly during the shoot and monthly during postproduction. It shows what's been spent, what is committed, and what is the predicted final figure for every category, adjusted on the basis of what happened that week. Its categories are:

a. actual dollars spent that week;
b. actual dollars spent to date;
c. purchase orders (money committed but not yet paid);

d. cost to date (total of a, b, and c);
e. estimate-to-complete – the PM's best guess on what further money will be spent;
f. estimated final cost (total of d and e);
g. the original budget;
h. variance – the difference between the original budget (g) and the final cost (f), expressed as a plus or minus.

When the estimate-to-complete begins to chew into the contingency, a lot of things happen. The producer calls a meeting with the department heads who are going over budget. The banker phones the guarantor. The guarantor confers with the producer, the PM, and maybe the director and AD. If the contingency invasion is alarming, the guarantor will need to be convinced that the damage can be contained. Essentially he or she will want to know what happened to the Business Plan. If it looks like the trouble will continue, or get worse, the guarantor will want from the producer a plan to reverse the trend. If the guarantor is not sure of the numbers, he or she will spot-check the accounting department to see how many unpaid bills are being carried around in pockets or hidden in drawers.

Because of the professionalism and high standards of virtually all production managers and production accountants, the cost reports can normally be relied upon. Once in a while, a producer may want to delay revealing the bad financial news, but of course it will come out eventually anyway. Production accountants generally refuse to participate in "delayed" reporting, partly because of their professional code and partly because they know they will be blamed at the end of the day, as the Israelis say. In one case, a production accountant who was handed more than $800,000 of late invoices labelled her next (shockingly increased) cost report not No. 14, as in sequence, but No. 13-A, as a kind of mute protest. In general, a movie production office is not a good place to try to keep secrets.

Surprisingly, the computer has become the ally of ethics in the production office. A proper software program leaves an accounting "trail", so that when, for example, an expense column goes down from one week to the next, the interested observer can trace where the missing expense items were moved to. Quite often they mysteriously move back where they came from after questions have been asked.

If any of the preceding remarks suggest that movie sets are riddled with corruption, let me state plainly that this is not the case. At least 95 percent of the professionals play it straight, and the Canadian film industry has established a reputation for fair and honourable practices, second only, in my experience, to the very high degree of honourable practice in Australia and New Zealand, where a handshake is still counted as binding.

"Goosing" the Budget

This was to be a section on budget padding, currency cushions, interest cadging, underheads and overheads, two-budget systems, and other exotica. But on second thought, those familiar with such devices are not in need of tutoring or exposure, and those unfamiliar will mercifully retain their innocence in the knowledge that in the fullness of time these devices are always exposed (if only to be replaced by even more exotic practices that will be exposed in their turn). A little diddling there will always be, but grand larceny leads only to more and more complex legal agreements which are merely set-ups for litigation, pushing the industry ever further from its real objectives and reason for existing – the making of moving pictures.

Allan King reminds me that Ingmar Bergman has said, it is not talent or art, but punctuality, which makes a great director. If so, then it might be as truly be said that what makes a good production manager (and a good budget) is meticulous regard for the details. Canadian production managers, perhaps because they had to do so much with so little for so long, have an enviable reputation worldwide for the detail called integrity. If one is permitted a personal note, this is a quality that has yet to be fully realized in the movies they make.

\						
PRODUCTION BUDGET SUMMARY						
ACCT	**CATEGORY**	**PAGE**				**TOTAL**
01	STORY RIGHTS/ACQUISITIONS	1				25,000
02	SCENARIO	1				74,642
03	DEVELOPMENT COSTS	2				50,142
04	PRODUCER	3				214,074
05	DIRECTOR	4				163,244
06	STARS	5				
PRODUCTION		**TOTAL "A"**				527,102
10	CAST	6				265,536
11	EXTRAS	9				45,580
12	PRODUCTION STAFF	10				169,150
13	DESIGN LABOUR	12				24,000
14	CONSTRUCTION LABOUR	13				35,400
15	SET DRESSING LABOUR	14				15,000
16	PROPERTY LABOUR	14				25,000
17	SPECIAL EFFECTS LABOUR	15				5,600
18	WRANGLING LABOUR	15				27,250
19	WARDROBE LABOUR	16				17,600
20	MAKEUP/HAIR LABOUR	17				11,000
21	*VIDEO TECHNICAL CREW*	18				
22	CAMERA LABOUR	20				68,448
23	ELECTRICAL LABOUR	21				33,550
24	GRIP LABOUR	22				23,100
25	PRODUCTION SOUND LABOUR	23				25,000
26	TRANSPORTATION LABOUR	23				13,000
27	FRINGE BENEFITS	24				74,698
28	PRODUCTION OFFICE EXPENSES	25				31,140
29	STUDIO/BACKLOT EXPENSES	26				4,100
30	LOCATION OFFICE EXPENSES	27				700
31	SITE EXPENSES	28				41,850
32	UNIT EXPENSES	29				19,450
33	TRAVEL & LIVING EXPENSES	30				276,191
34	TRANSPORTATION	31				73,467
35	CONSTRUCTION MATERIALS	32				25,200
36	ART SUPPLIES	32				1,000
37	SET DRESSING	33				15,800
38	PROPS	33.				18,550
39	SPECIAL EFFECTS	34				6,000
40	ANIMALS	34				5,000
41	WARDROBE SUPPLIES	35				26,500
42	MAKEUP/HAIR SUPPLIES	35				5,000
43	*VIDEO STUDIO FACILITIES*	36				
44	*VIDEO REMOTE TECHNICAL FACILITIES*	37				
45	CAMERA EQUIPMENT	38				72,900
46	ELECTRICAL EQUIPMENT	38				63,500
47	GRIP EQUIPMENT	39				23,000
48	SOUND EQUIPMENT	39				20,700
49	SECOND UNIT	40				9,156
50	*VIDEOTAPE STOCK*	41				
51	PRODUCTION LABORATORY	42				122,552
TOTAL PRODUCTION "B"						1,739,668

Note: All items set in italic are video budget accounts

			PRODUCTION BUDGET SUMMARY					
ACCT	**DESCRIPTION**	**PAGE**					**TOTAL**	
	TOTAL PRODUCTION "B" CARRIED FORWARD							
POST-PRODUCTION								
60	EDITORIAL LABOUR	43					67,250	
61	EDITORIAL EQUIPMENT	44					24,500	
62	*VIDEO POST PRODUCTION (PICTURE)*	45						
63	*VIDEO POST PRODUCTION (SOUND)*	46						
64	POST PRODUCTION LABORATORY	47					60,076	
65	FILM POST PRODUCTION SOUND	48					87,105	
66	MUSIC	50					100,000	
67	TITLES/OPTICALS/STOCK FOOTAGE	51					16,000	
68	VERSIONING	52						
69	AMORTIZATIONS (SERIES)	53						
TOTAL POST PRODUCTION "C"							354,931	
TOTAL "B" + "C" (PRODUCTION AND POST PRODUCTION)							$2,094,599	
70	UNIT PUBLICITY	54					50,000	
71	GENERAL EXPENSES	55					94,500	
72	INDIRECT COSTS	55					171,400	
TOTAL OTHER "D"							$315,900	
TOTAL "A" + "B" + "C" + "D"							$2,937,601	
80	CONTINGENCY 10% of $2,094,599	56					209,460	
SUB TOTAL							$3,147,061	
81	COMPLETION GUARANTEE 6 % of $2,975,661	57					178,540	
82	COST OF ISSUE	57					NIL	
GRAND TOTAL							$3,325,601	

NOTES:

All union cast and crew based on a 10hour day 6 day week

DOP/Operator combined

5 year all rights buy-out per ACTRA performer

All shooting on location

CHAPTER FOUR

Financing Your Production

*by David J. Patterson with additional
material from Michael MacMillan*

*D*AVID J. PATTERSON *is a co-founder of Filmline
International Inc., a Montreal-based film and television production company. From 1968 to the mid-
1970s, he was one of Canada's most successful television producers, creating hundreds of commercials for
such clients as Eaton's and Bell Canada. Later he co-
produced* Heartaches, *which won three Genie Awards,
and the film version of John Irving's novel,* Hotel New
Hampshire. *Filmline International's recent projects
include theatrical films (*Toby McTeague*), mini-series
(*Spearfield's Daughter*), and made-for-TV movies
(*Choices *and* Barnum*).*

*Michael MacMillan is President of Atlantis Films Lim-
ited, a film and television production company he
formed in 1978 with his partners Janice Platt and Sea-
ton McLean. Some of the award-winning programs produced by Atlantis over the past eight years are:* Boys
and Girls, *which won an Oscar in 1984;* The Painted
Door, *nominated for an Academy Award in 1985;* The
Ray Bradbury Theatre, *winner of three Ace Awards
(Award for Cable Excellence), Los Angeles in 1985, and
cited by* Time *magazine as one of the top ten programs
shown on U.S. television in 1985;* Brothers by Choice, *an
adventure-drama series set in British Columbia and
broadcast nationally on CBC in 1986; and* Airwaves, *a
CBC drama series.*

Introduction

Whether you are setting out to produce a theatrical motion picture, or a television program or series, you always have to begin with a great idea. Part of this great idea has to be your strategy for financing the production. No less creativity is required when building a financial structure than for any other aspect of developing a successful package.

You must tailor every aspect of the project to suit the financial realities of the market place in which you intend to distribute. Then you must not only raise the requisite amount of working capital, but raise it in such a way as to ensure that it will be available when you need it, and on terms and conditions that make the project financially viable for both you and the financiers.

We will be examining the methods of raising financing for three distinct phases of the project, all of which are integral to the creation of a well-packaged and potentially successful production.

Some Basic Definitions

Before we begin our examination of these activities, some definitions might serve us well:

a. *The Project.* A "project" is any production destined to be a feature-length theatrical motion picture, a feature-length television movie (a so-called Movie-of-the-Week), or a television series.

b. *Development Financing.* This is the cash financing required to package a project to the point where it is ready to go before the camera.

c. *Production Financing.* This is the cash financing required for preproduction, production (principal photography), and postproduction of a project; that is, for its completion and delivery.

d. *Direct Sales Expense Financing.* This is the cash financing required both to secure the best commercial release for the project and also to report on and disburse revenue to financiers.

Development Financing

Financing for the development stage of your project is often the most difficult to obtain. Development financing has sometimes been defined as the amount of money to be spent in order to determine that a project should *not* go into production. Do not undertake development of your project certain that it should and will be produced as you currently envisage. The development process itself should be designed to determine the form your project should take.

Your timing may be bad and your project may sit on a shelf waiting for a lucky break, or the market place may tell you that it's just not interested. Be tenacious but realistic. Finance the development stage so that minimum sums are being spent and all your financiers know the risks being taken. After all, you and they are setting out to determine the viability of your idea, not simply to promote its production without regard for the market place reaction.

Production and Direct Sales Expense Financing

Presuming that you have successfully completed the development phase on your project, you will of course have an immediate need for production financing. There is an important distinction to be made here: while development financing is available whether or not the project is completed, dollar one of production financing does not normally flow until *all* financing required to complete the project is irrevocably committed in a form acceptable to each financier.

The remaining financing category, direct sales expense, should actually be viewed as a subset of production financing, and should form part of the production budget of the project. This item is often overlooked, but is sometimes crucial to the successful commercial exploitation of the project and to the harmonious relationship between the producer and the financiers. Specifically, during the development phase, at which time the budget for the production is determined, you should take a careful look at what expenses will be incurred in marketing the film to its targeted market, whether this be television stations, television networks, pay-television outlets, home video distributors, foreign distributors in either theatrical or television, or theatrical distribution worldwide. (For more on distribution, see Chapters 6 and 7.)

If you are able to arrange distribution and the arrangement is at all successful, net revenue should be generated. On-going management and disbursement of these revenues – and reporting of them to the financiers of the project – becomes vital. Indeed, it is normal for financing contracts to stipulate a specific form of financial reporting, as well as stated intervals at which the producer must report to the financiers. This continuing responsibility will soon become onerous, unless enough financing has been provided for a trustee or disbursing agent who will act on behalf of both the producers and the financiers.

This chapter will examine in detail the financing of each of these stages of production, as well as highlighting some areas of particular concern to both prospective and committed financiers. The successful financing of a film or television program can take numerous forms. However, regardless of the size of the project in dollar terms, or the size of the market for which it is primarily destined, all financing in the end tends to be a hybrid, born of the same basic factors.

The Production as an Asset

Always remember that, in financial terms, when you undertake the production of a film or a television program, you are creating an asset. Initially, if all the financing for the creation of the asset has been your own, this asset resides unencumbered on the financial records of your company. However, as an independent producer, you will undoubtedly begin to trade in this asset with others. As soon as you do this, you give them some form of interest, lien, or encumbrance in the asset, in return for their financial participation in bringing your project to the screen. This financial participation by third party investors can take several forms, as the following sections will explain.

Equity Investment

A favoured method of film financing in Canada for many years has been by equity investment. Our federal government has ensured that Canadians investing in the production of certified Canadian films will enjoy certain tax advantages based upon this investment. In order to qualify for special tax benefits, the investor must be a qualified Canadian individual or corporation, and the project must be certified as a Canadian production. Later in this chapter, in the Production Financing section, there is a fuller discussion of tax benefits for private investors. (See also Chapter 9 for a discussion of tax shelters and a detailed description of qualification regulations.)

In an equity investment arrangement, a third party financier, the investor, actually acquires an ownership interest in your asset: the film or television program. This ownership interest can represent all or any portion of the asset in question. As part of the sale by the producer to the financier of this ownership interest, the producer is granted by the financier an entitlement to a portion of the revenues and/or profits derived from the commercial exploitation of the film or program.

In general terms, 100 percent of the money gets 50 percent of the action; that is, your investors will receive 100 percent of the revenues generated by the project until they have recouped the full amount of their investment. From then on, they will receive 50 percent of the profits. The producer receives the other 50 percent of the profits. Out of this share, however, the producer must pay any other profit participants, such as performers or the director, who may have acquired profit points in the production and are entitled to a specified percentage of the profits. Remember, profits are those revenues received by the production *after* deducting all the costs of production and distribution.

Broadcast and Distribution Deals

The second component in project financing is based directly upon the revenues that the distribution of the film or program will likely bring in. You, as producer, might enter into distribution licensing agreements with film or television distribution companies that advance cash sums sufficient to enable you to complete production. These cash advances are in effect prepayments of commercial exploitation revenue.

A second form of licence agreement involves a direct relationship between the producer and a broadcast outlet, wherein a licence fee is paid by a broadcaster in return for the right to broadcast the program on a specified number of occasions over a specified length of time on its own broadcast outlets. Such a licence fee is not an advance against future revenue, but rather a payment in consideration of the rights granted. A distributor or a broadcast outlet may make a firm contractual commitment to your project that is not in cash, or at least will not be payable early enough to be available as cash during production. In this instance, a third arrangement is required: a banking transaction that converts the contractual commitment into cash financing sufficient to complete production.

Broadcasters and distributors will also consider equity investment as a mechanism to acquire the rights to your project. Usually this arrangement is made to allow the distributor or broadcaster to supply more funding to the producer than that normally associated with the licence fee or advance, with the opportunity of recouping these additional advances from commercial exploitation revenue.

Fitting Together Financing Components

Needless to say, it is the clever combination of various kinds of financing that ultimately forms the financial structure of any given project. No equity investor is likely to be interested in acquiring an ownership interest in your property without some assurance that it has revenue producing potential. As a practical matter, this means you have to demonstrate to the potential investor that specific contracts with bona fide distributors or broadcasters are already in place, which will generate sufficient revenue for the investor to recoup his or her investment. This is usually a "post-tax" calculation, wherein the tax advantage of making the investment is also taken into account. Before your potential investors can make a decision, you will be required to supply the following specifics of recoupment to them:

a. identity of distributors making guarantees and their track record;
b. amounts of guarantees and when payable;
c. portion payable to investors; and
d. potential for revenue beyond the guarantees, sales fees, or commissions to be deducted from these revenues before payment to investors.

This is how your second kind of financing – the distribution advance or guarantee, and the broadcast licence – comes into play as part of the equity investment scenario. It is necessary for you, as the producer, to secure sufficient minimum distribution revenue guarantees for your project in order to succeed in putting together an equity investment package. It is usually sufficient if revenue guarantees of between 60 percent and 75 percent are acquired. The amount of the guarantee is dependent upon the competitive market situation and other offerings being made at that time to potential investors. A guarantee of 65 percent, for example, assures your investor that he or she will receive 65 percent of the investment back after a specified length of time, as well as tax advantages on the full investment. These revenue guarantees need not be in cash, if they are viewed to be bona fide. On this basis, it is often possible to put together an equity financing package that will generate 100 percent of the cash production financing required.

The Cost of Financing

Once you have arrived at a financial structure, be sure to examine in great detail all of the costs associated with this financing. Include in your calculations the on-going cost of reporting in accordance with your contractual obligations to each of the financiers and profit participants in the film. These costs usually appear after the above-the-line and below-the-line costs in the budget, and do not form part of the calculation of the 10 percent contingency nor of the 6 percent completion bond fee. (Both contingency and completion bond are explained in Chapter 3.) Your financiers will also require an estimate from you as to when you will require various portions of their financial commitment. This so-called "cash flow projection" is a document that should be based directly on your finalized production budget.

Be sure that you can justify each of your estimates in each of the categories, and that they tie in directly either with the contractual obligations you are undertaking, or with normally accepted industry practice as to when specific items are payable. All financiers attempt to advance as little money as possible as late as possible, so you can expect a certain amount of negotiation with them. It always helps to have a solidly documented cash flow projection to fall back on during the course of these negotiations.

Equity financing will tend to increase your budget significantly. The costs can include brokerage fees, which are usually 10 percent of the money raised; costs of issue; legal and accounting fees; trust administration fees; printing (and in Quebec, translation) of the prospectus; and so-called interim financing fees. The interim financing fees relate to the interest costs associated with receiving cash advances at the time of production. Although you may be shooting in the spring, your investors are not likely to write you a cheque until late in the tax year, since they do not realize a tax benefit until the end of the tax year. Because of the spread between the time you need the money and the time you receive it, you must obtain financing from another group, which will lend you the money and charge a fee for providing this interim cash. A commitment from your broker and your distribution contracts will be used as security. Your interim financiers will be repaid from your permanent financing. It should be stressed that none of these equity financing factors is unique to the film business, but rather forms a normal part of the equity financing market place in Canada and other countries.

Your investors' guarantees of payment at a later date also require certain banking mechanisms in order to "discount" the value of these guarantees and convert them into cash financing at the time of production. Telefilm is in the business of undertaking this kind of discounting under certain specified circumstances. They must determine the present-day value of a future contract based on the amounts, date of repayment, and interest rates, in order to calculate the discounted value and how much they will lend you.

Now let's go back to the beginning and examine in more detail some of the steps in making financing arrangements that you as the producer should undertake.

First Steps in Development Financing

How Viable Is Your Project?

We have so far learned that, to finance your production, you will need distribution agreements sufficient to ensure that the tax-shelter-eligible equity investment package you offer will be viewed as workable and interesting by the Canadian investment community. Therefore, your first priority must be to investigate the commercial viability of your project. Are the film and/or television industries interested? Let's examine some of the steps involved in finding out.

First, we assume that you have an idea, either developed by you or acquired from someone else. In either case, and no matter what form the idea may initially take (novel, play, screenplay, etc.), it is imperative that you be able to demonstrate that you control the "movie and allied rights" to this idea. Such a package of rights is normally referred to as "the property". The so-called chain of title to the property, which is explained in Chapter 9, is always a matter of crucial interest to anyone contemplating participating with you financially in any aspect of the production. Ensure from the outset that these rights have been unequivocally granted to you; that you are free to enter into the contractual obligations that will follow; and that you are able to make the representations and warranties that will be required of you as producer. Also be sure that your documentation quickly and clearly demonstrates these facts. (Hiring a lawyer to prepare such a contract just might be a good idea.)

Preparing the Development Budget

A crucial part of the financial structure at this stage will be the preparation of a detailed development budget for the project. This budget should include not only the costs of acquiring and maintaining control of the property, but also the costs associated with the screenwriting, breakdown and budgeting of the production, together with administrative costs such as clerical help for the production itself, legal fees, accounting fees, travel and living expenses, telephone, telex, and so forth.

This budget will have to be approved by each of the development financiers, and normally expenditures will only be permitted by the financiers in categories that they have approved. Think this budget through very carefully. It is often difficult to go back to financiers and request more money for unexpected costs and activities. It immediately makes them feel that they are dealing with a producer who cannot foresee factors that he or she *should* have foreseen. Remember, they are looking to you to control the project in their best interests, and they must be able to trust you to do so. (Chapter 3 tells you more about development budget preparation.)

Discussions with Broadcasters and Distributors

As the package develops and the screenplay reaches complete form, you will be concerning yourself more and more with the distribution potential of your project. Depending upon the market for which your project is destined, you may now be forced to consider the identity of your principal players, together with (perhaps) the identity of your director. At this stage, some projects are developed with a particular performer or director in mind. Although this is not normally the case, the involvement of such key personnel can sometimes be essential to the commitment of sufficient financing or distribution guarantees. This is the stage at which discussions must begin with these distributors and broadcasters so that you can tailor the package to suit them. Use their expertise and involve them intimately in the development of the project. Such foresight will pay dividends in the end.

Development Financing Sources

Approaching Telefilm Canada

It is highly probable that, in order to undertake step one, the investigation of your project's commercial viability, you have already made a cash outlay. This has been your first development expense. Many will follow. It is now time for you to take the second step: examining the development financing resources available to you as a Canadian producer. First and foremost on your list must be Telefilm Canada (formerly the Canadian Film Development Corporation). This federal government agency has been instrumental in the development of virtually every Canadian-originated film and television program since its founding some twenty years ago. Telefilm has a comprehensive development program, and is, in effect, willing to participate in as much as 50 percent of all the costs associated with developing your project, if you and your project qualify for their assistance.

Of equal importance is the *way* Telefilm is willing to participate: loans made to the production company are to be repaid, together with certain fees, on the first day of principal photography. By implication, should there never be a first day of principal photography, Telefilm's only option is to exercise its right as lienholder against the property. That is, Telefilm would be entitled to take possession of your property if you have failed to live up to the specified contractual commitments.

Telefilm is fairly specific about the kinds of development activities that qualify for its financial assistance, and the criteria to be met by a qualified project. It is imperative that the first thing you do is discuss your project with one of their representatives, making sure that you fully understand their rules and regulations. Then make a comprehensive written application to Telefilm, as specified on the many forms they will be happy to supply to you. Telefilm can be your greatest ally and supporter during this very difficult stage of development and preproduction. Their support is not without its price, however, which often takes the form of frustration with some of Telefilm's bureaucratic attitudes and procedures. In general, though, as long as the producer ensures that good will and good faith prevail, their support will always be there.

Provincial Aid

Depending upon your province of residence, a number of provincial governments also support the development of film and television properties. The Alberta Motion Picture Development Corporation has a strong assistance program, well financed and well run. The newly opened Ontario Film Development Corporation has a comprehensive screenplay development program for both television and feature films, with significant funding. The Société genérale du cinéma du Québec has for a number of years been supporting Quebec filmmakers with both a strong script assistance program and the possibility of equity financing and loans at the production stage. Manitoba has also developed a film assistance program that is currently being expanded. (These programs are discussed in somewhat more detail in Chapter 2.)

A certain amount of care should be taken when attempting to blend Telefilm involvement with provincial government assistance programs, so that the two do not end up running at cross purposes. Telefilm and the various provincial organizations have worked out a modus vivendi based upon their experience with past projects. Be careful about such items as priority of security interest to your property (that is, who among your development investors has the first right to seize your property if you don't repay your loans), entitlement to recoupment of their development loans, and credit. Be sure to inform both Telefilm and any provincial organization you approach of your intention to involve the other. In this way, any later conflicts can likely be avoided.

Distributors or Broadcasters

Development financing you require will often come from broadcaster involvement (if a television program is being developed) or distributor involvement (in the case of a theatrical motion picture). In fact, a certain minimum financial commitment to the development of your package by either the broadcaster or a Canadian film distributor is a prerequisite for Telefilm Canada's financial aid to your development budget.

Private Development Financing

Ideally, you would wish to have a relationship with a source of private financing committed to your project and to you personally as a producer, in order to ensure that you could always "step up to the wicket" and match the dollars available from Telefilm, broadcasters, distributors, and others.

Many clever schemes have been developed by many producers over the years to interest private money in this form of risk investment. It *is* a risk because, after all, the expenditure of these development funds does not ensure that the project will ultimately be produced. Such plans and schemes have always included the preferential treatment of these ground-level investors once the project is completed. Such treatment can take the form of additional profit point entitlement for these investors in any completed project, assuring them an increased percentage of the profits generated, or an actual repayment to them on first day of principal photography of an amount greater than their original investment and any interest thereon. Remember, however, that these investors are financing *you* in *your* participation in development costs. Therefore, in all probability, whatever benefits are to be payable to them will not be payable out of the production itself, but rather out of your entitlement to fees, revenue, and profit from the project.

In no scenario is it likely that you as producer will get off scot-free. Any form of investment always requires that the principals be involved financially as well. Be prepared not only to put in a lot of time and effort, but also to put up significant financial resources of your own, as may be required by your contractual relationship with Telefilm and other financiers.

Production Financing

The Production Budget

By the time you begin preproduction stages, if the creative processes have continued to keep pace with your financial packaging, you should have at least a first draft screenplay to show your financiers. It is crucial that at this stage a qualified assistant director and/or production manager review your screenplay, break it down into its component parts, plan a well-thought-through shooting schedule, and then prepare a detailed production budget. Initially, this budget should concern itself with all the "below-the-line" items: the direct labour and material costs associated with preproduction, production, and postproduction. (Chapter 3 gives more detail on these items, and Chapter 5 discusses your general responsibilities during the preproduction, production, and postproduction phases.)

One of the first questions you will be asked by any distributor or broadcast outlet seriously considering your project is your anticipated production cost. No doubt, you will quickly come to the conclusion that your target amount should match the amount of money your type of production can logically raise in the market place. However, make your first pass at the budget an honest assessment of the real costs associated with producing your screenplay properly. Add to this the costs associated with the above-the-line elements: specifically, your story and script costs, your own producer fee, fees payable to the director, and any allowance you wish to make for stars over and above the normal scale rates for performers. Finally, it is normal and accepted in the production industry to allow for a contingency of 10 percent of all the above- and below-the-line items, and normally one would also provide for a premium payable to a completion bonder equal to approximately 6 percent of the above- and below-the-line budget. The completion bond insurance allows you to assure your financiers that should it become impossible, due to unforeseen circumstances, to complete the project for the amount of money committed to it by the financiers, the completion bonder will see that the project is finished and delivered in its originally contemplated form. (Chapter 3 has more on this subject.)

Your production budget should also make certain allowances for the costs that will ultimately be associated with the marketing of the film. These "direct sales expense" items should be estimated, based upon your experience to date and the costs you have been incurring in order to market the film to the various distributors and broadcast outlets you have in mind. Remember that it will likely be necessary at a future stage to include certain public relations activities, the printing of material describing your project, and your travel out of town, either to film markets or to meetings with various distribution companies. Once again, a consultative meeting with Telefilm Canada's distribution department will undoubtedly stand you in good stead when making this estimate. Be sure that your budget includes *all* the costs to be incurred, including the fees and costs associated with the financing itself.

Be prepared to indicate which of the items within your budget could be deferred to a later date for payment. So-called "service deferrals" are often required of the producer and form part of the equity investment you are bringing to the table when negotiating with your financiers. Determine what within your budget can be paid for at a later date; that is, from revenue at a specific time. Can you, the writer, or the director defer part of your fees? Will the laboratory or the film equipment supplier accept payment from revenue, when and if it is available? In general, approach those who are closely committed to the project with you.

The Negotiation Stage

At this stage, you have a viable package, in which distributors and/or broadcast outlets have expressed great interest. It is *relatively* easy to get to this stage. It's the next stage that most often proves to be the undoing of many promising packages. Let's look at some of the factors to watch out for.

In the instance of a broadcast outlet, be sure that you are in a position to measure the fair market value of your property, and to determine whether or not the offer that has been made to you by the broadcaster conforms to that fair market value. Telefilm can be very helpful in this regard, because they have been party to virtually every broadcast agreement entered into by a Canadian producer with a Canadian broadcaster for a Canadian television program. They are willing to advise and, indeed, become actively involved with you in the negotiating of such a broadcast agreement. In any event, their financial involvement will be contingent upon their approval of such contracts. Telefilm is also in a position to advise you on the fairness of the distribution agreements you may be entering into with distributors, both Canadian and foreign, for the distribution of your property theatrically, on home video, and in every other respect, both in Canada and around the world.

In both the instances noted above, bear in mind that your need for financing in cash as opposed to contractual commitment for cash to be paid later will go a long way toward determining the terms and conditions you will be able to negotiate. Needless to say, any company required to pay to you its commitment in cash during the course of production and before the delivery of the program is going to ensure that it receives greater benefits than it might otherwise require. Money is a valuable commodity, after all.

The ability to negotiate these terms and conditions so as to arrive at a contractual relationship that is fair and equitable, not only for the distributor but equally for yourself and for the financiers of the balance of the production costs, is one of the trickiest parts of the packaging process. As mentioned, Telefilm can play a very significant advisory role. However, you should also consider retaining legal counsel or other consultative representation at this stage, to ensure that you are taking full advantage of the negotiating skills and knowledge of the film and television industry that are available to the producer, albeit at a fee.

Forms of Canadian Television Financing

Normally, the broadcaster (either a network or an individual station) will license the program for a specified number of airings over a defined period of time; for example, two runs over two years. For this privilege, they will pay a licence fee that varies from broadcaster to broadcaster. For example, in 1986, the CBC was paying $100,000 licence fees per half-hour episode of programming; $500,000 for a made-for-television movie; and $250,000 for a theatrical movie. At CTV, the licence fee range was $30,000 to $95,000 for half-hour shows, and up to $250,000 for movies of any description. Individual stations pay a fraction of this amount. This licence fee can be used as a source of production financing either by being paid to the producer during the course of production, or by being promised in a firm contractual format that the producer can "bank" at Telefilm or a private lending institution, or use as first revenues applied against equity investors' investment.

The other form of broadcaster participation is equity investment, which normally happens when a broadcaster is willing to pay more for a program than its normal licence fee. The broadcaster expects to get a return on this augmented amount of money by recouping from other commercial exploitation revenue.

Canadian Theatrical and Home Video Distribution Advances

For certain types of programming, particularly films with a theatrical possibility, Canadian theatrical distributors will sometimes make financial commitments in the form of distribution advances or revenue guarantees which, if not appropriate for use as direct financing to the production, can still be used as revenue guarantees to attract private and other sources of financing. Similarly, Canadian television program exporters are becoming more and more aggressive at foreign markets, representing Canadian productions of all sorts. These program exporters are now beginning to be a source of revenue guarantees or export advances.

Government Sources of Financing

Telefilm Financing. Let us assume that you now have specific offers on the table from distributors and/or broadcast outlets for the distribution of your film. It is now time to finalize your production financing arrangements with Telefilm. If it has been involved financially with you in development to date, Telefilm is aware of every aspect of your package. You now wish to move with them to the production financing level.

Telefilm has two specific programs that provide for their equity investment in your project: the Canadian Broadcast Program Development Fund (with approximately $65 million) and the Canadian Feature Film Development Fund (with approximately $33 million). The program for which you qualify will, in the first instance, be determined by the identity of the medium in which you will first distribute your film or program. Each is capable of supplying up to 33 percent of your cash needs, and in some exceptional cases, even 49 percent; to a maximum of $1.5 million. There are objective and subjective criteria to be met. Be prepared to review and defend every aspect of your package as part of this crucial negotiation. Of significance is Telefilm's willingness to allow Canadian private investors, who may constitute the balance of your equity financing, to recoup their investment in some preference to Telefilm's recoupment. Negotiate this one carefully with both Telefilm and any private equity groups you may be approaching.

It is now time for you to make a choice as to the financing method that will be employed to bring in the balance of production financing.

Provincial Financing. The Ontario Film Development Corporation will invest up to $500,000 in projects by Ontario-based producers with a broadcaster or distributor commitment. Low-budget productions (under $3 million) are preferred. In addition, Ontario production and distribution companies qualify for the Small Business Development Corporations Program (SBDC), created to encourage private development. Investors in these companies may receive a rebate of 25 percent on their investments.

The Société générale du cinéma du Québec will invest up to 60 percent of the budget to a maximum of $500,000 for feature films. It will also match broadcasters' investments up to 33 and one third percent of the budget, to a maximum of $150,000 for made-for-television movies, or a maximum of $250,000 for series or mini-series. Distributor or broadcaster commitments are required.

Film Manitoba will invest up to $200,000 in eligible Manitoba productions.

National Film Board of Canada. The NFB has a long track record of creative excellence, and their recent involvement with the private sector and co-production makes them an important potential participant in your production. If you think your project might in any way interest them, talk to one of their representatives about the possibility. The NFB works with long lead times, and so you should approach them about co-production at a very early stage of development.

Private Financing – Where to Look

Initially, you should investigate those companies in Canada that have traditionally been involved in the equity financing of film projects. If you are able set up meetings with these people, review with them your package and the financial commitments already made, in order to gain from them both their commitment to complete your financing package and information about the final form your distribution contracts should take to be acceptable to them. This is perhaps the most complex aspect of the financing structure. There are so many tax regulations and investor best interests involved that the producer will often feel that he or she is tiptoeing through a mine field. One false step might cause the entire deal to blow up! If you will be raising money on the equity market, you will either have to associate yourself directly with a broker who is licensed to do so, or with another producing company that may act as your executive producer and assist you in the packaging of the financing elements.

There is no limit as to the variety of private investment sources. Many productions have used private investment from rich uncles, business associates, and friends of the producer. It is important to note that the current Capital Cost Allowance rules permit revenue guarantees to be promoted as part of the prospectus or offering memorandum; indeed, such presales seem to be expected and are generally acceptable to sophisticated investors. "Revenue guarantees" refers to the revenues from a presale (usually to a broadcaster), which are not used to pay production costs but instead are reserved to be applied as revenue that ends up in the hands of the investors. Investment dealers who specialize in tax shelter investments for this type of offering will only become involved on the understanding that the producer will be able to provide as much as 50 percent to 75 percent coverage of an investment with presale or distribution contracts in place before the unit investment purchase occurs.

Private investment in Canadian films is encouraged by the 100 percent Capital Cost Allowance tax shelter for investments in a film or television production that qualifies under the Income Tax regulations as a certified Canadian film. The tax deferral benefits allow private investors to deduct their investments, over a two-year period, from their taxable income, thus lowering their effective tax rate. Eligible productions must be certified Canadian: in general, the producer must be Canadian; 6 "points" must be obtained for Canadian key creative personnel; and 75 percent of costs must be spent in Canada or on Canadians. (For more details on the certification system, which is administered by the Department of Communications, see the regulations at the end of this chapter.)

Public Offering. One way of securing private investment is by a public offering through an established brokerage house. It is designed to raise a large amount of money through the issuance of units of ownership in a film or television production. These units could range in value from $5000 to perhaps $25,000 and their total would equal the production budget. The budget would include financing, legal, and brokerage costs, which can amount to 30 percent of the production budget. The units must be offered via a prospectus that has passed the scrutiny of the appropriate provincial securities commission, and they must be sold by a registered securities broker.

The normal way for an investor to acquire these units is by making a cash contribution, which can be as little as 5 percent of the units' value, and providing a promissory note secured by a letter of credit for the balance of the purchase price, payable no later than four years hence. Obviously, in preparing a prospectus, the producer must seek legal counsel as well as a firm commitment from the broker embarking on this course of financing. The production's principal photography *must* be completed by the end of the tax year in which the units are sold.

Private Placement. This form of investment is similar to the public offering, except that the investment document is an offering memorandum (describing the project, the producer, and all the financial and other business aspects of the production and the investment) which can be prepared and sold directly by the producer. The producer may approach no more than 75 prospective investors, and may sell to no more than 50 of them. There are still regulatory requirements and statutory declarations required, but the regulation process is less onerous and complicated than for a public offering. The units sold can vary in value from $5000 to $100,000 or more. The investors, as with a public offering, acquire an ownership interest in the film or television property. This form of investment has become more frequently used in recent years.

Goods and Services Investments from Production Companies

Certain equipment suppliers, laboratories, and video editing facilities sometime will agree to contribute a portion of the facilities or services used to make a production, as an investment in that production. In such a case, a supplier or laboratory might receive a payment equal to its out-of-pocket costs as part of the production budget and may be prepared to accept an equity investment position in return for the remainder of its contribution.

Industry Deferrals

It is not uncommon for producers, artists, and technicians to defer part of their fees as an investment in the production, to be repaid out of revenue as and when it is generated. This source of revenue should *only* be considered when all other possible sources of funding have been exhausted. Successful producers have discovered that this is truly financing of last resort, because everyone would like to be paid for the work they do. Producers and production companies that wish to produce more than one film or television program need producer's fees to fund their continuing operations and to pay themselves during the time they are developing their next project.

Contra Deals Suppliers of props, vehicles, and accommodation will sometimes agree to provide these items or services in return for a promotional mention in the credits of the film or program. Obviously, for some productions made far away from city centres, the saving on travel and accommodation costs could be substantial. There are several companies that specialize in the arrangement of such "contra deals" for services. As well, these companies can sometimes arrange product placement in a film in return for a cash payment to the producer. This form of advertising is generally only applicable to big-budget films (such as the product placement of Reese's Pieces in *E.T.*). However, on a smaller scale, in certain specialized circumstances, such arrangements can be a source of funding for a resourceful producer.

Corporate Sponsorship and Barter Deals Often, for high-profile projects, serious corporate sponsors can be attracted to invest in the production as part of a barter deal with the broadcaster who will later be showing the production. In such a case, the broadcaster provides cost-free commercial time in which the corporate sponsor can run its own advertising, in exchange for the sponsor's investment in the production. This sort of corporate sponsorship needs to be worked out on a three-way basis by producer, sponsor, and broadcaster.

Foreign Financing for Canadian Productions

The largest market in the world for films and television programs is the United States. In fact, the U.S. represents approximately 70 percent of the revenues earned outside of Canada. The American market is very different from the markets in other countries, which usually have government-supported feature film industries and broadcast systems. Film and television in the United States are, by and large, corporate entrepreneurial activities.

There are two major sources of financing for your production in the United States; one is for theatrical production and the other is for television.

American Sources of Financing

Theatrical Distributors. The major American studios and some American independent distributors have worldwide distribution systems. They are the largest source of investment in high-budget Canadian feature films. Their investment, in most cases, is in the form of a distribution advance (that is, subject to both interest and profit participation in return for their investment). They normally request *all* rights in *all* media in *all* countries; however, the Canadian producer should be aware that, to receive money from Telefilm, the Canadian rights must be retained by the producer to be given to a Canadian distributor or broadcaster. Large distribution advances from American majors are not easy to come by and are only made on properties that the American distributor feels can be successful in the American and world markets.

Major benefits of this type of financing are: guaranteed access to the American market; the majors' ability to devise and carry out an aggressive advertising sales campaign; and ready access to videocassette distributors and American pay-TV networks. Of course there are strings attached to such deals. A producer will be asked to cede control, particularly in key creative areas such as casting and the choice of the director, editor, composer, and so on. There can be strong financial controls attendant upon investment from majors, and their investment may be costly, because of the interest charges that are often levied.

When dealing with majors, the producer hardly ever has to defer his or her fees; however, profit participation is seldom realized. The costs and interest charges often have the effect of reducing the producer's effective investment in the project and of discouraging other possible investors who do not wish their investment to be so diluted and delayed.

American Television Presale Licences. Presale commitments are rarely given to Canadian productions by the commercial networks in the United States. More commonly, American pay-TV channels, such as Showtime, Disney, and HBO, make presale licence or equity investment commitments in Canadian-initiated programs. PBS (the Public Broadcasting System) and its member stations and related program consortiums sometimes make similar commitments. American broadcaster participation can be a significant source of financing. Your deals with them can be structured in such a way as to involve Canadian investment as well, making it attractive for the American broadcaster. The latter can acquire the programming for a lower cost than a similar American program, because the Canadian producer's involvement means Canadian funding for a portion of the production budget. American broadcasters are interested in all formats of programming, from series to specials.

The advantage of this source of financing is that it is firm and securely bankable. As well, American involvement in the project guarantees exposure to a much wider market for Canadian projects. On the other hand, there are always strings attached to American broadcaster participation. Like all other end users, they will want approval of key creative elements, including your budget. You must also be aware of potential U.S./Canada border signal spillover problems. In cases where an American broadcast signal can also be received in Canada, and vice versa, the signal may be in conflict with the broadcast rights that have been sold to the broadcaster on the other side of the border. Therefore, in negotiating your contracts with the broadcasters, you must be careful to ensure either simulcast broadcast rights to the Canadian and American broadcasters, or to negotiate "windows" of use so that the broadcasts do not overlap.

Other Foreign Sources of Financing

Presales. Presales may be made directly to a foreign broadcaster (which are most often the Northern European broadcasters in Germany, France, and the United Kingdom). These sales are often used as part of the financing, and normally require that the producers or their sales agent make the rounds of each country in person. With the notable exception of the ITV network in Britain, these broadcasters are generally government owned.

Sometimes, a foreign broadcaster who has purchased the licence to broadcast your production may also be obtaining the rights to sell it in other territories. A foreign broadcaster's licence may also include the rights to make sales to other media, such as home video. The Canadian producer should be aware that such sales may risk foreclosing on other possible later sales. Foreign presales are, by and large, for dramatic or children's material. (More about sales to foreign broadcasters may be found in Chapter 7 by Jan Rofekamp.)

Co-production Treaties. Canada has negotiated official co-production treaty agreements with France, Italy, the U.K., Germany, Israel, Belgium, Algeria, and Spain, and is constantly working to negotiate new treaties with other countries. A film that qualifies as an official co-production under the terms of one of these treaties, whether it is a theatrical or television production (most of the treaties started as theatrical treaties and are now being broadened to include television productions), has the benefit of qualifying as an "official film of dual nationality." This makes it eligible for government financing and investor benefits in both countries.

The primary benefit of official co-production status is that potential revenues are enhanced with access to two domestic markets. The producers also have greater flexibility in selecting their key creative personnel and cast from both countries involved. The percentage of personnel from each participating country should, by and large, parallel the percentage of financing generated from each country.

There are, of course, difficulties associated with official co-productions. There is yet another bureaucratic procedure that the producer must familiarize himself with. Each treaty has its own set of restrictions and regulations concerning the use of foreign talent. You must always be aware that you are dealing with two regulatory bodies, not one. You will also require a lot more legal work.

Joint Ventures. A production undertaken with a partner in another country that does not have a co-production treaty with Canada is called a joint venture. The most common joint ventures are between Canada and the United States. A joint venture may qualify as Canadian if it meets CRTC regulations and their definition of Canadian content. However, a joint venture does not usually qualify for Capital Cost Allowance benefits or Telefilm investment, unless it meets the criteria required of indigenous Canadian productions. Telefilm may, however, invest in a percentage of the Canadian portion of the financing, under certain circumstances.

As with official co-productions, there are benefits and disadvantages of joint ventures. A major benefit is the simplification of the bureaucratic procedures associated with official co-productions. One difficulty of international joint ventures is that the projects need to be attractive, from a content point of view, to two countries. Producers often find that their efforts result in a project which is too hybrid for its own good. It may be an artistic and / or commercial failure because unrealistic "deal" points have been imposed (as a hypothetical example, a foreign star unconvincingly playing a Saskatchewan famer) in order qualify it as a domestic production in the countries of both joint venture partners. As with indigenous Canadian productions, most of the key creative personnel must be Canadian and 75 percent of the money must be spent in Canada or on Canadians, eliminating a major benefit enjoyed by the official co-productions.

Twinning (Pairing). Recently, some producers have attempted to overcome some of the problems associated with international joint ventures by "twinning" or "pairing" two productions. In the twinning process, each country involved originates a production which is indigenous to that country and is contractually linked to the other production. The onus is on the Canadian producer to sell both the Canadian and the other project in Canada. If Telefilm investment is desired, a Canadian broadcaster or distributor must be committed. The Telefilm investment, and any other investment, can be cross-collateralized across the two productions involved. Both productions will also qualify as Canadian when submitted as a package to the CRTC. Only the Canadian production, however, will qualify for CCA benefits.

Twinning ensures that the productions need not be compromised by artificial casting and crewing in order to qualify them for the benefits available in each country. However, the producers must ensure that both projects are attractive to both markets. Ideally, the projects should be similar in size and budget, and should commence production at roughly the same time. Investment in twinning packages is often conditional on both parts of the package actually being produced.

Successful producers have discovered that there is no limit to the range and number of financing sources available to the creative producer. When the probability of finding successful financing appears daunting, new producers can take some solace from the fact that it *is* possible – the sheer volume of recent Canadian production attests to this.

Appendix: Capital Cost Allowance Certification Requirements

Legislative Requirements

The following are excerpts from the Income Tax Regulations, subsections 1104(2) and 1104(10) which define the requirements of the certification process.

Certification Requirements: Subsection 1104(2) and (10)

1. Features

"Certified feature production", in respect of a particular taxation year, means a motion picture film or videotape certified by the Minister of Communications to be a film or tape of not less than 75 minutes running time in respect of which all photography, taping or art work specifically required for the production thereof and all film or tape editing therefore were commenced after May 25, 1976, certified by him to be a film or tape in respect of which the principal photography or taping thereof was commenced before the end of the particular taxation year or was completed no later than 60 days after the end of the particular taxation year and certified by him to be

a. a film or tape, the production of which is contemplated in a co-production agreement entered into between Canada and another country, or
b. a film or tape in respect of which
  i. the individual who performed the duties of producer was a Canadian,
  ii. the Minister of Communications has allotted not less than an aggregate of six units of pro-

duction, not less than two of which were allotted by virtue of clause (A) or (B) and not less than one of which was allotted by virtue of clause (C) or (D), for individuals who provided services in respect of the film or tape, in the following manner:

A. for the director, two units of production,

B. for the screenwriter, two units of production,

C. for the actor or actress in respect of whose services for the film or tape the highest remuneration was paid or payable, one unit of production,

D. for the actor or actress in respect of whose services for the film or tape the second highest remuneration was paid or payable, one unit of production,

E. for the art director, one unit of production,

F. for the director of photography, one unit of production,

G. for the music composer, one unit of production,

H. for the picture editor, one unit of production,

shall be allotted, provided the individual in respect of such allotment was a Canadian,

iii. not less than 75 per cent of the aggregate of the remuneration paid or payable to persons for services provided in respect of the film or tape (other than remuneration paid or payable to, or in respect of, the individuals referred to in subparagraphs i and ii or remuneration paid or payable for processing and final preparation of the film or tape) was paid or payable to, or in respect of services provided by, Canadians, and

iv. not less than 75 per cent of the aggregate of all costs incurred for processing and final preparation of the film or tape, including laboratory work, sound re-recording, sound editing and picture editing (other than remuneration paid or payable, to, or in respect of, the individuals referred to in subparagraphs i, ii and iii) was incurred in respect of services provided in Canada,

other than a film or tape
c. acquired after the day that is the earlier of
   i. the day of its first commercial use, and
   ii. 12 months after the day the principal photography or taping thereof is completed,
d. acquired by a taxpayer who has not paid in cash, as of the end of the particular taxation year, to the person from whom he acquired the film or tape, at least 20 per cent of the capital cost to the taxpayer of the film or tape as of the end of the year,
e. acquired by a taxpayer who has issued in payment or part payment thereof, a bond, debenture, bill, note, mortgage, hypothec or similar obligation in respect of which an amount is not due until a time that is more than four years after the end of the taxation year in which the taxpayer acquired the film or tape,
f. acquired from a non-resident, or
g. in respect of which certification under the definition has been revoked by the Minister of Communications as provided in paragraph (10)(b).

2. Shorts

"Certified short production", in respect of a particular taxation year, means a motion picture film or video-tape certified by the Minister of Communications to be a film or tape of less than 75 minutes running time in respect of which all photography, taping or art work specifically required for the production thereof and all film or tape editing therefore were commenced after May 25, 1976, certified by him to be a film or taping thereof was commenced before the end of the particular taxation year or was completed no later than 60 days after the end of the particular year and certified by him to be

a. a film or tape that would be certifiable under the definition "certified feature production" if that definition were read without reference to the words "of not less than 75 minutes running time"*, or
b. a film or tape in respect of which
    i. the individual who performed the duties of producer was a Canadian, and
    ii. not less than 75 per cent of the aggregate of all costs incurred in respect of producing the film or tape, including remuneration and processing, was paid or payable to, or in respect of services provided by, Canadians,

other than a film or tape
c. acquired after the day that is the earlier of
    i. the day of its first commercial use, and
    ii. 12 months after the day the principal photography or taping thereof is completed,
d. acquired by a taxpayer who has not paid in cash, as of the end of the particular taxation year, to the person from whom he acquired the film or tape, at least 20 per cent of the capital cost to the taxpayer of the film or tape as of the end of the year,
e. acquired by a taxpayer who has issued in payment or part payment thereof, a bond, debenture, bill, note, mortgage, hypothec or similar obligation in respect of which an amount is not due until a time that is more than four years after the end of the taxation year in which the taxpayer acquired the film or tape,

* In the event that a film/videotape of less than 75 minutes does not meet the criteria of a certified short production, a producer may apply using the definition of a feature production.

f. acquired from a non-resident, or

g. in respect of which certification under this definition has been revoked by the Minister of Communications as provided in paragraph (10)(b);

10. *[Definitions]* For the purposes of subsection 1100(21) and the definitions "certified feature film", "certified feature production" and "certified short production" in subsection 2;

    a. "Canadian", means an individual who was, at all relevant times,

        i. a Canadian citizen as defined in the Citizenship Act, or

        ii. a permanent resident within the meaning of the Immigration Act, 1976, other than a permanent resident who has been ordinarily resident in Canada for more than one year after the time at which he first became eligible to apply for Canadian citizenship;

    b. a motion picture film or videotape that has been certified by:

        i. the Secretary of State; or

        ii. the Minister of Communications

    as a certified feature film, certified feature production or certified short production, as the case may be, may have its certification revoked by the Minister of Communications where an incorrect statement was made in the furnishing of information for the purpose of obtaining that certification and a certification that has been so revoked is void from the time of its issue;

    c. "remuneration" does not include an amount determined by reference to the amount of income from a motion picture film or videotape;

    c. 1. "revenue guarantee" means a contract or other arrangement under the terms of which a taxpayer has right to receive a minimum rental revenue or other fixed revenue in respect of a right to the use,

in any manner whatever, of a certified feature film,
certified feature production or certified short production;

c. 2. a screenwriter shall be deemed to be an individual who is a Canadian where

    i. each individual involved in the preparation of
the screenplay is a Canadian, or

    ii. the principal screenwriter is an individual
who is a Canadian and

        A. the screenplay for the motion picture film
or videotape is based upon a work authored
by a Canadian,

        B. copyright in the work subsists in Canada,
and

        C. the work is published in Canada;

d. "unit of production" means a measure used by the
Minister of Communications in determining the
weight to be given for each individual Canadian
referred to in subparagraph (b)(ii) of the definition
"certified feature production" in subsection (2)
who provides services in respect of a motion picture film or videotape; and

e. where each individual who performed a service in
respect of a motion picture film or videotape as
the

    i. director,

    ii. screenwriter,

    iii. actor or actress in respect of whose services
for the film or tape the highest remuneration
was paid or payable,

    iv. actor or actress in respect of whose services
for the film or tape the second highest remuneration was paid or payable,

    v. art director,

    vi. director of photography,

    vii. music composer, or

    viii. picture editor

was a Canadian, the Minister of Communications
shall be deemed to have allotted six units of

production in respect of the film or tape for the purpose of the definition "certified feature production" in subsection (2)

Section I is applicable in respect of a motion picture film or videotape, the principal photography or taping of which commenced after 1981.

CHAPTER FIVE

Preproduction, Production, and Postproduction

by Martin Harbury and Bob Wertheimer

*M**ARTIN HARBURY has been in the film business for eleven years. He has produced two television special dramas:* Clown White *(fully sponsored by Trans Canada Telephone System) and* Hockey Night. *He has had two books published on wild horses and produced several smaller films. Recently he produced and directed a half-hour television documentary,* The Making of Anne of Green Gables. *He has also just completed production of a one-hour TV drama* Counter Play *and, as Executive Producer, a feature documentary on comic books, with Ron Mann. Additionally, Martin Harbury is on several industry committees, as well as serving on the Board of Directors of the Academy of Canadian Cinema & Television.*

*B**OB WERTHEIMER'S production credits are legion – he has worked on over 20 Canadian feature films, including* Meatballs, The Brood, Atlantic City, *and* The Haunting of Hamilton High. *Active within the industry, he is currently on the National Executive Board of the Directors Guild of Canada.*

No matter what type of film you may be about to produce, most of the planning principles are the same. In this chapter, we will attempt to cover all of the many stages and factors to be considered, planned for, and achieved in an independent dramatic film production. If you are mounting a less complex production, the areas that do not apply to you should become fairly self-evident. On the other hand, if you are mounting a more complex production than that contemplated in this chapter, and you are not already an experienced producer, we suggest quite strongly that you reconsider whether you are ready to do so. Almost certainly, you are not.

The Stages of Production

Whether the film you are going to produce is an industrial, a documentary, or a drama of any length, you should understand that preproduction, production, and postproduction are three distinct phases. Each phase has different concerns and priorities, as well as its own specific objectives.

What's Preproduction?

In current usage, preproduction is certainly the least definable phase. As reference to any trade paper will reveal, some films have been in "prep" for several years. (This early and often protracted stage of preproduction is also called the development or negotiation phase. Normally it is considered that the development phase is over when you have secured the financing commitments you need to produce your project.) Films with some complicated production aspects (particularly unusual special effects) may be in prep for months. Most dramatic films, however, prep for a few weeks, the length of time being dictated by budget size and script requirements. During this period of time, activities may include:

a. financial arrangements, including: preparing the budget, establishing a company structure and arranging separate incorporation; and later: finalizing financing contracts, making cash-flow adjustments and arrangements, and placing bonds of tens or even hundreds of thousands of dollars;

b. hiring personnel, including: casting, crewing, negotiating with stars, arranging insurance, negotiating deals and contracts with unions and guilds, and arranging work permits for non-Canadians under the Federal Immigration Statutes;

c. logistical arrangements, including: preparing breakdown and boards, shot lists and storyboards (these will be defined and discussed later in the chapter); carrying out location searches, building sets in studios or backlots, acquiring or creating props and costumes, arranging travel, accommodation and catering for large numbers of people, and renting crew and picture vehicles.

Even this list is not exhaustive, although it should give you a broad impression of the variety and complexity of activities that the producer must oversee at this stage. Later in the chapter we will return to these tasks in more detail, since every step of prep is so vital to what will follow.

What's Production?

The preproduction phases are over and production begins when everyone has been hired, schedules and locations are locked, the money is in place, and everyone is working towards the same end. Shooting is underway. From here on, we believe that it is the producer's job to stand back as much as possible, and trust in the team that he or she has selected. Nevertheless, the producer must monitor the situation constantly, to make sure that they are working smoothly together.

The producer must tread a fine line between, on the one hand, allowing creativity to run rampant, with its inevitable, dire consequences, and on the other hand, firing people or throwing tantrums every time things go a little awry. An atmosphere of fear and tension is totally inconducive to the creative process. More than anyone else, the producer can create the environment that will determine the quality of the final film. It is a significant responsibility.

Under ideal conditions, when the right mix of people is working together on a project in which all of them have confidence, a high level of communication and trust is established. In these circumstances, the fortunate producer will be warned of impending problems and, with enough time and expert advice, will be able to take the right steps to correct them. However, if there is an uneasy, mistrustful atmosphere on the project, or if the producer is not readily accessible for consultation, problems can worsen until they cost a lot of money to rectify or, in the worst cases, result in lawsuits and / or physical injury.

As an analogy to the producer's job during production, imagine riding a surfboard along the crest of a tidal wave, with another, bigger one just behind you. Stay calm, look calm, and concentrate.

What's Postproduction?

A rule of thumb of postproduction is that you're on your own, not only because your entire production crew are now working on their next film, but also because even if you budgeted for postproduction co-ordinators or other help, you may no longer be able to afford them. And so, even though the tidal waves have passed, you must keep running for higher ground.

Your editors, with constant supervision from your director – "Go back to the outtakes (the discarded pieces of film), I *know* he / she did it better!" – spend their time trying to make sense out of everything that's usable. They put the scenes and shots together to tell the story, while meeting your stringent deadlines. Your own priorities, apart from making sure that the editor has a chance of meeting those deadlines, include arranging for the stages that must follow: the rough-cut and fine-cut screenings, the music, the sound editing, effects, Foley, ADR or looping, mixing, negative cutting, slash prints, titles, opticals, answer print timing, interpositives and internegatives or CRIs, versioning, video transfers and dupes (we will discuss these technical terms at greater length later in the chapter), as well as screenings, premieres, publicity, and delivery deadlines.

At the same time, you are probably taking care of audit requirements and Canadian content certification, retrieving performance bonds from the guilds and unions (the bonds were posted to guarantee their members would be paid); closing off the various accounts, arguing with locations about late charges and damages, and with vehicle rental companies about accident claims and parking tickets; selling off props, wardrobe, and other such minor irritants; as well as trying to develop your next property – and plan a vacation!

While the greater part of what will be discussed in the following pages relates most specifically to larger dramatic productions, we hope that the topics covered will help the reader through most production situations he or she may encounter. It may also help to remember that this is an industry in which nobody knows anything for sure, and that even the most meticulous planning can never prepare you for every eventuality. There is no substitute for experience and the acquired nose for impending disaster. As much as anything else, producing successfully implies an instinct for when to make the inevitable compromises, while leaving yourself enough time and resources to make the result look as if no compromise were involved.

Preproduction

Company Structure and Separate Incorporation

Although there are no rules, it is probably true to say that most feature-length films are produced through companies especially incorporated for an individual production. The purpose, simply enough, is to streamline company structure and bank accounts and to reduce liability. Thus, when the production is over,

you can simply close the books and start over. This structure is even more important when a public stock offering is floated, since it allows the investors' ownership of the completed film to be clearly limited to the company's sole asset. Most often, the new company will be a numbered company or one that bears the name of the film being produced, established by the principals of the parent producing company with officers and signing authorities often separate from the parent. The system, although not obligatory, certainly simplifies the process, allowing for a structure to be established that best suits the needs of a given production and its financing fabric. (For more about the incorporation process, see Chapter 9.)

Preproduction Financing

The point at which the development phase ends and preproduction commences is somewhat nebulous. The various possibilities and limitations of development financing are described elsewhere in this book (particularly in Chapter 4). The nature of the production and the sources of financing will most often dictate how much can (or must) be achieved in development and how much may be deferred to the preproduction phase. Suffice it to say here that just to raise the development money necessary to produce a high-quality script and to link the script with a package (including, for example, stars and a noted director) attractive enough to bring in production financing is a significant achievement. Development money is the hardest to raise.

Let's assume, however, that you've managed to get through the various hurdles of development. You are now ready to start into official preproduction, making ironclad commitments with signed contracts. This is the time of the "closing", when all of the production contracts and financing are locked in place. At this stage, you hope that all of your careful planning, preliminary budgeting, and negotiation has put you in a position where your cash flow and schedule projections will match up with your real needs. Interim financing is both difficult to find and expensive.

Cash Flow

The ideal situation would be to have all of your production budget in your bank as early as possible, earning maximum interest rates and available to you as and when you need it. Dream on! The normal situation is that, before signing production financing contracts (with anyone except investors), you will have to plot out the amounts of money you will need from week to week. Funds will then be released to you, on an arbitrary basis, at various stages during the production, when you have achieved certain, predefined objectives.

Cash-flow planning involves assessing your needs in relation to these arbitrary fund-releasing points. These points may vary, but generally occur at signing and proof of financing, commencement of principal photography, approval of rushes, approval of rough cut, and perhaps at several other points up to final delivery and final cost reports. The early stages of preproduction generally require little in the way of cash payouts, while the last week of prep necessitates large bond payments before principal photography begins.

The cash-flow calculations for the period of production should include all cast and crew weekly rates, along with budgeted overtime allowances, location costs, per diems (when applicable), and all the other regular costs amortized across the shooting schedule. In almost all instances, the toughest time, from a cash-flow point of view, will be the last week or so of shooting and the first week or two of postproduction. This is just prior to the release of the performance bonds. Release is triggered by payment in full of all outstanding obligations to the members of the guilds or unions.

The Closing

In the best of circumstances, the closing will take place before preproduction commences. Unfortunately, this is not always the case, and so the line between the end of development and the start of prep is often quite fuzzy.

The more financing sources that exist for a production, the more complex the contract negotiations and the closing. Until all the parties are satisfied as to their own contracted position and the way it is related to the other participants, no production funds can be released to the producer. The financing sources may have the right to approve stars, principal crew, script, schedule, Canadian content, completion guarantor, bank arrangements, trustees, interim financing (if needed), and so on.

For the producer, this can result in a few days when feet never seem to touch the ground: running from office tower to office tower, spending endless, nail-biting moments in elevators, making frantic phone calls and trips to photocopying machines, arguing, pleading and wheedling with an unending stream of stony faces in an attempt to pacify and satisfy them, and trying to meet the precise and exacting demands of the government agencies, the broadcasters, the banks, the trustees, the lawyers, the last investor, and the completion guarantor.

As nightmarish as the closing can be for the producer, it helps to remember that all those concerned are simply ensuring that the relevant contracts and other documents agree with each other, are correctly signed, dated and sealed, and that everyone's liabilities are clearly defined relative to their involvement, responsibilities, and potential benefits. This adds up to a huge volume of paper.

Banks

In the late 1970s, the Canadian banking and investment community, spurred by the 100 percent Capital Cost Allowance for investment in Canadian films, poured large amounts of capital into a bonanza of production. In many cases, in order to help the films into production before the sale of all the investment units, the banks took the position of interim financiers. If, in the end, the issue was not fully subscribed, the banks were left holding the baby. Inevitably, the results were messy.

Not surprisingly, the banking and investment communities lost their enthusiasm for Canadian film production, and the repercussions of that mess have been slow to fade. Today, no matter how good your relationship with your individual bank manager, the head office policy of most chartered banks in Canada dictates that interim financing for a producer, against the latter stages of a standard production contract from either Telefilm or the CBC, is virtually impossible to obtain. Any contract with any conditions of payment that are not ironclad guarantees has, for our chartered banks, an all-too-familiar soggy smell.

There are exceptions to the rule, but few producers are able to run a sufficient volume of productions and cash through their banks to generate even a fraction of the enthusiasm and support that once existed. Gradually, though, as more productions are achieved that perform as well as the producers told their bank managers they would, the situation may be improving. In smaller matters, good relations with your bank manager certainly do help. For example, co-operative bank managers will open the doors for their customers outside of normal hours, or give a producer breaks on the rate being charged for foreign currency exchanges. If part of the production budget is coming from the United States, this may provide benefits against the rates allowed for in the budget. Whatever the specifics, your relationship with your bank manager is one that requires, and will benefit from, careful nurturing.

Budgets

At some point during the development stages, varying according to the financing sources, the producer must declare the proposed budget for the production. Invariably, this point comes too soon. The ideal point at which to lock the budget would be at the end of preproduction, when the final shooting script is ready, talent negotiations are complete, and locations are contracted for.

Although it is vital for a producer to know his or her way around a budget form, as well as the various price lists and union and guild collective agreements, there are very few producers who do not need the services of an experienced and busy production manager (PM). Budget preparation is a highly specialized skill. (See Chapter 3 for more – much more – on this subject.)

The basis of all budgets is the script. An analysis of

the script – called a breakdown – will identify and list locations, studio sets, characters, character / days, and so on. All of this information must be known before an accurate budget can be prepared. The PM will also question the producer and director about the "above the line" costs (story, script, development, producer, director, and stars) because all of these are fixed costs, unaffected by the exigencies of production. The PM will also need to know if there will be special effects or other anticipated extraordinary costs, as well as the overall amount that the producer believes can be raised for the production. Armed with this information, the PM will know, for example, whether the production can afford to sign union contracts for technical crew. More about this later.

Before production begins, everyone concerned – producer, director, PM, director of photography (DOP), first assistant director (1st AD) and editor – must agree that the schedule provided for in the budget can be made to work. When everyone is satisfied, the budget figures are then transferred, by category, into the budget column of the master cost report form. From this point on, the PM prepares weekly cost reports until the end of production. Copies of the cost reports, after careful examination by the producer, are forwarded to the completion guarantor, the bank, Telefilm (if they're involved), and to any other major investor who demands them. A sample cost report is included at the end of the chapter. (See Chapter 3 by Douglas Leiterman for a full description of the cost report.)

Breakdown and Board

Another of the vital concerns during preproduction – earlier if possible, although delay in preparing the final script can often be a major obstacle – is the script analysis known as the breakdown and the creation of the board. Simply put, the breakdown is prepared by listing the characters in each scene, and noting details of location, interior / exterior, day / night, special equipment needed, and so on. Then the scenes can be grouped to make the most efficient, practical, and economical use of the resources, human or otherwise. (For example, all scenes to be done in the churchyard location would be grouped; all scenes featuring the high-priced star would be grouped.)

All these decisions are displayed on a large board, which is covered with thin, flexible coloured strips that can be slotted in and removed. Each strip, about one-quarter inch wide, designates a scene, and contains all relevant information about location, characters, number of pages of script, number of extras required, and any other special requirements of the scene. The colours of the strips have their own meaning. Usually, these are:

white	day exterior
yellow	day interior
blue	night interior
green	night exterior
black	divider between scheduled days
others	special effects

Once a preliminary board is completed, with additional input from the director, the designer, the art director, and the production and location managers, the first assistant director can finalize the production board. When it is completed, adjusted, and readjusted (many times) to come as close as possible to meeting everyone's needs, the board becomes The Bible. From the moment that the board is locked, everything else hinges on it, and every department builds its own priorities around it. From this point on, almost any change is likely to cost a lot of money.

The board, the prime responsibility of the 1st AD, forms the basis for the production schedule and the day-out-of-days which, combined, are the basis for all production logistics.

The Day-Out-of-Days

Simply put, the day-out-of-days is a calendar cross plot. It involves grouping together those scenes that will be shot on the same day or in the same location, and plotting in the characters required for each scene / day. One hopes that the total number of days matches the budgeted number of shooting days.

Location vs. Studio

Most films produced in this country are shot on location rather than in a studio. There is a limited number of studios available, and most are in the major production centres of Toronto, Montreal, and Vancouver. In some circumstances, production companies take over warehouse space to create their own studios. In general, however, the choice between studio and location is made on the basis of the availability of suitable locations, the dictates of the script, and cost.

Anne of Green Gables, set at the turn of the century, was shot largely on location, although the interior of Green Gables was shot in a temporary studio (a warehouse close to Highway 401, east of Toronto). The script of *Atlantic City* called for windows in two apartments facing each other across an alley. Suitable apartment buildings were found, and their exteriors, entrances, and stairways were all shot on location. The interiors of the apartments and their facing windows were, however, shot in a studio.

The permanent studios, at base costs of perhaps $3000 per week *before* you build anything, are too expensive for many productions, despite the enormous freedom and flexibility that they offer. Everything you could possibly need is there: production office, photocopying equipment, phones, power, prelit sets, carpentry shop, wardrobe and art departments, dressing-rooms, toilets, and restaurant. Your sets can be designed and built to allow for "wild" walls that can be "popped" (removed) for reverse angles. Flat floors allow for dolly shots without the necessity for laying and leveling track.

Studios also allow the use of the "French Day" provision which, with prior agreement, permits a seven-hour work day, with no provision for overtime or meal breaks, but with an all-day buffet to which cast and crew can help themselves whenever they wish. The short day and the non-stop momentum are generally very good for both morale and productivity in the studio. And finally, the studio has lock-up security, so that when you are finished for the day, you can just switch everything off and walk away.

Location shooting, on the other hand, can cost you a great deal of money in travel expenses alone, especially on those days when you have a number of short scenes, each in a different location. You may lose up to half of your work day just in travel. To this you must add the fact that logistical problems, both of production and of support, are exponentially increased on location: timing relative to sunrise and sunset; making the moves; co-ordinating actors and extras; creating, printing, and distributing maps to each location; making arrangements for meals; providing an alternative communication system if there are no telephones; and checking out the locations of the nearest hospitals and gas stations. These and many other organizational complexities mean that location shooting stacks up quite poorly against the compact convenience of the studio.

Casting Major Roles, Star Contracts, Buyouts, and Points

In the Canadian film industry there are several conundrums. None of them is harder to deal with than the fact that, although there are no rules for how to make a film, we operate in what is perhaps the most over-regulated industry in the country. These regulations may frequently impinge on the casting of major roles, limiting your choices and sometimes precluding the casting of the ideal performers. (See Chapter 9 for more on the Canadian certification systems.)

Generally, casting decisions for major roles are collaborative ones made by producer, director, casting director, and some other interested parties: broadcaster, distributor, foreign partners, or anyone else with a negotiated say in the matter. Although it doesn't happen often in this country, the biggest star involved, once contracted, may also have a voice in casting decisions. As you can see, the producer must walk a very fine line in order to satisfy all interested parties.

In the best of all possible worlds, the producer – or his or her representative – starts to approach actors and actresses on the basis of script requirements, the markets for which the film is intended, the box office drawing-power or TV "Q" rating (by which American broadcasters assess the likely audience of a show with a given performer) of those being approached, and the budget.

The script may well be the principal deciding factor in the actor's response to your blandishments, although this is something you may not know at the time. He or she may love the script or hate it, but if it is not a part that suits career plans, the performer is unlikely to accept the role for love or money. There are also those actors and actresses whose agents start from the position that they will not even look at a script until a basic minimum fee has been negotiated, which fee may be the only deciding factor. Alternatively, you may find that your timing is perfect, and the part you are attempting to cast is perceived to be an ideal match for the personal ambitions of the performer. Under these circumstances, a major star may agree to take a role for a reduced fee.

In fact, the permutations are innumerable and the possibilities endless. The only limitations are your imagination, your courage, and your timing. The producer has to be aware that many people have an opinion about casting, and some of them may have the power of veto. Government funding agencies have some very strict rules as to Canadian content. What is truly important is to obtain the committed participation of a professional who can put the performance on the screen within the dictates of the budget, the script, and the schedule; and, one hopes, whose name will help to sell the film and bring in the audience.

Star contracts can include some very strange items, from the power of veto of other cast members, director, and crew to script approval; from demands to bring along personal makeup and hair people to requests for personal Winnebagos or drivers and cars permanently at their disposal; from demands for specific hotels and airlines to the assumption that the expenses of spouses, children, agents, managers, or even pets will be paid – nothing should surprise you! Often, stars are contracted for your production by letters of agreement or deal memos, pending fully documented contracts that may be negotiated subsequent to the work, in minute detail, over a period of several years. Alternatively, the final contracts may never be signed. (See Chapter 9 for more on letters of agreement.)

Buyout decisions are complicated. All of the money in your budget for talent – all the performance fees (scale), all the overtime, travel, wardrobe, makeup, and other items that may be calculated and paid – buys you *only* the performance and the time. The rights that you may have to use that performance; for example, to show the film publicly or to license others to show that film, are very tightly defined. Reference to the ACTRA Independent Producer Agreement (IPA) is mandatory in calculating the amounts you need to pay performers, not only for their performance, but also to acquire the rights you need as economically as possible. Failure to pay buyouts at the time of production may cost you very dearly down the road or, in the worst instances, may even make some sales impossible.

At budget preparation time, you often start by allowing buyouts that will purchase rights for five years in every market, worldwide. By the time you start signing performer contracts, circumstances may have changed so that you are only willing, or able, to buy out the minimums to cover the known markets sold. A forty percent buyout is the very least (under the current ACTRA Agreement) that common sense dictates. Any smaller buyout would cost the production exorbitantly in residuals (payments to performers for additional exhibition rights not previously contracted for) when further sales are made. It is vital for any producer working in drama to be thoroughly conversant with the ACTRA contract book. The ramifications of the proposed buyout, the declaration of use (which must be specified on the individual performer contracts), and the timing are crucial considerations that may either cost or save you a lot of money and may, in the long term, spell the difference between the profitability and financial failure of your production. None of these decisions can be made realistically until you know the potential of your film to be sold in any given market. It's worth getting expert advice.

In the case where a producer is attempting to obtain the services of a star whose value far outstrips the capacities of the budget, the producer's main bargaining chip is the offer of points of profit participation. Since the producer has 100 percent of the points with which he or she can survive after the financing, the writer, and the director are taken care of, there is generally a fair degree of negotiating strength available. If the actor truly believes in the script, then accepting part payment in potential profit should make a lot of sense. For the producer, this kind of deal can greatly stretch the budget available to enhance production values, as well as putting a cap on overtime for the highest paid member(s) of the cast.

Crewing and Casting

No matter how good your script, how lavish your budget, and how talented your director and stars, if you don't have a committed, happy crew, and solid supporting actors, you are not going to have much of a finished product. A positive approach, a carefully selected crew, and attention to the small things will pay huge dividends down the road, when straitened circumstances may demand that you ask people to waive certain rights which they may have under the collective agreements. The crew and the actors, if they sense that they are being unfairly squeezed, will respond in kind. If, however, they know that you have made every effort to plan properly and to treat them as well as you can, then generally, in our experience, they will come through for you in the crunch.

In Canada, you have the option of signing a Letter of Adherence with ACTRA and contracting with experienced, professional actors, or of not signing with ACTRA, and trying to get performances out of amateurs.

For crews, depending upon where you are shooting, you have numerous options. Vancouver-based technicians are exclusively under the aegis of IATSE (often referred to as IA – it is the International Alliance of Theatrical Stage Employees and Moving Picture Machine Operators) and the Teamsters. Nor is this situation confined to the technicians. IA also claims jurisdiction over art departments, editors, production co-ordinators, production secretaries, accountants, and bookkeepers. This situation has probably developed through the number of foreign-financed films that have been shot in Vancouver since the early days of Canadian production. It means that, in the west, shooting non-union is difficult, although a few people have managed it.

In Montreal, likewise, the non-union option is limited. Everyone there is under the auspices of STCQ (Syndicat des techniciens et des techniciennes de cinéma du Québec), including unit managers, location managers, and assistant directors. (This situation, in which managers are members of the same union as the people they manage, can lead to some serious conflicts.)

Toronto offers the producer the greatest flexibility in choosing crews. There are a number of well qualified non-union technicians, and there are several union possibilities including IATSE, ACFC/Camera Local 81, ACFC/NABET, and NABET straight. (ACFC stands for Association of Canadian Film Craftspeople and NABET stands for National Association of Broadcast Employees and Technicians.)

It is probably fair to say that these options are equally viable, but that the differences will be most apparent when you have established the specifics of your own production and have started looking at the current contracts of the organizations, the availability of crews, the flexibility of the rates, and other major deal points as they relate to your needs. Since most production in this country (at the time of writing) is for television, the flexibility of the organization and its members is often of paramount importance. None of this is meant to suggest that the producer is ever in a position where he or she can dictate the terms and rates under which the production will operate, especially financially. If you are working under union contracts, there are always absolute minimum rates and other conditions that no amount of negotiation can change.

When the decision has been made and you are ready to crew up, your approaches to the various department heads and the way in which you have prepared your budget become vitally important to the production. Ideally, each department head should be presented with as many options as possible within the structure that already exists. Once they have agreed to perform their jobs within the constraints of your budget, schedule, and whatever collective agreements you may have signed, we feel that they should be given a large degree of autonomy about whom they hire and how they administer their own budgets. In this way, they bring with them not only their own creative and technical expertise, but also the people with whom they have found they work best and a measure of pride in running their own show. These factors create a strong sense of commitment to seeing the job done properly. The benefits to the production of this kind of approach, and the resulting team spirit, can mean more to your production in time, aggravation, and money saved, than all the high-priced brilliant individuals that a fat budget can buy, or than constant overbearing supervision can possibly produce.

The peculiarities of your script will likely dictate the order in which you bring people onto the production team. When you, as the producer, have decided on your director, and jointly decided on your stars (compromised is more likely), then there are many more appointments to be made. Some will be made jointly with the director, but some will be your own decisions. The production manager, preferably the same one who prepared the budget in the development stages, is necessary from the beginning of preproduction, and the first assistant director should certainly be hired soon after that, as should the art director and / or the production designer, the location manager, the costume designer / wardrobe mistress, and the director of photography. Obviously special effects, if any, should be set in motion at the earliest possible date, most likely before commencing prep. The office staff, production secretary, production co-ordinator, and accountant should also come on payroll very early on.

The earlier you can decide on your editor, the more smoothly the shoot can go, because production meetings and planning sessions, storyboards, and shotlists will all benefit greatly from the editor's input. Within their budgets, department heads will start to bring their own people on as necessary. It will pay dividends to ask department heads to submit their own budget estimates on a weekly basis. This helps to keep them fully aware of their own spending vis-a-vis their overall budget, and thus helps to keep the entire film budget on track.

Directors of photography (DOPs) often work with

the same people all the time; indeed, some come complete with camera, lighting, and grip departments. They are a ready-made, cohesive team for whom words seem to be virtually superfluous. It's a joy to watch such a team in action, and it makes for a serene set when all those people walk quietly but purposefully around, moving lights and assorted pieces of equipment, communicating as if by telepathy. It is also not uncommon to find Canadian production crews in which a complete department speaks French while the rest speak English, or vice versa.

In general, the longer people work together in a positive environment, the better they will perform. Within the confines of your budget, therefore, it is preferable to hire people as early as possible, allowing the teamwork and communication lines to be established and strengthened before the controlled chaos of actual production.

Insurance for Creative Personnel and Talent

Film insurance, generally speaking, is not cheap, and it represents a large lump payment to be included in the budget and early on in the cash-flow projections. The major insurance categories, other than for the key creative personnel, are simply arranged and contracted for: negative insurance covers the entire results of the production from the moment you expose the raw stock until the picture is finished and there is more than one printing element (protection) of the finished product; equipment and liability insurance are straightforward (although liability rates have been going through the roof recently), as is insurance for vehicles.

But the million dollar question is this: whose incapacity or demise would most severely damage your ability to finish the picture, on time and on budget? It would be easier to ask: whose wouldn't? The problem is that you can't cover everybody. You are generally limited to a specific number of people (the "named insured") within a normal film insurance package.

Every additional person will cost you more. Generally, producers decide to insure the director and the highest-paid actors. Then they lose sleep worrying over those whom they decided they could not afford to cover.

For the insurance company, should the unthinkable happen, the claims can be enormous. If one of your named insured, for whom you have to arrange and pay for medical examinations, is in some way stricken, then the insurance company will have to pay the cost, no matter what it may be, of replacing that creative element. If that means recasting and reshooting the entire picture, with all associated costs (less your deductible), then that's what they will pay. Less onerous variations could still end up costing many hundreds of thousands of dollars. This insurance is vital, even though you may feel that it doesn't cover enough of your people.

Unions and Guilds

Although the basic contracts of the film industry unions and guilds define the terms and conditions considered by their members to be the minimums under which they will work, it is highly advisable to maintain good relations with them. No matter how much time you may spend poring over the lengthy and unwieldy contracts, you would have to be both a lawyer and a very experienced producer/production manager to spot all of the permutations and combinations of the clauses that may be interpreted or applied to help or hinder your own project. Where the good relations come into play is in the natural course of frank discussion about your project and the contract with the representatives of the association(s). To the extent that it does not conflict with their priorities, they may like your project and wish to see it made, but the work opportunities that represents to their constituents will always be their bottom line.

Your record of dealing fairly with these constituents, of making prompt payment, and of generally doing what you said you would, will determine the amount of co-operation that they offer you. As a producer, your own reputation for straight shooting and fair dealing is important, but so is the reputation of your production manager. The combination of two strong reputations will ensure that the deal you get from the national business executive of any union or guild is as good as that given to any other producer.

Further, as a measure of support for indigenous Canadian productions, when crews' past experiences with a producer have been positive, they may show some degree of flexibility about travel, overtime and turnaround (hours of rest between one day's work and the next), and about some of the areas of the contract that do not directly relate to the hours or basic conditions of work. If you negotiate in good faith, being open about your budget and the deals you are striking elsewhere, you will usually find that the guilds, the unions, and their members will respond in kind and do whatever they can to ensure that the needs of your production are met.

Certainly, any collective agreement imposes limits, which at times complicate your life. The positive thing to be said about collective agreements is that they establish basic working conditions – pay, length of work day, and so on – which are known and agreed to before work begins. Everyone is then able to concentrate on the work itself and ignore the smaller, irksome details that, without the contracts, might cause stoppages and grievances.

Caps, Flats, Deferrals, and Investment Deals

The opportunities here are endless; the only limits are your imagination and your powers of persuasion. The object is to make a film. The problem is that, to one degree or another, you lack sufficient funds. The solutions discussed here are all ways of getting the production made that defy the normal precepts of budgeting. Implicit in these solutions is the idea that people who work on your production are willing to do it for reasons over and above the direct salaries they will earn.

"Caps" refers to payment schedules that limit, or put a cap on, the amount of money to be paid to cast or crew, no matter how long the days. "Flats," somewhat less attractive to the hiree, differ from caps in that there is no hourly rate established, just a flat daily rate. "Deferrals" generally split the pay so that the hiree receives a portion in cash and the remainder is deferred until some point in the future. At this time, depending on deals the producer may have made previously, the hiree may start to share in profits, or revenues, until the deferred portion of income is paid off. "Investment" deals, however structured, mean that the hiree actually owns some equity, in perpetuity, in the production and, if the production is really successful, may expect revenues, over and above the recoupment of the investment, as long as the film continues to have a market value. (Deferrals and investments are discussed further in Chapter 4.)

There are no rules as to how such deals may be structured. As a general rule, however, the worse the deal is for the people you hire, the greater the likelihood that you will have a group of burnt-out and frustrated individuals on your hands.

Hiring Non-Canadians	The reasons that a producer would like to hire non-Canadians, either for cast or crew, may be quite simple or very complicated. The circumstances vary enormously. At the beginning of the film boom, in the late 1970s, there were frequent instances of Canadian technicians and key creative personnel being hired, with foreign "consultants" or "supervisors" also in place. So that the productions could be certified as Canadian films, the Canadians would be paid and accorded credit while, in reality, their functions were performed by the foreign advisors. Technically, this satisfied the

requirements of certification and, at the same time, met the conditions laid down by the foreign distribution or presale deals. This is now both harder to get away with and, with rare exceptions, unnecessary.

The volume of film production in Canada over the last few years has grown to a point where, on several occasions, few fully experienced crews have been available for all of the productions that were financed and ready to start. This high volume of production has served both to increase the number of crews available and also to produce crews of sufficient experience that Canada can now boast creative and technical people as good as those found anywhere.

By the same token, especially in countries with many more years of high-budget feature film production experience than Canada has, there are exceptional individuals, companies, and facilities whose expertise may be indispensible to a particular Canadian film. Clearly, budget notwithstanding, certain films could never have been produced in Canada. Mostly, these films have special needs in the areas of special effects and computer animation (*Tron* and *Star Wars* spring to mind) for which the facilities and expertise do not exist here. Certain films transcend nationalism.

Actors present a somewhat different case. No matter what levels of talent and skill exist among Canadian performers, film and television are still one big numbers game. There are times when those numbers demand a performer whose name attached to a production will make a significant difference to its financial returns.

The numbers break down as follows. The United States represents approximately 70 percent of the world market and the contingent audience and cash return potential for both feature films and television. Canada represents approximately 5 percent. It follows that, if your production is not able to come very close to a break-even point in Canada, you, as a responsible, business-oriented producer, need to guarantee revenues from other markets.

Television presales, advance distribution guarantees, and international co-productions are dealt with in Chapters 4, 6, and 7 of this book and are, even for the most experienced producers, complicated to arrange. In order for your production to break even, or perhaps make a profit, you need something else to stack your deck. The box office or television "Q" rating of stars help to create an audience, and thereby a market, for your film. Canada has its own stars, to be sure, and some of them, for certain periods of time, have been stars of international magnitude. This small group, however, is very busy; further, they may not be right for the roles in your production, even if they are available when you need them.

Although these numbers and the box office realities are recognized throughout the industry, there are times when you will run headlong into a wall of resistance if you try to cast a non-Canadian in a role for which the performer may be ideally suited. Reference to the current ACTRA Agreement will show that, from their perspective, there are no objections to the casting of at least one foreign actor and, under specific conditions, a second. Your dilemma, in the casting stages, is to find the balance between the requirements of aesthetics, production financing, and the potential of the production to repay its financing from sales revenues. Potential profits are a further consideration. Certification of your production as Canadian remains the key to financing and selling in this country. (Chapter 9 provides details on this certification.) Hiring of non-Canadians remains a contentious issue that causes the producer many headaches. However, if it's necessary, and you know you're right, persist.

Child Labour Laws While Canadian labour laws relating to child performers are considerably less stringent than those operating in the United States – particularly in California and

New York – the scheduling restrictions of a film with children in major roles can quite seriously affect your budget and planning. In the United States, from the moment you pick up the child – including all travel time, makeup, wardrobe, time on-camera, meals, and mandatory tutoring – to the time you deliver the child home, the working day may not exceed eight hours. Canada's laws are somewhat more lenient: the eight hours allowed do not include travel time or meal breaks, within city limits. No overtime is allowed, and there are provisions about the length of uninterrupted time the child may spend in front of the camera, scaled according to the age of the child. In addition, tutoring may be required.

Study the ACTRA book carefully, make adjustments to your script if necessary, and be prepared to make adjustments to your schedule. There's never enough time or money, but careful planning can solve most of your problems. Abuses of the rules pertaining to minors could shut down your production more quickly than just about anything else.

Casting Directors

Casting is a highly specialized area. A good casting director, no matter what your budget, will almost invariably save you untold quantities of time, money, and problems. The earlier the casting director is brought in, the more time will be available to ascertain, discuss, and share in the visions of the producer and director. Once everyone is agreed on what they are seeking, experienced casting directors will only involve the producer and director in casting sessions when convinced that someone who really fills the bill has been found.

The impact of a smooth casting operation will be felt throughout the other departments and will be evident as soon as shooting commences. A rough casting job, on the other hand, may well produce a domino effect through all departments. Imagine, for instance, the problems for the wardrobe department and the unanswerable scheduling questions of the ADs if major casting decisions were to be delayed to the end of preproduction!

Specialized Computer Services

Computer services to production companies are relatively new and, like much else in the area of computers, still very much in the throes of development. Services available range from companies that will simply do your payroll for a fixed percentage of your budget to systems whose software can take a word-processed script and automatically prepare as many variables as you can dream up of budget, breakdowns, day-out-of-days, schedules, and boards (as well as handling your payroll).

Some systems may make you feel that you've lost the direct, hands-on control that you're used to and some may suit your needs perfectly. What is certain is that, if you're already using a computer, and if you buy appropriately, these services can speed up your production planning and accounting exponentially. There are companies in Canada developing and supplying software that is at the leading edge of what is available anywhere.

From the production manager's viewpoint, the advantages of a computer system in preproduction can be enormous, as things get juggled and shuffled from one budget to another, and schedules are changed on a daily basis, if not even more frequently. Figures can be manipulated electronically and the resulting option spat out almost before you've warmed up your calculator.

Script Revisions

From a production viewpoint, script revisions after the beginning of prep are totally undesirable: necessary evils that always go on long after they should. The longer they do go on, the greater the repercussions will be, unless they can be limited, after the preparation of the schedules and other breakdowns, to dialogue changes. The fact that they rarely are is the prime cause of the avalanche of paper that has been known to burn out many good copying machines and production co-ordinators. The co-ordinator is the poor unfortunate upon whom falls the responsibility of disseminating all information to all concerned as fast as it becomes available.

Originals of anything are always published on white paper. Generally it is eight and a half by eleven inch paper with three holes punched for easy storage in a three-ring production binder, as well as for easy removal and replacement by new versions as they come, on (in order) pink, green, blue, orange, and canary yellow paper, and then back to white again.

"As they come" refers to the ability of the production co-ordinator to stay on top of all this, and to make sure that, at the very least, all of the department heads and the actors get the new versions immediately. If you're not all working with the same information, if some people get their copies late and fail to insert them in their binders, you're courting disaster.

Shot Lists and Storyboards

"Shot lists are dream sheets"
— B. Wertheimer

With sufficient time and money, a production may be able to afford the costs of a full shot list and storyboard for the entire shoot. The value of the shot list is considerable, *if* the script remains intact and the production remains on schedule. It also implies that the director doesn't come up with some new ideas as he or she goes along.

The value of the storyboard in a dramatic film is questionable. In a commercial, almost every shot is exactly to storyboard. This is one of the reasons behind the huge costs of commercials. A comparison of shooting ratios and shooting time per finished minute of product explains why commercial and big-budget feature films can afford to shoot storyboards, and why low-budget features and television films rarely can. A big feature, or a commercial, may do ten camera and lighting set-ups in a day of shooting, and produce 30 seconds to a minute of finished product. A production in a lower budget category, in that same day, might average well over 30 set-ups and shoot five to eight minutes of end product.

A storyboard artist may cost in the region of $1000 per week. Storyboard panels average around 200 per half hour of film. Every time there are script changes or location changes, the storyboard will change. The costs, for a low-budget production, are extremely high in relation to the value.

The Contingency Fund

Nobody, at the time when the budget must be locked, can ever be prescient enough to cover everything that needs to be in that budget. The purpose of the contingency fund, then, is to give you money for expenses you could not have foreseen. Conventional wisdom says that the preparer of the budget is not right more than nine times out of ten. Hence, the contingency fund is generally equal to 10 percent of the budget. You generally assume that it will be spent, and you hope that the results will be noticeable on screen. The key is in knowing how and when to spend contingency funds in small packets in order to *save* large amounts. (We'll have more to say about the wise use of the contingency fund in the Production section of this chapter.)

Production

The Role of the Producer during Shooting

In principle, if everything has been well prepared, and if nothing goes awry, then the producer's role during production is minimal. The prime function is to monitor everything that is going on, to appear everywhere and talk with everyone daily, to be available to trouble shoot, to keep visitors to the set out of everyone's hair, to anticipate, and to worry.

Everyone else involved in the production has his or her own specialized and – by virtue of the pressures of time and money – tightly defined role to perform. The producer is the only person whose job it is to maintain a complete, objective overview and to remember why everyone else is there. The style you employ to achieve this objective is highly personal, but one element is paramount to a successful production: an early warning system.

The process of putting together a production – from the decision about the story, through to the script, the casting, and the crewing – is the creation of a well-oiled machine, to do one job extremely efficiently. Systems must be built in so the operator of the machine – in this analogy, the producer – will receive a warning about any potential breakdown while there is still time to fix it without disrupting the process. The essential element, the early warning, derives from the levels of trust and communication that the producer has taken care to establish with everyone who joins the production team from day one. Like any good manager, the producer must create a working environment in which both cast and crew know that their abilities and their professionalism are acknowledged. If you don't give them that, you risk stifling initiative and, probably, creating tension and resentment.

Nevertheless, remember that no matter how good your people are at their jobs, and no matter how close a friendship you have with them, they are still your employees. The final responsibility for the production is yours. Talk to everyone, listen to what they have to say, but never put the PM or the AD in the position of pulling the plug or committing the production to major overtime, or meal or turnaround penalties (contractual penalties incurred for servicing meals late, or leaving too few rest hours between one day's shooting and the next). That's *your* job.

The Relationship between Producer and Director

Ideally, the relationship between producer and director should be (and in rare instances is) a form of partnership. Imagine a framed picture: two rectangles, one inside the other. The producer starts with the raw materials for the frame. Each decision that he or she makes determines its size and shape. The story and script, the budget, the schedule, and the choice of director, cast and crew make up the four sides of the frame. Within the frame will go the picture. This is the director's area of influence, his or her prime responsibility. As long as the director concentrates on the picture, he or she should be left alone. When the director wishes to make a change in the framing materials, though, negotiation will ensue.

Directors often say "I don't shoot schedules, I shoot pictures." That's true, but pictures aren't made without money, nor are directors paid without money, and making sure that the money is available is a major function of a producer. Although it may often seem that the producer spends much of his or her time trying to meet the director's needs, the fact is that the director works for the producer. While it is to be hoped that it does not have to be stated in such blunt terms, the producer does have the final call, the final cut, and the responsibility to deliver the film contracted for, at the budget agreed upon.

In the best of circumstances, producer and director can work well together, despite the seemingly contradictory nature of their two positions. The director must push for the best moment, the best shot, the best location, the best of everything; the producer must encourage and support that creative enthusiasm, but must also contain it and, if necessary, curtail it.

Wise Use of the Contingency

There are no rules, and there is only one goal: to spread the contingency fund out, reasonably, through the production and postproduction stages, in a way best calculated to give the finished film the highest possible production values. It may appear overly simplistic, but it is worth stating that 95 percent of a brilliant product is not good enough. One hundred percent of a good product, with moments of brilliance, while not the ideal, is certainly much better.

Bear in mind that the people working on the film, if

you have hired well, are professionals who have accepted the work, based on the script and the budget, and are committed to bringing in the best product they can. Their concerns and their priorities are yours, and their requests for more money are not made frivolously. Your job, faced with the deluge of requests, is to remember what you are making (a television drama does not have the budget of a theatrical feature), and to make decisions accordingly.

In the past, many producers offered their PMs an incentive cash bonus, based on a percentage of whatever portion of the contingency they managed to save. This is often an unwise incentive if it causes the PM to chip away at nickels and dimes, creating an atmosphere of distrust with the crew, and a lot of extra work, for very small savings. A more productive use of the contingency (apart from covering an unforeseen but unavoidable day of shooting) occurs, for example, when the crew has worked long days or nights, and a temporary crew, brought in for a few hours or a couple of days, pre-rigs a large set-up, or wraps at a location, thus saving the energy of the main crew.

Anticipate problems, and reserve a percentage of your contingency fund that is somewhat greater than the percentage of shooting which remains to be completed. Try to leave a good proportion of your contingency for postproduction. Not only will you be glad you did; so will your completion guarantor! Under ideal conditions, your original budget would contain, within each budget code, enough funds to cover everything. If production were truly predictable, though, you would never need your contingency.

Travel Days, Holding Days, and Weather Cover

In this grab bag of items are things which the producer likes to think will be covered by the initial budgeting process but which frequently end up as contingency items. Travel days for performers are usually paid up to eight hours at straight time, and the first two holding days are paid at 50 percent of the daily rate, with all subsequent idle days at the full rate. Since the initial budget will be done before most decisions are made concerning locations, casting, or schedule, travel and holding days are hard to allow for at that time. As the realities become clearer, you will have to decide which is more expensive: to keep the actors hanging around in hotels, paying them their fees and per diems, or to pay for airfares, taxis, and so on, so that they can travel to and from locations as needed. Holding days are generally cheaper than travel days. One way of protecting against this kind of contingency, at the time the original budget is prepared, is to allow some overtime for every performer day.

Weather days are often major problems, especially in films with a large proportion of outdoor scenes. It is generally wise to load the exteriors on the front end of the production schedule, where location and travel permit, but to have options available ("weather cover") for both locations and talent should the weather turn against you. You are still, of course, left with the need to go back to the planned location later, but at least you have kept the film in production. You have not paid everyone to sit idle and, apart from the location costs and any other cancellations you may have to pay for, you are still on time and budget. The best insurance you may have, apart from a direct connection to Him-up-There – which some ADs claim to have – and a bottomless contingency pot, is accurate weather prediction! Weather Consultants of Canada have survived in this chancy business for a good many years, so they must be right more often than not.

Feeding and Housing of Cast and Crew

Start by checking the basic minimum requirements as laid down in the union and guild contracts and don't even consider taking an entire crew into a major city. The cost will kill you. If you have hired an experienced production manager and co-ordinator, they will know the kinds of deals that can be made and will get the best group rates available. Out-of-town shoots invariably cost you more than you think they will, so pull every deal possible.

As a rule, the production pays one week ahead, taking care of rooms, breakfasts, and lunches, and giving the crew cash for the dinner meal. When the day is over, they're on their own. No matter how well you plan, though, the additional costs of vehicles, gas, mileage, and trips to bars, restaurants, and grocery stores all seem to end up on your tab, no matter what is laid down in writing and no matter how tight your controls.

Catering

It is amazing what a salutary effect good food can have on the morale and enthusiasm of the cast and crew. When you find a good caterer, you've found a goldmine. The best caterers understand and can cope with the nature of film production: the late schedule and location changes, the sudden extra mouths, and the weird and wonderful circumstances under which they must often present their offerings. Apart from the price (at present the norm in a city is about $9.50 to $12 a head and lower in smaller towns) the key considerations when choosing a caterer are versatility, flexibility, and variety.

Call Sheets

Every production generates vast piles of paper. From the last day of preproduction through to the last day of shooting, every member of the crew and all cast members who are involved in the next day's shooting receive a call sheet. It is prepared by the assistant directors and, depending upon what happens between the time of preparation (usually over the lunch break) and the end of the day, it may need to be revised and re-issued, sometimes more than once. The call sheet lays out all of the next day's activities. The information, drawn directly from the most up-to-date version of the production schedule, is a specific set of instructions which ensures that everyone is working towards the same objectives for the day. (A sample call sheet can be found at the end of this chapter.) The following information will always be included in the first section:

the day number in the shooting schedule; office address and telephone number; call time; the location; contact name at location; a list, by name, of producer(s), director, PM, unit PM, and 1st AD; and the weather forecast and time of sunrise and sunset.

The second section lists:

scene, set, description, day / night, script day, cast, pages, and locations; followed by artist, character; pick-up time, time due on location, in make-up, in wardrobe, and on set.

Also listed on the call sheet are ADs' telephone numbers; the advance schedule for two days hence; transportation notes, specific reminders for each department about schedule requirements: for example, special effects, warnings to craft services and caterers of likely numbers to be fed or complications on the location such as crowds of extras; time of breakfast, proposed lunch time, and so on. In short, the call sheet contains all information that can be specified about what the next day's work is to accomplish. It may also contain some kind of reference, often humorous, to previous days' work. Once established as a convention, humour is quite a good way of ensuring that everyone reads every word of the call sheet, searching for some hidden gem. (It is also a way in which ADs with writing aspirations may be discovered!)

Rushes

The screening of the rushes is an extremely important part of the day for everyone, and is generally held as soon as possible after wrap. There are many different theories about who should attend. The collective agreements and the budget should be consulted before asking people to attend. The presence of certain people at rushes (such as the DOP, the continuity person, and the art director) is mandatory, while others attend as a matter of professional pride.

Some directors like to have actors at rushes, despite the inherent danger that the actors may not like the performances they see and begin to modify their characters. Most directors prefer to discuss the actors' work with them personally, thus maintaining their own vision and a consistent performance. Obviously, this can be a delicate subject for negotiation. For the producer, a good measure of the morale of the crew is the number of people who attend rushes voluntarily after the initial zeal during the first few days.

Daily Production Reports

As a weekly cost report is to the overall financial picture, so the daily production report is to the state of the production as a whole. The schedule, the amounts of footage (raw and exposed), timings of scenes shot, overtime, meals, sickness, vehicles, shooting ratio – every possible detail of the production is covered in the report. An informed and experienced eye, going over such a report, can rapidly evaluate the status of the production. Think of the production report as a vital tool.

Daily Reports to the Completion Guarantor

The job of the completion guarantor, for which he or she receives a bond of 6 percent of your budget, is to ensure that your production is completed at no additional cost to the investors, broadcasters, or other financial participants and interested parties. Implicit in this are certain rights, access to anything relevant, and a requirement that the producer satisfy the guarantor's demands and answer any pertinent questions.

Although you are paying for the service, you are not directly the recipient of the benefits. In fact, if things do not go as they should, the completion guarantor can take over your production. This will be done if you are unable to demonstrate, early enough, a comprehension of the problems and an ability to come up with practical solutions.

Before the completion guarantor takes over, he or she will generally do anything possible to find a way for the existing producer and director to complete the production. But the process is very painful. Meetings are held; questions are asked as to how and why things happened; and options, such as cutbacks and new controls, are discussed. The producer's options at this stage are to make cutbacks in the postproduction budget, or cut his or her own salary, or cut the salary of the director. Quality will suffer along with your reputation, but the picture may be saved this way.

The importance of regular communication with the completion guarantor is clear. The guarantor must be kept informed of every major development, and copied on every report and call sheet. It is in your interests to keep the guarantor as up to date as possible so that he or she is exposed to as few nasty surprises as possible, and thus has no reasons for giving you grief. A good relationship with the completion guarantor can, in fact, give you an extra resource person to help deal with logistical problems.

Personality of the Set

From the very start, with your first selection of the people you will hire, you are setting in motion the process determining the personality of your set. It's your decision as to the type of set you will run, but it's preferable that the choice be made by commission rather than by omission. Your choice is to drive as hard as possible, pushing and squeezing to get the maximum out of your crew or, having decided that people give more in response to a happier atmosphere, to do what you can to make the working situation pleasant. In our view, the latter approach will bear more fruit.

Keep your people involved in all major decisions, ensure that they have the best possible equipment, that their vehicles are good ones, and that the environment in which you are asking them to perform minor miracles on a daily basis is as comfortable and professional as you can make it. Wrap time pools (bets on the time the working day will end) and a case of beer at rushes provide a little break from the pressure. Well-catered sets and ones in which craft services (the people who provide coffee and snacks) are always there are sets where everyone responds with just a little extra effort. These are all small things that may not seem worthy of a producer's attention, yet the payoff can be phenomenal.

Editing during Shooting

Where possible, and especially on a low-budget, tight-schedule production, it is highly desirable to have the editor(s) assemble the material as you shoot. If this is being done, you will know, almost as you go along, *exactly* what inserts (shots of important details), or lines of extra dialogue you are going to need. This will save you a fortune in the postproduction phase. On the days when, for whatever reason, you have a second camera to help cover big, expensive, or unrepeatable scenes, consider having the editor direct the second unit. On many productions, while the director and main unit are busy getting the overall scene and action, the second unit is left to grab whatever it can within fairly vague guidelines. It's much more efficient if the editor can use the time to provide you with options such as detailed cutaway shots. (For example, if the main action of your scene is a hockey game, you might have cutaways showing the scoreboard or the crowd's reaction.)

"It's Lonely at the Top"

A prime given of the film industry is that no matter how good your story, script, or director, no matter how talented or famous your cast, no matter how well you have hired all of your production department heads and crew, no matter how meticulous your budgeting and planning to take care of every conceivable contingency and emergency, something else will go wrong.

How you will react when things do go wrong depends on how well you have prepared for it, by creating a good working environment, by building solid working relationships with all the people involved (including script writers, agents, investors, broadcasters, and completion guarantors), *and also depends on your own personality and self-confidence.* You have hired people. You can fire them. How you wield that particular club is your decision. Show it only when you must use it, but don't underestimate the effect of using it. Remember that those who work for you are freelancers, people whose next job depends on this one. So does your own.

If you create tension, it will show in the product. If you are cavalier in the use of your club, remember that this industry is like a small village, with a very efficient bush telegraph. When a dramatic production gets off the ground, that alone is a small miracle. When it comes in on time and on budget, that's a bigger miracle. If it's good too, then it represents the state of the art of talent, communication, organization, and committed enthusiasm and sweat. As a producer, you have pulled together all of the elements to create the environment and tools to let that happen. A lot of other people have worked very hard and very long hours to make that happen. They're also human, with all that that implies.

As producer, you are the one person who knows how important any given thing is to the end product that you have contracted to deliver. Your job is to keep things moving and in perspective. Panic spreads rapidly, and can never help your production. If there is a solution to a problem – and there almost always is – then you must use your resources to find it. If there isn't, you must recognize that, and act appropriately.

Keep your eye on the goal, trust the people you've hired until they've proven untrustworthy, and take the necessary action.

Postproduction

Approvals of Cuts

There are few rules here, except to say that he who pays the piper calls the tune. Almost invariably, the director has contractual rights to what is known as the director's cut. The editor assembles the footage according to the script and according to what has been shot. Generally, shots are selected on the basis of performance and dramatic effect. When the editor has completed the first assembly, the director has the opportunity to work with the editor to put together the film that he or she envisioned at the time of shooting. This is generally the time when the editor or assistant editor is driven crazy trying to accommodate the director's demands for the take he or she *wishes* were there.

The next formal step, in terms of approvals by broadcasters or completion guarantors, is the approval of the rough cut, which is generally a trigger point for the release of further funding. Problems can become apparent here, when everyone – those who have been in daily contact with the production and those who have seen virtually nothing – sees the entire production in one run and has the opportunity to judge how well the story is told.

Many methods may be used at this point to solve the perceived problems. Sometimes, these problems may be limited to specific scenes. Perhaps lines are delivered badly or there are moments that don't work well dramatically. The solutions may lie in voice looping for better readings or changed lines, or in reordering some scenes to produce the right build-up of dramatic tension leading up to the problem scene, or in changing the length of some scenes. The one thing you *don't* want to have to do, unless you've budgeted or planned for it, is to reshoot. Trying to bring back the necessary team is hard enough. Trying to get all the locations, sets, wardrobe, props, and vehicles together can be a major headache. Add to this the almost infinite variety of changes that may have taken place with your actors – suntans, haircuts, injuries, beards or moustaches, weight loss or gain, moves to L.A. or Europe – and you can see that reshoots are a daunting prospect.

At some point, the producer will start to take a more active role in the editing. This will often be determined by the relationship, contractual or otherwise, that the producer has with the director and the level of confidence that he or she has in the editor. No matter what deals have been made regarding cut approvals, the producer's responsibility for delivery, be it to studio, broadcaster or distributor, will demand that the director, unless he or she is in total accord with the producer, yield control over the final shape of the picture.

Choice of Music

Each production will call for its own set of decisions about the music that might be best for it. That could boil down to a decision about which composer to hire, leaving it to him or her to look after hiring musicians, copyists, and studios. Or you might prefer to look after the details yourself, working with the composer only on creative and artistic matters.

Musical talent abounds in Canada. In the three or four largest Canadian cities, there is no shortage of outstanding composers, songwriters, instrumentalists, singers, recording engineers, and editors. Recording and mixing studios are also first-rate and readily available. If you are not familiar with the world of composers and musicians, the Guild of Canadian Film Composers or the Canadian Music Centre may be of help to you.

The kind of music your film requires is generally a subjective decision of your creative team. If you step out of the bounds of more conventional music, you may run into problems. In recent years, some film

soundtracks have become hit records, tempting producers into leaping on the pop/rock bandwagon.
Here you enter the world of music publishers and
record companies, which may add to your worries
and consume a great deal of time. Some of the largest
music companies are "vertically integrated", meaning
that a parent company might control a film production company, a record label, a music publisher, an
artist agency, a concert promotion firm, musical
instrument rental operations, sound studios, and any
other potentially profitable part of the music business.
Such companies can afford to have exclusive contracts
with composers, songwriters, and performers, which
can make deal-making complex and costly when it
comes down to the ownership of ancillary rights.

The budget available for music is obviously a prime
consideration. The ability to satisfy some needy aspect
of the score, such as having larger orchestras, a greater
variety of sounds, or an extensive musical background
requiring additional recording sessions – all of these
things will cost money. Unfortunately, the budget for
music is usually established early in the game, while
the score itself is one of the last elements to be tackled.
This increases the temptation to nibble away at the
music budget during the earlier production stages, a
temptation to be resisted valiantly, especially since the
allocation was probably too low to start with. Better by
far to make the music budget generous, leaving the
producer with an unexpected but welcome sum in
hand if, by some good fortune, it should not all be
needed to finish the music job.

There are clearly good reasons to deal with your
musical questions early on and to find your musical
collaborators as soon as possible. Listen carefully to
their views and advice; they can help save you money.
Most important of all, they can provide you with a vital
ingredient of your production, which contributes
greatly to its artistic effect.

Sound Editing　　A good sound recordist on set can save you enormous trouble and time in postproduction. Although, in the crunch, location sound always seems to come second to picture (you can't do anything about picture, but sound can always be played with later), the best recordists are always looking for ways to improve on the situation. They will take the time to get better readings of wild lines (off-camera dialogue), and make sure that they cover the live effects separately or on another track, to give the sound editor the greatest number of options.

Sometimes, where time allows, picture editors look for the opportunity to do the sound editing as well. There are various pros and cons. Sound editing is a very specialized field and, in many cases, a specialist is necessary. On the other hand, where delivery schedule and the relative complexity of the sound required allow it, the picture editor may be a good choice since nobody knows the picture and planned effects better. You must weigh your own needs in making your decision.

If your film is for television, no matter what you may do with the soundtracks, the end result will be heard, for the most part, on the very cheap speakers built into most TV sets. Since subtle effects will not be heard, television sound does not need the same time, attention, or money as does sound for theatrical films. This is not to suggest that you cut corners. Sound editing is an art as valid as any other technical function in film production and can contribute enormously to the end product.

ADR and　　The process of recording new line readings in post-
Looping　　production used to be called looping because, when dialogue replacement was necessary, the scene to be changed was cut into a small, endless loop, and run through a projector in sync with a section of sound tape of identical length. This process has largely been

replaced by Automatic Dialogue Replacement (ADR), which achieves the same results without having to cut the loops. The film is run and rewound in sync with a magnetic sound dubbing machine until the director, producer, editor, performer, and engineer are all satisfied with the new performance. In both systems, the picture is marked with grease pencil, so that the actor is properly cued and can time the readings accurately.

Labs

Labs frequently seem to be on the short end of many peoples' sticks. They are certainly most vulnerable to criticism (when they're not there to defend themselves) if the rushes don't look quite right, or they're delayed, or the colour timing is off, or the sound transfers are screwed up, or a machine broke down. The possibilities for dissatisfaction are almost endless.

A good lab is a priceless ally, often bending over backwards to help you, re-processing or timing or printing or mixing – whatever it takes to process the film to your satisfaction. You may also be able to make some savings from your budgeted list prices by negotiating discounts with a lab. In addition, a lab may be able to provide you with many ancillary facilities, including office space, editing space, video services, ADR, Foley, mixing studios, and so on. (Foley is a studio sync sound effects system, employing a variety of built-in surfaces, such as gravel, creaking floorboards, etc.)

Despite the number of good lab facilities in Canada, it will probably be a long time before our production volume can support the elaborate facilities that exist in some other countries. It is more likely that we will be continuing to seek ways to save money on the basic services. One way to cut costs, only viable in 35 mm, is to print only selected takes. The risk to your more fragile negative in selecting takes on 16 mm is not worth the savings. Every time your originals are touched, moved, or run through a machine, the risk of damage increases. Whatever the lab may advise to provide some form of protection for those original elements will cost you money, but you should listen carefully to their suggestions.

From Work Print to Negative Cutting

So, your picture is locked (everyone's agreed that there's no more time to tinker and, short of re-shooting, it's as good as it's going to get), the sound editors and Foley people are hard at work, and your music composer is working from a videotape copy of the fine cut. Now you have to steal the cut work print away from the sound people long enough to get a slash print made from it. The slash print – a contact print, often done in black-and-white, and generally of very poor quality – is what the sound people will have to use, from this point on, right through the mix.

The cut work print is turned over to the negative cutter (often called the "neg" cutter). Neg cutting is one of the most isolated functions in filmmaking. He (or, more often, she) works in a dust-free room, wearing white cotton gloves, matching edge numbers on the negative to edge numbers on the work print. The neg cutter rarely even knows what the film is about as he or she painstakingly matches, frame for frame, cut for cut, the decisions you've been arguing back and forth for many weeks.

Titles and Credits

In the meantime, as you co-ordinate all of this, there are a few other things to keep you busy. Apart from the normal bill paying and trouble shooting, you must prepare, proofread and crosscheck all of the titles and credits for your film, making sure that they fulfill all contractual obligations. Then you have the art work designed to match the credit sequences (which you have asked the neg cutter to assemble first so that you can get the negative over to the optical house). At the optical house, the titles will be shot and either super-imposed on your footage or left on black, if that is what is required. When your title and credit sequences are completed to your satisfaction, then you must get them back to the neg cutter for inclusion in the body of the film.

Mixing

By about this time, you hope that the sound editors have completed their preparations in time for your scheduled mix. You may have a large number of tracks by this stage: several dialogue tracks, several effects tracks, at least a couple of music tracks, and any number of effects loops.

The music is generally recorded during several sessions onto multi-track machines, mixed down onto a two-inch tape (mono or stereo, according to your requirements) and then delivered on quarter-inch masters, which are subsequently dubbed to sound stock and cut, in sync with the picture, into the music tracks, in preparation for the mix.

Depending on your budget and the time and equipment available, you will probably proceed to a premix, separately mixing all of the dialogue, the effects and the music to their own appropriate levels. As with most things, the longer you can spend in preparation, the easier and quicker it will be when you get to the final mix. At a cost of around $250 per hour for mixing, you want to be well prepared. At the end of the process, you will have a master tape with three tracks on it from which you will be able to create your final soundtracks – in 16 mm, it is usually an optical track and in 35 mm, it is more commonly magnetic – while retaining the ability to separate out the music and effects tracks to create the inaterntional track. This, together with a copy of the original language version and a dialogue transcript, will be needed for foreign versions. (More about the importance of all this is found in Chapter 7.)

If everything has been well scheduled and smoothly executed, you hope that about this time, your neg cutter will be finished and that the resulting cut negative will go back to the lab for timing in preparation for the answer print (the best print that will ever exist of your film). Timing is the process by which skilled technicians go through the negative, scene by scene, shot by shot, and produce a tape of instructions to the computerized printing machine, to adjust the colour balance and light density of each shot as it passes through the printer. If everything has gone according to plan, your soundtrack will be ready to print along with the first answer print, so that you can now go into a screening room and, for the first time, see your completed film.

Frequently, adjustments must be made to the timing in some scenes, or, occasionally, throughout the entire film. You want to minimize such work because of the increased hazard to your precious negative each time it is handled. Your final protection is in the creation of your masters for reproduction: the CRI, the interpositive and internegative (all of these are defined in the glossary), and/or the videotape master. Once these are satisfactorily achieved, the original elements should be stored in a climate-controlled, fire-protected storage vault where, you hope, they will stay. You will only need to remove them if your printing materials are damaged and need to be replaced. The printing materials should be left in the lab vault where they can be accessed as needed.

Videotape Options

Videotape was originally designed for news, current events, and sports. Gradually, its quality has been improved to the point where it can be used for almost everything except, in the opinion of most who work in film, to replace film for drama. Videophiles will certainly tell you otherwise, especially in the light of some recent developments. It is a moot point.

You have (depending on the markets for your production) several options to explore:

Shoot film – finish (that is, edit and postproduce)
on film – deliver film and tape
Shoot film – finish on tape – deliver tape and film
Shoot tape – finish on tape – deliver tape

If your reproduction is only going to television, then any of the options are viable, limited only by the facilities and budget available to you. If your finished film might receive theatrical exhibition, you are limited to the first two options. If you take the first option, then it may well be in your best interests to include the transfer to videotape in your broadcast contract and budget, and supervise it yourself. In this way, you can use your answer print, together with your three-track master mix, to create a tape of the highest quality.

Choices:
16 mm, Super
16 or 35 mm

The bigger the frame size, the higher the potential quality of the end product when projected. Relatively few productions in this country, however, can afford to shoot in 35 mm (especially without a theatrical distribution guarantee). In the hands of a good cinematographer, 16 mm is excellent for most television productions, and lab facilities exist in some numbers. If you know you will never need a 16 mm print, and that all distribution will be done either on videotape or after the film has been blown up to 35 mm, then you can consider using Super 16. The additional 25 percent of frame size (no sound track) will give proportionately higher quality, although the system does have its disadvantages. The camera has to be converted, lab facilities are limited, and the editing machine, too, must be converted. Although 35 mm is bigger and better, it is also considerably more expensive and, because of its bulk, takes longer to shoot. Lab facilities are readily available. Other options, such as 70 mm or anything even more exotic, are probably not appropriate for discussion until you have made a film on 16 mm or 35 mm.

Summary

It is our personal belief that there are only two good reasons for making a film, especially from a producer's viewpoint. One is that you feel passionately that you *must* make the film. The other is that you want to make money. These two reasons need not be mutually exclusive. No other reason is compelling enough to carry you through all of the ups and downs that you will inevitably encounter. A common consensus seems to be that it takes, on average, about two years to put a production into motion. For the producer, who must finish the film, deliver it to prime markets and arrange distribution, sales promotion, enter it into major festivals, arrange a première, wrap up the books and the audit and the certification applications, there may well be an additional year of his or her life taken up by the film.

Planning and forethought are everything, but it's just as important for you to know *why* you are doing this work. This sense of purpose, as well as the enormous sense of achievement and pride in putting together and being part of a team of dedicated, smart, and talented people all working together towards a common goal – these things make it all worthwhile.

Imaginary Productions
Toronto

CALL SHEET

DATE: WED. NOV. 19/86   DAY: __4__
UNIT CALL TIME: __08:00__
ON CAMERA: __08:30__
SPEC. CALLS: 06:30 CRAFT SERVICE
                        MU/HR/WDB - 07:00

PRODUCER: R__ N____
SUPERVISING PRODUCER: H__ B_____
PRODUCTION MANAGER: S___ F_____
DIRECTOR: W__ M____

LOCATION: 1) Shore Breeze Motel
                2175 Lakeshore Blvd. W.
                Rm. 201, 202
CONTACT: __251-____

WEATHER: _____ Partly cloudy, no
rain, no snow - 10% chance precip.
SUNRISE: 7:18   SUNSET: 4:50
TOTAL DAYLIGHT HOURS: HRS 9 MIN 32

SCENE	SET/DESCRIPTION	D/N	CAST	PGS	LOCATION
Sc. 21,22pt.	EXT: MOTEL CU Gilchrist Room. Gilchrist & Julie appear in window. Freelong appears in his window.	D	2,8,9	-	1
3A	INT/EXT: MOTEL OFFICE Freelong talks to Gruber	D2	1,9	-	1
4	EXT: MOTEL Gruber crosses from office to rooms	D2	1	1/8	1
4	VTR EXT: MOTEL Simultaneous coverage of Sc.4	D2	1	-	1
5	EXT: MOTEL Gruber collects rent from mousy woman. Freelong goes to car.	D2	1,9, 16,17	2	1
8	EXT: MOTEL RM. 104,105 Gruber confronts skeletal woman, Sax man splits.	D2	1,18 19	3/8	1
7	EXT: MOTEL RM. 204 Gruber enters Rm. 204	D2	1	1/8	1
10	EXT: MOTEL RM. 205 Gilchrist pays Gruber	D2	1,8	1 1/8	1
32	EXT: MOTEL Man on balcony, goes into 206. Gruber slides on up and into 204.	N3	1,29	2/8	1
36	EXT: MOTEL Gruber descends stairs, confronts Saxman.	N3	1,19	6/8	1

ARTIST	CHARACTER	PU	MU	ON SET	REPORT TO
P__ P_____	1. GRUBER	07:45	08:00	08:30	1
C____ R____	2. JULIE	07:15	07:30	08:30	1
	8. GILCHRIST	-	08:00	08:30	1
	9. FREELONG	-	08:00	10:30	1
	16. MOUSY WOMAN	-	10:00	10:30	1
	17. SHIRTLESS MAN	-	10:00	10:30	1
	18. SKELETAL WOMAN	-	11:00	11:30	1
	19. SAXMAN	-	11:00	11:30	1

EXTRAS
Sc.32: balcony man on location 08:00 (8 hrs.)
        balcony woman on location 08:00 (4 hrs.)

1st A.D.	2nd A.D.	3rd A.D.	Unit/Location Manager
M___ F___	L___ P___	S_ W___	D__ P_____
421-	925-.	365-	783-

NOTES OF NOTE:

SET DEC./PROPS:
Sc.4: receipt book, money case, pen, keys
Sc.5,8,7: per Sc.4
Sc.10: per Sc.4 and new bills
Sc.32,36: briefcase, duffel bag

PICTURE CARS:
Sc.3A: Gruber's van, Freelong's car
Sc.4: Gruber's van, Freelong's car, Gilchrist's car, ND cars
Sc. 5,8,10: per Sc.4
Sc.32: per Sc.4

M/H/W:
Sc.32: Julie in disguise (with glasses)

FX:
Wetdown ready at 08:00

SP. PERSONNEL:
07:30 - Paul French and video crew

TRANSPORT:
MU/Hair unit warm by 06:45
PU P___ P_____   @ Sutton Place Hotel - 955 Bay St. - 07:45
PU C_____ R _____ @ Sutton Place Hotel - 955 Bay St. - 07:15

CRAFT SERVICE:
06:30 on location
06:45 coffee hot n' tasty
11:00 walking breakfasts for 40

LUNCH:
14:00 - 15:15 - on your own

SECURITY:
20:00 on location

HOSPITAL: Queensway General Hospital
          150 Sherway Dr.
          259-6671

ADVANCE SCHEDULE - THURSDAY, NOVEMBER 20, 1986 - DAY 5

Sc.69	EXT:MOTEL - man on balcony watches couple kiss, goes down to 101 - 15,24,29	
Sc.15A	EXT:MOTEL - cleaning woman exits #204 - 18A	
Sc.16	EXT:MOTEL - Gruber changes bulb - 1,3,18A	
Sc.38	EXT:MOTEL - Gruber parks in front of office - 1	
Sc.73	EXT:MOTEL - Gruber & Adele go to car - 1,3	
Sc.32	EXT: MOTEL	

WEATHER COVER

Sc.22B, INT: TV. ROOM STORAGE ROOM - Gruber extracts brass cases and and cardboard box - 1
Sc.37 INT: SHED - Gruber rigs telephone tap - 1
Sc.135 INT: T.V. CAMERA ROOM - Gruber dismantles camera - 1

PRODUCTION TITLE:_____   COST REPORT

CODE	ACCOUNT	PAID THIS WEEK/PERIOD			PAID TO DATE			PAYABLES		
01	STORY RIGHTS ACQUISITIONS									
02	SCENARIO									
03	DEVELOPMENT COSTS									
04	PRODUCER									
05	DIRECTOR									
06	STARS									
	TOTAL 'A'									
10	CAST									
11	EXTRAS									
12	PRODUCTION STAFF									
13	DESIGN LABOUR									
14	CONSTRUCTION LABOUR									
15	SET DRESSING LABOUR									
16	PROPERTY LABOUR									
17	SPECIAL EFFECTS LABOUR									
18	WRANGLING LABOUR									
19	WARDROBE LABOUR									
20	MAKEUP/HAIR LABOUR									
21	VIDEO TECHNICAL CREW									
22	CAMERA LABOUR									
23	ELECTRICAL LABOUR									
24	GRIP LABOUR									
25	PRODUCTION SOUND LABOUR									
26	TRANSPORTATION LABOUR									
27	FRINGE BENEFITS									
	SUBTOTAL									

COST TO DATE	ESTIMATE TO COMPLETE	TOTAL COST	BUDGET	(OVER)/UNDER

CODE	ACCOUNT	PAID THIS WEEK/PERIOD			PAID TO DATE			PAYABLES		
	SUBTOTAL BROUGHT FORWARD									
28	PRODUCTION OFFICE EXPENSES									
29	STUDIO/BACKLOT EXPENSES									
30	LOCATION OFFICE EXPENSES									
31	SITE EXPENSES									
32	UNIT EXPENSES									
33	TRAVEL & LIVING EXPENSES									
34	TRANSPORTATION									
35	CONSTRUCTION MATERIALS									
36	ART SUPPLIES									
37	SET DRESSING									
38	PROPS									
39	SPECIAL EFFECTS									
40	ANIMALS									
41	WARDROBE SUPPLIES									
42	MAKEUP/HAIR SUPPLIES									
43	VIDEO STUDIO FACILITIES									
44	VIDEO REMOTE TECH. FACILIT.									
45	CAMERA EQUIPMENT									
46	ELECTRICAL EQUIPMENT									
47	GRIP EQUIPMENT									
48	SOUND EQUIPMENT									
49	SECOND UNIT									
50	VIDEOTAPE STOCK									
51	PRODUCTION LABORATORY									
	TOTAL PRODUCTION 'B'									

COST TO DATE	ESTIMATE TO COMPLETE	TOTAL COST	BUDGET	(OVER)/UNDER

CODE	ACCOUNT	PAID THIS WEEK/PERIOD			PAID TO DATE			PAYABLES		
60	EDITORIAL LABOUR									
61	EDITORIAL EQUIPMENT									
62	VIDEO POST PROD. (PICTURE)									
63	VIDEO POST PROD. (SOUND)									
64	POST PROD LABORATORY									
65	FILM POST PROD. SOUND									
66	MUSIC									
67	TITLES/OPTICALS/STOCK FOOT.									
68	VERSIONING									
69	AMMORTIZATION (SERIES)									
	TOTAL POST PROD. 'C'									
	TOTAL B&C PROD. & POST PROD.									
70	UNIT PUBLICITY									
71	GENERAL EXPENSES									
72	INDIRECT COSTS									
	TOTAL OTHER 'D'									
	TOTAL 'A'+'B'+'C'+'D'									
80	CONTINGENCY									
	SUBTOTAL									
81	COMPLETION GUARANTEE									
82	COST OF ISSUE									
	GRAND TOTAL									

COST TO DATE	ESTIMATE TO COMPLETE	TOTAL COST	BUDGET	(OVER)/UNDER

CHAPTER SIX

The Domestic Market

Part 1 by Daniel Weinzweig
Part 2 by Ralph C. Ellis

*D*ANIEL WEINZWEIG is President of Norstar
Releasing, a Canadian theatrical, television, and
video distribution company. He has years of experience
as a distributor, booker (for Cineplex Corp., where he
was later Senior Vice-President), and producer (he was
Executive Producer of Pinball Summer, 1979). He has
been actively involved in a number of industry organizations, including a term as President of the Association of Independent and Canadian-Owned Motion Picture Distributors, and as Secretary of the Motion Picture Institute of Canada. He is on the Board of Directors
of the Canadian Film Institute, is a member of the Academy of Canadian Cinema & Television, and is Co-
chairman of the National Association of Canadian Distributors.

*R*ALPH C. ELLIS, through two associated companies,
Key Productions Ltd. and Manitou Productions
Ltd., has created and produced many nature documentaries and two outdoor adventure drama series. He
founded Ralph C. Ellis Enterprises in 1964, one of the
leading television program distributors in Canada,
which pioneered in international marketing of Canadian TV programs. From 1979 to 1982, he was President
of the Canadian Television Program Distributors' Association, and he has been a member of the Academy of

*Canadian Cinema & Television since its inception. In
1984, he won the Jack Chisholm Award from the Canadian Film & Television Association for his "outstanding
contribution to the industry."*

Part 1: Feature Film Distribution

"So who needs a distributor anyway?" you may ask.
"Why should I pay those guys outrageous fees and
probably never hear from them again? Besides which,
with the telephone and a few good lunches, I could do
it myself."

Well, let's face it, you can. But would you attempt to
fix your new $40,000 Mercedes-Benz yourself or would
you take it to a dealer who specializes in luxury auto-
mobile repairs?

You, as a film producer, have made enormous
efforts in financing and producing a multi-million dollar motion picture. But your responsibility does not
stop there: you must now ensure that your picture
returns the greatest possible revenue from the market
place, in all media, both here and abroad. It is therefore extremely important that you select the appropriate distributor in each territory. Some of the criteria
you will wish to consider are:

1. Is your picture appropriate to the distributor
   under consideration? If your picture requires a
   slow, careful, and selective release in the best
   quality cinemas in the country, then you should
   choose a distributor who has a reputation for distributing art or specialty pictures; an understanding of the need for getting your film screened at
   film festivals and critics' screenings; and knowledge of the best time of the year to open the picture. If, however, your film is a wide-release action,
   comedy, or exploitation film, needing saturation
   bookings in each market and appropriate electronic media advertising support, then you must

make sure that your distributor has the financial strength and exhibitor relationships to achieve these ends.

2. Can you work with these people? This industry is very much a people business, and it is extremely important that the producer and distributor trust and respect each other. This will ensure that the distributor feels confident that you're not going to "take the money and run" if he or she goes out into the market place and does a superb job.

3. Does the distributor have a reputation for honesty? Yes, there is such a thing in the film distribution business! You should check with other producers and suppliers of your chosen distributor to find out how they have run their business in the past. Have they paid their bills? Are their accounting practices (including regular and accurate financial reporting) consistent with the industry's standards? Ask television buyers or the head buyers of the major theatre chains how they would rate your distributor. Do not underestimate the importance of this research in determining who your distributor should be.

4. How crowded is the release schedule of your chosen distributor? It is possible that the distributor has committed to too many pictures and will not be able to give your film the amount of attention or financial commitment that it deserves.

5. Should you sell your picture to a "major"? Of course it is the dream of nearly all film producers to have their films distributed by Paramount, Warner Bros., Universal, MGM-UA, Columbia Tri Star, Twentieth Century-Fox, Orion Pictures, or the Walt Disney Company. Such distribution lends a good deal of prestige and importance to both picture and producer. These companies also have the financial and market clout to release your picture in the maximum number of theatres, supported by the greatest amount of advertising pos-

sible. They also have the ability to pay the largest advance guarantee for your picture, if they like it. However, it is also historically accurate to say that 60 years of creative accounting practices will probably ensure that (unless you're Woody Allen, Steven Spielberg, or George Lucas) whatever advance guarantee you receive will be *all* you receive. This, of course, depends on (a) how much money your picture ultimately grosses in all markets and (b) what type of deal (net or gross, described later in this chapter) you have structured.

Selling Your Film to a Major

The most common deal with a major has both your advance and all distribution expenses cross-collateralized in all media. This means that any unrecouped advances or losses from the theatrical distribution of your picture will be recouped and off-set against any revenues from other media such as television and home video distribution. There are as many deals as there are pictures, and how good a deal you strike with the major will depend upon how badly they want your picture and how good a negotiator you are.

Selling Your Film to an Independent

There has been a proliferation of independent film distributors in the last five years, in part because of the burgeoning new technology that has created powerful after-markets for the theatrical film: pay cable, syndicated television and, in particular, home video which, at this time, threatens to eclipse theatrical box office in gross revenues.

There is usually much more flexibility in negotiating a favourable deal with an independent producer, which might include splitting off rights (for example, selling home video or cable TV separately); non-cross-collateralization (an arrangement whereby the distributor is prevented from recouping losses from theatrical release with income from any of the other rights sold – for example, home video); a gross deal from the first dollar; and possibly more marketing input than you would receive from a major. It is also true that, because most independents do not have a guaranteed flow of product from in-house production, they may work harder to ensure a successful distribution of your picture and a more lasting relationship with you as an independent producer. On the other side of the ledger, it is probable that you will receive a smaller advance guarantee from an independent distributor and/or a lesser commitment towards prints and advertising of the theatrical release.

As a Canadian producer, and particularly if you are using the Telefilm Fund or other government production funds, you may be compelled to use a Canadian-owned independent distributor to release your film in Canada, while making a separate deal with a major or independent distributor in the United States. Even if you are not compelled to do it, it may be in your best interest to use a Canadian independent distributor, for other than nationalistic reasons. Independent distributors in most parts of the world are more knowledgeable about releasing pictures in their own market, and may be more committed to producing a profitable result in the territory where they work and live. In addition, Canadian independent distributors are eligible for financial assistance from Telefilm and other government agencies to offset distribution costs, which encourages them to develop a more ambitious publicity campaign for your film.

There have been many examples of Canadian-produced feature films that received distribution in Canada by a Canadian-owned distributor and distribution in the United States by a major. For example, *Tribute* was distributed by Pan-Canadian in Canada and by Twentieth Century-Fox in the United States; *The Bay Boy* by Pan-Canadian and Orion; and *Dancing in the Dark* by Norstar and New World.

The Mechanics of Theatrical Distribution

The logistics of theatrical film distribution are as complex, time-consuming, and expensive as preparing for a climb to the top of Mount Everest – and just a little less challenging. Once the contract between producer and distributor has been signed and a release date established, the distributor must go into action to acquire all the necessary materials to support a successful theatrical release. They include, but are not limited to, the following items.

Release Prints

The 35 mm release prints must be ordered from a lab chosen by the distributor. The lab will manufacture the necessary number of prints from original materials supplied by the producer. The materials that the producer turns over to the distributor typically include:

1. One first-class 35 mm composite positive print fully cut, titled, and with the soundtrack in perfect synchronization throughout. The print shall not contain any physical damage – including, but not limited to, spots, scratches, abrasions, dirt, cracks, or tears. Quality of the picture image and quality of the soundtrack image shall conform to the average quality established by current practice in the motion picture industry.
2. The original 35 mm colour negative to the picture and an interpositive made from the original picture negative.
3. One 35 mm master magnetic combined music and filled effects track assembled in synchronization with the original picture negative (or the original sound negative in cases where magnetic recording facilities are not available) and optical sound track fully synchronized with original negative and interpositive.
4. One English language dialogue continuity script and music cue sheets.
5. A 35 mm internegative of the backgrounds to the main, credit, insert, and end titles of the picture.

6. Six sets (or as many as available) of black-and-white still photographs comprising production, publicity, and portrait photographs together with their negatives. Each of the prints should have an explanatory caption.
7. Press kits – synopsis of the picture and biographies of the individual producer(s), director(s), stars, and leading players.
8. The complete statement of all screen and advertising credit obligations, together with a layout of the proposed screen and advertising credits, and a statement of all dubbing obligations, if any.
9. Distributor's right of access to all foreign language versions prepared with respect to the picture, as well as access to all key art advertising materials and promotional materials prepared with respect to the picture; the licensee shall have the right to duplicate and utilize any such material at no cost or expense to licensee.
10. One print of the theatrical trailer, if it exists.
11. A copy of producer's errors and omissions insurance, naming the distributor as additionally insured.
12. A certificate of nationality and certificate of origin issued by local authorities; or copies of the United States and Canada copyright registration certificates filed with the American and Canadian copyright offices.
13. Canadian Certification number, given by the federal Department of Communications.

The number of 35 mm release prints required, in most cases, will match the number needed to open the picture simultaneously in all theatres or markets where the picture has been booked. In Canada, on a limited run or specialty picture, this could mean anywhere from 6 to 10 prints; on a very commercial, wide-release picture, it would range from 30 all the way up to 100 prints.

Trailers

A trailer (an assemblage of scenes from the film designed to make it look as enticing as possible) is an extremely important tool for publicizing your picture to the very audience that you hope will eventually pay to see it when it opens. The earlier your trailer gets on as many screens as possible, the better chance you have to build a favourable awareness of your picture. It is important that your trailer be put in theatres exhibiting the type of film that will attract an audience appreciative of the film you have produced. In other words, you would not put the trailer for *Dancing in the Dark* in a cinema showing *Aliens*. Nor, conversely, would you put the trailer for *The Fly* in a theatre where *The Decline of the American Empire* is playing.

The distributor should order between three and five trailers per 35 mm release print. For example, if a distributor is opening the film in 10 theatres across the country, he or she should have a complement of 30 to 50 trailers on screens in advance of the opening. Additionally, once your picture has finally opened, trailers should still be playing in cinemas in the same locale as the cinema playing your picture. This is known in the industry as "cross-plugging".

Most territories have centralized services (such as Consolidated in Canada and National Screen Service in the United States) that handle, on behalf of distributors, the distribution of trailers and accessories. However, it is increasingly common for distributors to handle the shipping of these materials themselves, at least to the most important first-run theatres. In this way, they can ensure timely delivery, well in advance of the picture's opening.

Print Advertising Materials

The following are standard advertising materials required for proper distribution to theatres and the media:

a. one-sheet posters;
b. 8 x 10 stills (black-and-white and colour);

c. transparencies (slides) – best for reproduction purposes;
d. film clips (highlights from your movie for showing on television);
e. ads (glossy and various-sized ads for reproduction in newspapers);
f. press kits – a minimum of five stills from the movie; synopsis; biographies of the key cast and producer, director, and screen writer; and any other additional and pertinent information such as critical reviews, film festival showings, etc.

TV Advertising

TV advertising to publicize your picture will be arranged by a media buying service or advertising agency, working under the direction of your distributor. (The ad itself, which is often different in content from the theatrical trailer, is normally prepared by the distributor.) Appropriate programs are chosen in accordance with the projected audience for your movie. For example, a 30-second spot for a teen comedy would be directed to programs appealing to teens aged 12 to 17, during "late fringe" (after school 4:00 to 6:00 P.M.) or early prime time (7:00 to 10:00 P.M.). Television spots are generally purchased so that they start running on the Sunday or Monday before a Friday opening and continue through the weekend of the picture's opening. The frequency of such spots and the number of prime time spots are determined by the total advertising budget which, in turn, is decided by assessing a number of factors, including:

a. the number of screens set to open in each territory where television is being bought;
b. the potential gross of the picture in those theatres, as assessed by the distributor;
c. the terms (60 percent or 50 percent or 35 percent) that the exhibitor has agreed to pay the distributor for playing the picture; and
d. the quality or selling impact of the TV spot itself.

Radio Spots

Radio advertising is now used for very few types of movies. Movies with popular sound tracks or musical themes are most effectively advertised on radio stations whose listeners match the movie's projected audience. Since motion pictures are a visual medium, most distributors will choose to advertise their pictures on television and use radio sparingly.

Newspaper Advertising

Audiences today have been educated to refer to the entertainment pages of their local newspapers when deciding which movie they will attend. Therefore the quality and size of the movie ad on the newspaper page is extremely important to the picture's success.

Promotion and Merchandising

This is an area of increasing importance in today's competitive market place. You must never forget that you are working in an industry that has built and maintained itself with a strong infusion of showmanship. There are many factors in the effective promotion of a motion picture, such as tying in the elements of a picture with its appropriate merchandising counterparts. For example, *The Care Bears Movie* was promoted by both the distributor and the toy company that manufactured the Care Bear plush toy. Working together, they created a more effective, less costly campaign (including in-store, toy-package, and media advertising) than either could have mounted alone.

Promotion might also involve ticket give-aways on appropriate radio stations and arrangements with newspapers for free advertising in exchange for having the newspaper be co-presenter of the movie's première engagement. Usually the distributor will rent a theatre for the night before the film's official opening, in order to accommodate the recipients of the ticket give-away. In addition to the free exposure given to the picture by the radio station and the newspaper, a special screening has the added advantage of creating (you hope) positive word-of-mouth that will carry into the film's first week engagement and beyond.

Merchandising can be a hugely lucrative aspect of a successful theatrical release, and may include such items as T-shirts, toys, or soundtrack albums. In fact, the only limit to a successful cross-pollination of promotional and merchandising gimmicks is the imagination itself. (See Chapter 8 for a full discussion of publicity and promotion by David Novek and Kevin Tierney.)

The Theatrical Distributor's Duties – a Summary

Various mundane but essential aspects of theatrical distribution, such as shipping of prints and trailers, and arranging for viewing by various provincial censorship boards, are carried out daily by the distributor. But you can count on a good distributor to be a lot more than a well-organized shipper and receiver, as important as these functions are. The theatrical distributor's expertise is called for in the following ways:

a. acquiring playdates in the best possible theatres, in the greatest possible numbers, and on the best possible terms;

b. giving a good campaign to every release, with first-class publicity and promotion for each picture, irrespective of whether or not it is a box-office smash;

c. supplying exhibitiors with a consistent flow of good-quality product throughout the year;

d. maintaining a knowledgeable and experienced office staff consisting of (at least) a highly respected sales manager, a first-class booker, a top-quality publicist and advertising person, and an efficient and responsive accounting department;

e. providing expertise not just in theatrical distribution, but in all the important after-markets such as pay cable, network and syndicated television, and home video distribution. The distributor must follow consistent and orderly release patterns for your picture in each of these markets in order to maximize the return.

The Release Schedule

Although the vagaries of the industry may change the rules in the future, there exists today a standard and accepted rule-of-thumb for the orderly release of a theatrical motion picture. This is how it goes:

a. theatrical release – six-month window (a window is a period of time in which the purchaser has the exclusive right to exhibit the production);
b. home video release – six-month window;
c. available to pay-TV – twelve-month window plus three-month blackout period (a blackout period is a time during which the program will not be shown);
d. available to syndicated television (a syndication sale is one made on a station-by-station basis).

If there is no pay-TV sale and the picture goes directly to network television, then the following pattern may be established:

a. theatrical release – six-month window;
b. home video release – six-month window;
c. network TV – two-to-three-year window;
d. syndication.

The Contract between Distributor and Producer

"It's probably the only industry in the world where a contract just gives you the right to argue." This comment, credited to an unknown distributor, has a certain wry truth to it. There can be as many deals as there are pictures, and the permutations of terms and conditions in a distribution agreement are virtually unlimited. The major deal points, as outlined in such an agreement, may include, but are not limited to, the following items.

The Picture

In this clause, the licensor will warrant that the picture is of first-class technical quality and that the running time shall be not less than "x" minutes nor more than "y" minutes. Additionally, details such as the names of the producer, writer, director, and stars of the picture may be set out in a schedule attached to such an agreement.

Grant of Rights

In this clause, the licensor sets out and grants to the distributor (licensee) the exclusive rights to rent, lease, license, exhibit, distribute, and deal with the picture "in standard and sub-standard gauges" (that is, 35 mm, 16 mm, video, etc.) and for any and all purposes whatsoever. Subject to negotiations between the distributor and the producer, the rights included in this clause may include any combination of the following: theatrical, non-theatrical (16 mm, schools and film societies, armed forces and airplanes, etc.), and television broken down into the following categories: pay cable, network, syndication, videocassette, and video disc. This clause may also cover other-language versions of the film, which the distributor will have the right to make and distribute in his or her territory, subject to the same terms and conditions.

The Territory

The territory will be defined specifically. In the case of Canada, it is generally stated as follows: "Dominion of Canada including its territories, possessions, dependencies; military camps, government installations and schools; Canadian Red Cross; Canadian United Services Organization (CUSO); veterans' hospitals and similar facilities; ships at sea and planes in the air flying the Canadian flag; and oil company and construction company campsites in Canada." Many contracts for the territory of Canada will specify "French and English Canada" or, if only English-language rights are granted, then "English-speaking Canada" may be specified.

The Term of the Agreement

The term of the agreement will generally be for a minimum of seven years, and it may be negotiated for a term that extends as far as "perpetuity". At the expiration of the negotiated term of the agreement, the rights revert to the copyright holder – usually the producer.

Delivery

The producer will be required to deliver any and all necessary printing materials for the picture to the distributor, on or before a specified delivery date, including any negatives, interpositives, internegatives, sound tracks, or any other materials required for the manufacture of prints. All such elements should be sent to a laboratory designated by the distributor, together with a "laboratory letter" that gives the distributor legal access to these materials for the purpose of ordering prints, trailers, video masters for television broadcast, or other required materials for the distribution and exploitation of the picture.

Licensor's Warranties and Representations

In this clause, the producer must warrant and represent that he or she owns and controls all rights granted to the distributor and that there are no claims, liens, or encumbrances against the picture which might in any way interfere with the distributor's granted right to distribute the film in his or her territory. Additionally, the producer must warrant that he or she owns or controls the music and performing rights within the film, and that the distributor will not be responsible for any payments or royalties due from the production company for these rights. Finally, the producer must indemnify the distributor against any trademark, copyright, or slander violations that may result from the distribution and exhibition of the picture. (For more on the legal ramifications of the producer's dealings with distributors, see Chapter 9 by Douglas Barrett.)

Licensee's Rights and Obligations

Concerns outlined in this clause include the distributor's rights to transfer or sub-distribute the picture through corporate subsidiaries, affiliates, or third-party companies; title to the material; treatment and disposition of prints during the term and at the expiration of the agreement; and the right to make deletions in the picture for the purposes of censorship and broadcast standards.

Accounting and Auditing

This paragraph in the contract deals with the distributor's obligations and accounting practices, and it should include a description of the form the statement of accounting will take. The statement will show details relating to the period to which it pertains, including, among other things, gross receipts and the sources thereof (theatres, towns, TV stations, radio distributors, etc.); and a description and breakdown of any deductions and any money owing to the producer. Such statements of accounting may also be accompanied by backup materials, such as remittance slips, contract forms, or box office statements, as well as proof of any major deductions in the form of bills, statements, or invoices.

This paragraph of the contract will also specify how often statements should be sent to the producer; for example, monthly during the first six months following release of the picture, quarterly for the next eighteen months, and bi-annually thereafter. Such a clause should also include the producer's right to audit the distributor with appropriate notice of this intention.

Default

This clause protects the producer and / or the distributor by setting out certain default provisions (actions that would nullify the contract) such as:

    a. if the producer fails to deliver the picture within a certain time period;

b. if either producer or distributor becomes insolvent or files for bankruptcy; or if a receiver, trustee, or liquidator is appointed;

c. if any of the provisions set out in the distribution agreement are breached.

In all of these cases the contract may be deemed in default and therefore terminated.

Producer's Share of Receipts (the Deal)

This key clause sets out the financial terms and conditions agreed to by the producer and the distributor. It will, among other things, set out the amount of advance or guarantee (if agreed to) that the distributor is going to pay the producer for the right to distribute the film in the territory. If it is an advance, then this money is paid to the producer "up front" and before the theatrical release of the picture. If it is a guarantee that has been agreed to, then the distributor has promised to pay the producer the agreed-upon amount of money over a period of time not to exceed, for example, three years (if the agreed-upon amount of money has not already been remitted to the producer as his or her share of the distribution proceeds). Whether it is an advance or a guarantee, it should be understood that this money is simply an advance against the producer's share of distribution rentals of the film and is fully "recoupable" by the distributor from the distribution income.

Additionally, the producer's advance or guarantee may be fully "cross-collateralized". This means, for example, that if the money advanced to the producer and the distribution expenses are unrecouped after theatrical distribution has been completed, the distributor may retain the producer's share of revenues from *other* rights (for example, a television sale or home video release) until the distributor's share is fully recouped.

The Main Types of Distribution Deals

There are almost as many deals as there are pictures produced, and it falls upon the producer and distributor to work out a deal acceptable to both parties. There are, however, two main types of financial arrangements: the net deal and the gross deal.

The Net Deal

A net deal represents a sharing of the "gross receipts" (those monies received from all sources for the rental of the picture), *after deduction* of the following items:

a. distributor's distribution fees;
b. distribution expenses in connection with the distribution of the picture, generally on a cross-collateralized basis; such expenses should be specifically outlined in a distribution agreement, under the heading "Distribution Expenses", and generally include the cost of prints, trailers, advertising, publicity and exploitation, censorship, and dubbing costs;
c. any advances paid to the producer, again, recouped on a cross-collateralized basis.

Here are some examples of the range of income splits between producer and distributor in a typical net deal:

	Distributor's Fee	Producer's Share
Theatrical	20 – 50%	50 – 80%
Non-theatrical	50%	50%
Network TV	10 – 15%	85 – 90%
Pay Cable	20 – 30%	70 – 80%
Syndication TV	25 – 40%	60 – 75%
Home Video	Producer receives 20 – 30% of distributor's wholesale price.	

In the home video market, the distributor must sell to the wholesaler, who in turn sells to the retailers of home video. The ever-changing complexities of this market dictate that the producer's interests are best served by taking either a percentage of the wholesale price or a flat amount of money per videocassette, no matter what the ultimate sale price of that cassette will be.

The Gross Deal

The gross deal is a much simpler formula, but for the producer the most difficult and problematic to obtain from a distributor. In this case, the producer would receive his or her percentage of the *gross* receipts derived from the distribution of the picture from first dollar, *without* deductions of any kind (other than the advance, if there has been one). Here, the producer would be receiving a significantly smaller piece – usually in the 20 to 30 percent range – of a much larger pie, as opposed (in a net deal) to a larger percentage of a smaller or perhaps non-existent pie. This puts the distributor, however, at considerable risk, since the distributor must absorb 100 percent of the "distribution expenses" and hope that the amount of film rental generated by the picture exceeds not only distribution expenses but also the distributor's fee.

A "gross deal" is, of course, much desired by producers, because it *guarantees* them revenues from the distribution of their picture, regardless of how much it cost the distributor to release the picture. However, generally speaking, only the most powerful and successful producers are able to strike this type of deal with their distributor.

The distributor has two main (and inseparable) functions in life: one is sales and the other is marketing. Without the first, the second is redundant. However, without the latter, the former will not achieve the desired results. I will now discuss in detail how a distributor will present your film to each potential mar ket place in order to achieve the highest possible dollar returns.

The Theatrical Market Place

The distributor may or may not operate with branches outside of the home office, strategically located in key areas of the country. Generally speaking, the majors operate with branches, while the independent distributors handle all territories out of their home offices, possibly using sub-distributors in other parts of the country. The main benefit of branches or sub-distributors is to achieve the maximum number of bookings to smaller, independent theatres who are not associated with a theatre chain or booking service, and who are reluctant to deal with a distributor who may be thousands of miles away.

It is to the benefit of both the producer and the distributor that a deal be struck between the two at the earliest possible time, preferably before or during the production of the picture. This will enable the distributor to plan the sales and marketing strategy that best suits the picture. Too often, the producer will not make a deal with the distributor until the film is in the can, demanding that the distributor release the picture to theatres two or three months thereafter. This is not an efficient way to maximize revenues, since in all likelihood the proper materials (for example, ads and posters) will not be available; the best theatre screens will already be taken for that date; and publicity and promotional efforts will not be maximized because the lead time is too short. As soon as a print is made available to the distributor, he or she will screen it for all important exhibitors and immediately begin discussions to select the best available date and most appropriate theatres in which to play the picture.

Here I want to say a few words about "bidding": the practice by which theatres and theatre circuits in competing geographic areas of a city offer guarantees

of film rental terms in order to win the exclusive right to play a particular motion picture. Bidding is an American phenomenon – in Canada such competition doesn't take place. Canada has only two major coast-to-coast theatre chains, Famous Players and Cineplex Odeon, which form, in effect, a duopoly.

As of late spring 1987, Cineplex Odeon owns approximately 550 screens in 170 locations across Canada, while Famous Players has approximately 470 screens in 177 locations. They have developed a policy of non-aggressive competition for pictures. The result of this, at the time of writing, is that each circuit has aligned itself with and receives 100 percent of the product from specific distributors, whose loyalty is, without exception, to that one circuit. This means that Famous Players plays *all* the pictures from Paramount (its parent company), MGM-UA, Twentieth Century-

Fox, and Warner Bros. Cineplex Odeon, meanwhile, exhibits the total output of pictures from Universal (a major shareholder in that corporation), Columbia Tri Star, and Orion. The same loyalties are now demanded of the independent distributors. These loyalties have, in fact, been one of the principal causes of the controversial distribution problems faced by Canadian producers. With "the majors" booking the majority of Canadian screens and optimum screen times for packages of films, Canadian independent producers have in the past had very limited access to the screens. Canadian independent distributors are now overcoming these accessibility problems by establishing their own strong ties with exhibitors.

Since the United States represents approximately 70 percent of potential world revenues for films and videos, and represents the most accesssible market for Canadian productions, it is useful to understand how the distribution system works there. In the United States, the distributor sends out to all competing exhibitors in each territory a letter which may read as follows:

> We enclose our request for your offer and a contract form for your convenience in submitting an offer for the production *XYZ*. Deadline is 2:00 P.M., September 22. Playing time: 8 weeks minimum; suggested guarantees: $50,000; suggested terms: 90/10 with the following weekly minimum – first week 70 percent, second week 60 percent, third week 50 percent, balance 35 percent.

The 90/10 arrangement means that the distributor will receive 90 percent of the gross receipts *after* the exhibitor has first deducted and retained his or her disclosed house expense. The exhibitor's expenses include: rent, light, heat, salaries, advertising, and everything involved in running the theatre. It is accepted practice in the industry, however, that the exhibitor does have some built-in profit in the stated overhead. If the house expense is $3000 and the exhibitor takes in $10,000 at the box office, the exhibitor has $7000 over house expense. The distributor gets 90 percent of the $7000, or $6300. If $8000 is taken in and the house expense is still $3000, only $5000 is left, of which $4500 belongs to the distributor.

However, the distributor's letter also asks for further guarantees. The exhibitor is asked to guarantee that the film will play for a minimum of eight weeks. The bid request also demands minimum percentage terms or a "minimum floor," whereby the exhibitor guarantees that he or she will pay no less than the specified percentages for each week of the engagement. For example, in the second week, the minimum floor is 60 percent. Under these minimum terms, the house expense is *not* deducted first for calculation purposes. Therefore a box office gross of $8000 will net the distributor $4800, or $300 more than would be yielded by the 90/10 split of the basic contract terms.

In Canada, although the 90/10 deal is sometimes available for the most commercial films, most pictures receive more conventional terms, which may not include any guarantee of length of playing time, and terms that start at 50 percent tops for the first week, scaled down in subsequent weeks to a minimum floor of 30 percent or even 25 percent of the box office.

After screening the picture for exhibitors, the distributor will negotiate various items, such as:

a. the best and most appropriate theatres available;
b. the opening playdate in each key city;
c. the maximum and minimum terms for each particular week on a descending scale;
d. the exhibitor's share and distributor's share of the advertising budget.

Once these essential questions are answered, the distributor can confidently order the required number of release prints, trailers, and advertising accessories necessary to get the picture opened.

The Right Theatre – and the Right Opening Date

It is absolutely crucial to the success of a theatrical release that the correct decisions have been made about the most appropriate theatres for the picture and the most appropriate opening date. A distributor would not be in his or her right mind to insist on opening *Porky's* in a single theatre in Toronto, nor *The Grey Fox* in a multiple booking using 30 prints with a TV saturation advertising campaign that was beamed mostly toward rural towns. It is important to know whether the picture will play best to a sophisticated, up-scale, urban moviegoer, in which case it should be booked in one to three theatres, primarily in the downtown core of a city like Toronto; or whether the picture will appeal to a wider, more youthful, commercial movie audience, in which case it needs a broad-release multiprint booking.

It would also be a mistake to take a film that required special handling, was relatively little-known, or required a slow build and word-of-mouth to succeed, and open it at a time when competition is most keen. For films, the largest target audience is between ages 13 and 24. The theory is this: when children become adolescents they want to get out of the house, away from their parents. By the time people are in their mid-twenties, though, many of them are married with families, and for them the cost of moviegoing becomes a luxury item (with babysitters, parking, and so on adding to the cost). That is why the most lucrative times for moviegoing are Christmas, the summer, and Easter, when school is out and the greatest number of potential moviegoers is available.

For the same reason, however, this would not be the best time to open adult-oriented and more specialized pictures requiring a less competitive market place and the maximum media coverage possible in order to achieve success. Pictures such as *My American Cousin* or *Joshua Then and Now* should open in the months between September and November or between January and May. There are obvious exceptions to this; you would not open *One Magic Christmas* at Easter! In any event, these are extremely important decisions that should be made in consultation between the producer and distributor.

The last thing that must be understood is that *most movies lose money theatrically*! This is an unassailable fact, although I have never met a producer yet who thought that this would be the case with his or her movie. Nevertheless, theatrical exposure of a feature film will likely enhance its value in other markets such as home video and pay television. Both these potentially lucrative markets are tied directly to the success a feature film achieves during its theatrical run.

The Non-Theatrical Market Place

This is, in fact, not one market place, but many – the 16 mm and videocassette non-theatrical market includes all those types of exhibition that do not compete with normal theatrical exhibition. This includes showings at schools, universities, institutions such as prisons or hospitals, lumber camps, oil rigs, military camps, government installations, and ships. Additionally, film societies and commercial airlines may be two important sources of revenues.

In recent years, 16 mm rentals have been on the decline, as videocassettes and VCR units have become widely used. In many cases, it is cheaper and easier to rent or buy a tape than to go through the often complex and costly procedure of renting 16 mm.

Network Television

Network television is potentially the most lucrative of all forms of television exhibition for your feature film, because it can reach the largest number of viewers. However, in recent years, broadcast television has moved away from showing theatrical motion pictures and now lists its programming priorities in the following order:

a. series;
b. mini-series;
c. made-for-TV movies;
d. variety shows or specials;
e. theatrical feature films.

The rationale behind this ordering is the need for competing networks to build audience loyalty by showing popular series on a weekly basis. Further, in recent years, many theatrical films have received mediocre or poor ratings, while mini-series and made-for-TV movies received higher ones. (For a discussion of the marketing of programs specifically made for TV, see Part 2 of this chapter.)

There are exceptions, of course. Most networks do broadcast a small number of theatrical feature films, usually those that have enjoyed significant theatrical box office success. For Canadian networks, the Canadian content of a film is an additional criterion. It is a distinct advantage if your film is scheduled for broadcast on one of the three major American networks, because this will encourage a Canadian network to precast or simulcast that film in Canada and thus benefit from any advertising and publicity provided by the American network. By and large, however, do not count on a network sale for your feature film. In the new market place, you are more likely to make a sale to pay-TV.

Pay Cable TV

Pay-TV has become the new domain for the theatrical feature film, representing, in most cases, its initial TV exposure. The largest pay-TV services in Canada are primarily movie channels. Here all but a very few theatrical feature films appear after their theatrical and videocassette release. (Usually they show up about twelve months after the initial theatrical opening, but sometimes sooner.)

In Canada, at the moment, there are three pay-TV services: First Choice-Super Channel in Eastern Canada; Super Channel-First Choice in Western Canada and the Quebec-based French pay-TV service Super Ecran. In all, about 700,000 subscribers receive these services. The fledgling years of pay-TV in this country were difficult ones and nobody is sure about the future of this service, given the extremely competitive market place represented by home video, satellite, and specialty services as well as conventional network TV. However, one thing seems certain, and that is that this will remain for some time to come the primary market for theatrical feature films to be shown on television.

The distributor negotiates one of two types of deals with the pay-TV service: a flat fee (the typical range is $100,000 to $150,000 for Canadian films) regardless of what the subscriber base might be; or a cents-per-subscriber arrangement, which may range from one or two cents per subscriber at the low end to as high as 25 or 30 cents per subscriber, depending on the theatrical box-office success of the picture being negotiated. For example, if the average subscriber base over a 12-month licenced period is 500,000 and a 20 cents-per-suscriber arrangement is made, then the total licence fee paid to the distributor over the 12-month period would be $100,000.

Syndicated TV

Syndicated TV sales represent the last phase in the exploitation of the film and the final source of revenue. Films become available for syndication when they have completed prior licence periods with pay and/or network television showings. Although fees are generally lower than in the latter markets, syndication can represent a lucrative additional source of income.

Fees charged by the distributor for sales of syndicated television are generally higher than either pay-TV or network commissions, because of the higher costs of selling, servicing, and collecting from a much greater number of independent television stations, often located in remote areas of this huge country.

Syndicated television sales are made in "packages", whereby the distributor puts 10, 20 or more films in a group and sells them to the TV station. By doing this, the distributor compels the station to purchase *all* his or her product – good, bad or indifferent – at one package price that the distributor will subsequently allocate according to the individual values of each picture. The licence period for syndication is generally between three and five years.

Home Video

The fast-growing market for videocassettes is the newest and most exciting source of revenue for theatrical feature films, but home video is also the most mercurial of the new technologies. At the time of writing, video rentals represent by far the largest share of the consumer market. However, as the price of tape and packaging comes down and competition increases, it is predicted that more people will buy films instead of renting them.

Logistically, here is the arrangement the distributor makes. Approximately six months following the initial theatrical release date of the film (sometimes earlier if the picture has been a flop), the distributor will designate a "street date" for the picture's availability to retailers and wholesalers. Before the street date and following the distributor's announcement of the picture's availability, a "cut-off date" will be set, by which time retailers must have their orders in to the wholesalers so that copies can be made and shipped to their ultimate destination. This method ensures that the distributor and wholesaler do not duplicate or stock more copies of the film than are actually required by retailers. Additional orders may be received in the weeks and months following the initial cassette release; however, it is generally acknowledged that 80 to 90 percent of all orders received on the picture occur within 30 to 45 days of the availability date. The wholesale price of cassettes is generally based on demand (with more popular titles carrying a higher pricetag). Wholesale unit prices to the retailer may range from $49.95 to $99.95. The distributor's share may be based upon a specific amount of money per cassette sold or, more commonly, a percentage of the wholesale price, ranging from 20 to 30 percent, on average.

It is significant to note, at this time, the explosion of the home video rental market. North American wholesale sales of pre-recorded videocassettes passed the fifty million unit level in 1985. Revenues remitted to distributors of videocassettes have reached a value of 1.5 billion dollars (according to *Variety*, January 8, 1986). Home video players are now in approximately 30 percent of North American households, with the prediction that, by 1995, when VCR penetration will reach 85 percent of households, 16 billion dollars of the total projected revenues of 23 billion dollars realized by film producers will derive from the home video market.

From a Canadian film producer's perspective, the sale of 1000 cassettes in Canada (easily reachable) typically generates approximately 10 to 15 thousand dollars in revenues to the producer. (The videocassette of *My American Cousin* has sold about 5,000 copies in Canada; *The Grey Fox* has sold about 4,000; and *Porky's* has sold about 10,000.) However, home video foreign markets, which are easier to crack than foreign theatrical release, can increase the revenues tenfold or more. Videocassette sales in the U.S. market were worth 3.3 billion dollars in 1985, which represented 27 percent of revenues from feature films, compared to 28 percent generated by domestic theatrical release (*Variety*, January 8, 1986).

To date, producers have not shared in the bounty of the video rental market, since they claim a share only of the initial purchase price paid for the cassette, not of the subsequent rental revenue. Recent break-throughs in videocassette retailing, with prices for consumers pegged as low as $24.95 to $29.95, hold out promise that more revenue might begin to return to producers, as sales become a larger factor in the video market.

**The
Exhibitors**

Exhibition is the backbone of the theatrical motion picture industry. Exhibitors are the "retailers" who put in their windows a commodity known as motion pictures. Most movie theatres in Canada, particularly in the larger centres, are part of theatre circuits or booking collectives known as booking agencies. Most of the major functions of theatre operations – such as booking and buying, advertising and publicity, concession supplies, and theatre supervision – are done out of the head office of these organizations.

Most movie theatres being built today are "multi-plex" (multitheatre) operations, containing from three to ten screens per complex, with seating ranging from 100 seats in the smaller auditoria to a maximum of 500 seats in the largest. This multiple cinema concept has revolutionized the motion picture theatre business, by allowing the exhibitor to open a new picture in his largest auditorium while the demand is greatest and then to move it down into his smaller auditoria as he holds the picture in subsequent weeks and the demand for it diminishes. While this is being accomplished, the exhibitor may open a new top grossing film in his largest auditorium and follow the same pattern. This process provides the exhibitors with economies of scale, minimizing the number of potential empty theatre seats at any given time.

The cost of operating a theatre can be broken down as follows:

a. rental costs of the motion picture;
b. advertising costs for the motion picture;

c. operating costs of the theatre, including: salaries to employees; property rent and taxes; amortization of theatre fixtures such as seats, projection equipment, screen, concession equipment; concession items, supplies, tickets, and so on;

d. operating costs of running a theatre circuit, including executive management, bookers, and accounting department.

When a picture is first released in theatres, advertising costs are generally shared between distributor and exhibitor, in accordance with the percentage of film rental earned on a motion picture. For example, if the deal is a 90 / 10 over house expense, the distributor will pay 90 percent of the advertising costs. Alternatively, when a picture is licenced to a theatre or group of theatres on a straight percentage basis, the advertising may be shared on a 50-50 basis between the distributor and exhibitor, up to a maximum of an agreed-upon limit. Anything spent by the distributor over that limit must be absorbed 100 percent by the distributor. Although advertising costs vary with pictures, approximately 10 to 15 percent of the theatre's box office grosses are expended in advertising dollars.

Theatres must be booked in accordance with their geographic location, taking into consideration various economic and demographic considerations, including average age, income, and education of the residents.

I would be remiss if I did not let you in on the unspoken, dark secret of the success of motion picture theatres throughout North America. It's ... yes, you guessed it, popcorn! The problem is that, in order to sell tremendous amounts of popcorn and cokes, you must fill those seats with warm bodies. Movie theatres often lose money or break even from the showing of movies, after the cost of showing those movies is taken into account. The real pure profit of the theatre business comes from the concessions! Each year, several major conventions with intriguing names such as Showarama, Show West and NATO (North American Theatre Owners Association) are meccas for exhibitors from all over North America. They gather to learn about the latest "state-of-the-art" popcorn machines and drink dispensers, as well as new and imaginative taste sensations with huge mark-ups to be foisted upon the unsuspecting moviegoer!

The future of the motion picture theatre, despite doomsayers, is probably secure, since the bulk of the moviegoing audience is young. These are people for whom staying at home on the weekends is cruel and unusual punishment. No matter what new and wonderful technology emerges for home viewing, the social experience, presentation, and excitement of going *out* to a movie is hard to beat! It is not enough, however, for theatre owners to sit back, content that business is good, and await the next blockbuster. Instead, theatre owners must constantly upgrade their facilities, creating new and exciting environments of picture and sound, in order to compete with the ever-changing competition for the entertainment dollar.

Part 2: Television Distribution

It has been said that there are five stages in the development of any television project. First there is total enthusiasm, followed by total chaos; next comes the search for the guilty, followed by the persecution of the innocent and, finally, the rise of the incompetent!

In many cases, it is only after all of the above has happened that it occurs to someone in the production company that it might be a good idea to market the TV program or series in Canada and around the world. This leads to the question of how to choose a distributor.

Why Have a Distributor? There was a time, before the proliferation of TV services around the world, when producers could be their own distributors, simply by making a few trips to the more lucrative world markets. Now the field of distribution has become much more complex and the task requires a specialist. Conditions in the television market place are constantly changing. In recent years, we have seen the introduction of pay services and videocassette sales.

Further, there has been overlapping satellite penetration via cable of what used to be exclusive markets for programs. For example, in the Canadian market there are American pay-TV services such as Arts And Entertainment, which reach only a small Canadian audience and hence pay a minimal amount for Canadian rights. A first sale to this service in advance of a Canadian sale could jeopardize a major Canadian sale. Similarly, four Detroit TV stations, the three major American networks plus PBS, are picked up now via CanCom's satellite to cable service in many parts of Canada. The timing of a program sale to Detroit stations, therefore, is subject to prior sales in Canada to ensure maximum return in each situation.

What can an effective TV program distributor accomplish for the producer? To summarize, the distributor can prepare a sales plan both nationally and internationally to launch the producer's program. In Canada, this means taking into account many of the following opportunities:

1. *Home video release* (sometimes involving a TV release hold back). Feature films and programs released for home video distribution are usually held back from TV release for certain periods. The logic is simple. If a program is available freely from other sources such as TV, it can be taped off the air at home rather than rented from video stores.

2. *A pay-TV window.* Pay-TV companies are in the retail business of selling a product to which they must have exclusive rights for their market. Their programs are only attractive if they are not otherwise available on TV. Thus they will demand a period of from months up to perhaps two years before programs or films they buy become available to free TV. This period is known as a window.

3. *Negotiating a network release.* This should be done with provision for as short a play-off period (that is, the length of time during which the program can be telecast) as possible in order to sell local markets repeat showings (syndication). Obviously the number of telecasts and the period granted for play-off will have an effect on re-run sales of the program on a market-by-market basis.

4. *Adapting or creating a French version.* This would be prepared for release as in points 1, 2, and 3 above.

5. *Providing a similar plan on a territorial basis for TV services around the globe.* For more on international marketing of television programs, see Chapter 7 by Jan Rofekamp.

The Canadian TV Market

You, as a producer, may have a certain skepticism about the need for a distributor in the Canadian TV market. Often heard is the remark "Why should I pay a distributor 35 percent for distributing my program?" In fact, in most instances, the producer pays nothing, because the distributor is working on a commission basis. If there are no sales there is no income, either for the distributor or the producer. In other words, the distributor obtains his or her income through successful sales efforts and not from the producer (except indirectly from the producer's program). In addition, the distributor's experience and business relationships are the keys to success in the TV market place.

Generally speaking, the sales of TV programs only come about by day-to-day contacts between the buyers (TV station executives) and the seller (the distributor). In the Canadian TV market, for example, with vast distances to cover and differing conditions in each market, the distributor must travel on a regular basis to keep up his contacts with the buyers. This is an expensive but necessary part of the work of all successful TV distribution companies.

The Canadian TV market is made up both English and French sectors. A distributor will analyse and get maximum revenues from both language sectors. In Canada, the main avenues open to the distributor in the effort to generate monies for the producer are: pay-TV, network TV, and syndication (that is, station-by station) sales. Pay-TV includes, at the moment, First Choice-Super Channel in Eastern Canada, Super Channel-First Choice in Western Canada, and Super Ecran in French Canada. In addition there are specialty services for music (Muchmusic) and sports (The Sports Nework) programming. The distributor can determine which of these services might be interested in the content of the producer's program. In some instances, it may be possible for the distributor to negotiate a pay window (a period before release to regular TV) that could be financially advantageous.

The TV networks in Canada include CBC and CTV, with headquarters in Toronto, and Radio-Canada, TVA, and Radio Quebec, with headquarters in Montreal. In addition, there are informal groupings of individual stations that from time to time purchase national rights to programs. These include Global TV, CHCH-TV Hamilton, CFTO-TV Toronto, and CITY-TV Toronto. Each of these stations then re-sells to other Canadian markets the show or shows on which they have national rights.

There are also regional services such as Global TV and TVOntario in Ontario, the Access Network in Alberta, and the Knowledge Network in British Columbia. A new Montreal-based French network, Quatre Saisons, began operations in most major French Canadian cities in Quebec in September 1986. TVO launches a French service for Ontario in January 1987, broadcasting from Toronto.

Any sales outside of network contracts are classified as syndication sales. These sales may involve first-run or second-run programming, but in general the term means selling on a regional or station-by-station basis across Canada.

The Importance of a Distributor in the Planning Stages

Most successful distributors like to be involved at an early stage. In general, producers need not worry that their creative freedom will be under assault, since distributors are interested in practical matters rather than interfering with production. For example, if you are planning a Christmas special, your distributor may point out that the Middle East and China will probably produce not much income. Your distributor can assist you with specific marketing knowledge that can sometimes save you a great deal of money. Here are some points the distributor may raise:

1. *Running time.* Half-hour shows should generally be no longer than 24 minutes and hour shows should be no longer than 50 minutes, to allow for the insertion of commercials.
2. *Commercial placements within the program.* This should be worked out with your prospective purchaser, but would normally include three breaks per half hour with appropriate placement. In a film program, it is best to fade to black for a few seconds rather than put in a "place commercial here" slug. The slug will create problems outside Canada with foreign language versions as well as in English language territories where the entire program is run without commercials, since it will have to be physically removed. In a film production, the footage removed will then cause your

picture and sound tracks to be out of sync, creating the unnecessary expense of having a dubbing studio re-sync that section of the film and the music and effects track.

3. *Textless Title Backgrounds.* Always make provision in your planning for textless title backgrounds, to be available for titling in French and other languages. For French Canada, it is generally necessary to render all opening and closing titles, credits, and so on in French. Failure to do this will mean expensive retitling at a later date before the program can be accepted.

4. *Music and Effects Track.* Always ensure that, if your program has international appeal, there is a music and effects track available for it. Having a separate music and separate effects track is best but a mixed M / E (Music and Effects) track is often acceptable for foreign versioning. In a dramatic video-taped production, if your action sequences and dialogue on location are shot at the same time, it will not be possible to separate background sounds from dialogue for your effects track. Instead, for example, if a conversation is taking place by a waterfall, it is easy and less costly to make a separate recording of waterfall sounds on the spot and rebuild a full effects track later.

It is essential for the producer, as early as possible in the production phase, to plan a comprehensive promotional campaign on behalf of his or her program(s). Black and white stills and colour transparencies, a poster, press kits, on-air promos, and bios of cast and creative team should be prepared. Keep in mind that every TV show is competing for audience attention. Make it easy for the network or sponsor to promote your program. (For more on this subject, see Chapter 8 by David Novek and Kevin Tierney.)

Contractual Relationship with Distributors

Legend has it that there used to be a contract in use by one of the American major program distributors which producers using its services were required to sign. It included a first paragraph that forbade the producer to read any further. The producer was simply directed to sign on the last page! Needless to say, Canadian agreements have far more respect for the producer. A standard contract between a producer and distributor will cover the most important points. The following is not a definitive list of contractual conditions but rather an explanation of important items that *should* be covered in the contract.

1. *Granting of rights.* The producer will have to certify that he or she has the sole and exclusive right to exploit in the media of television broadcasting, pay television, videocassettes, etc. the program(s) being offered to the distributor for specified territories. (See the section on chain of title in Chapter 9 for more about this topic.)

   The producer will also have to agree that the distributor will have the sole and exclusive right to distribute the programs in the territory specified and to act as the exclusive representative of the producer in the promotion and sale of the programs.

2. *Term.* The distributor's contract period will have to be decided. This might be, for example, a period of from three to seven years commencing at a given date, with a provision that the terms of the agreement shall continue from year to year unless cancelled by either party, giving a mutually acceptable term of notice.

3. *Best efforts clause.* A producer often asks the distributor to agree to use his or her best efforts to actively promote the sale of the programs in the territory that the producer has licensed to the distributor.

4. *Consultation.* The distributor frequently agrees to consult with the producer before entering into any commitment with a prospective licensee in respect of any sale of the programs, and to seek the prior approval of the producer as to the terms and conditions and the form of the proposed contract. It is understood that the producer will not withhold approval without good and sufficient reason.

   For purposes of clarification, while the term "sale" is used except in rare cases, contracts are for *lease* of the programs to a TV station for specified telecasts over a period of time. The actual ownership of the programs is never in question; it is vested in the producer.

5. *Publicity and Promotion.* The producer is usually asked to supply at least two or three viewing cassettes and 25 brochures about his or her programs in order to promote sales. The producer also usually provides any material on tape or film that is technically acceptable for approved contracts for the programs.

   It is understood that all publicity, audition, and transmission (i.e. telecast) material supplied to the distributor is on loan and remains the property of the producer, who will provide instructions for final disposition at termination of the contract. The producer may ask for their return or have them destroyed (in which case the producer will receive a certificate of destruction). Usually the distributor is responsible at his or her own expense for the safekeeping of all publicity, audition, and transmission material supplied by the producer, and will insure that material at its replacement value.

6. *Disposal of copies.* When videotape copies of the programs are required for servicing approved contracts or for the telecasting of the programs by a

licensee of the distributor, the distributor ensures that an account is kept of all copies and that their erasure is arranged promptly after use.

7. *Sponsorship.* If the distributor enters into an approved contract with a television sponsor, the distributor makes it a contract stipulation that it shall not be implied or suggested in connection with any associated publicity, advertisement, or transmission that the licensed programs were produced by arrangement with the sponsor or that the producer or any artists associated with the programs recommend any products publicized in this connection.

8. *Percentage.* The distributor receives a percentage of all licensing fees derived from the programs and deducts all such fees from the rentals *actually received.* The distributor is usually not liable to the producer for any loss sustained as a result of non-collection of licensing fees. The terms of any distribution contract will vary according to the financial potential of the programs being offered to a distributor. A made-for-TV movie or a TV series, for example, may have different terms from those for a single half-hour or hour-long program. Further, the distributor will receive higher fees if he or she pays the producer an advance or if the distributor guarantees a minimum return. The following rates are just a guideline for the benefit of novice producers, and they would apply to contracts with no advance or guarantee from the distributor.

Negotiated fees for a Canadian distributor might be:

a. 15 percent of revenue derived from licensing national television rights;

b. 25 percent of revenue derived from licensing rights in the French language;

c. 35 percent of revenue derived from licensing rights for regional television and in individual local markets; and

d. 50 percent of revenue for licensing video-cassette rights.

9. *Reporting.* The distributor usually makes payments to the producer according to the provisions of the contract, at monthly or quarterly intervals for the first few years from the date of commencement of the agreement. After this, again according to the contract, payment may be made semi-annually or annually.

10. *Representations and warranties.* The producer must warrant and represent that he or she owns or controls the complete, entire, and exclusive television exhibition rights being granted, and that the producer has the right to grant to the distributor an exclusive licence to sell the programs. The producer must also warrant and represent that he or she has the full right and authority to enter into the agreement and must confirm that there is no contract with any other person, firm, or corporation that would in any way interfere with any rights granted under the agreement. The producer must further warrant that the programs are free of all encumbrances of any kind that might be inconsistent with the rights granted to the distributor. Finally, the producer must warrant that the programs do not violate the private, civil, or property rights, or the right of privacy of any person.

The producer must warrant that the performing rights in any musical compositions contained in the programs are:

a. controlled by the Composers, Authors & Publishers Association of Canada, Ltd. (CAPAC), Performing Rights Organization of Canada Limited (PRO Canada), or their affiliated societies; or

b. in the public domain; or

c. controlled by the producer.

The producer must indemnify the distributor and hold the distributor harmless from and against any damages or expenses that might arise out of the broadcasting of any music in the programs by any person, firm, or corporation to whom the distributor may lease or license the programs, the performing rights of which come within category (c) above.

The producer agrees to furnish the distributor with all necessary information concerning the title, composer, and publisher of all such music contained in the programs. The producer must indemnify the distributor against any damages or expenses that he or she may suffer as a result of any claims based upon any alleged breach of the warranties and representations provided by the producer.

11. *Termination.* When the agreement is terminated and all the contracts for the programs have been fulfilled by the distributor, all publicity, audition, and transmission material provided by the producer will be returned to him or her, or be disposed of as the producer directs.

12. *Bankruptcy.* Usually, if the distributor becomes bankrupt, or if there is a voluntary or involuntary dissolution of the distributor, the producer has the right to terminate and cancel the agreement by written notice to the distributor.

Services Supplied by the Distributor – Summing Up

In general, the distributor will be responsible for selling, scheduling, and servicing (that is, providing tapes, film, music cue sheets, etc.) TV programs to networks and stations. Selling is really leasing and is arranged through a contract between distributor and user. (See the copy of the program leasing contract at the end of this chapter.) The distributor will also provide proper publicity, invoice and collect monies on the producer's behalf, and report and remit funds to the producer on a regular basis. The distributor has developed a special expertise about the business and a rapport with customers, which are the producer's best reasons for using the distributor's services. In addition, since success for both the producer and the distributor is inextricably tied with sales, the motivation is always there for the distributor to get the maximum number of sales and best price possible for the producer's program.

Where does a producer find a distributor for his or her programs? One way is sure fire. If you see a distributor in a crowd, the crowd stands out! (Well, not really. But modesty prevents me from saying that distributors are highly visible anywhere.)

PROGRAM RENTAL AGREEMENT | No.

AGREEMENT MADE THIS

BETWEEN	AND
HEREIN CALLED "DISTRIBUTOR"	HEREIN CALLED "LESSEE"

WITNESSETH

1.

Upon the terms and conditions set forth herein, Distributor hereby grants to Lessee under the respective copyrights on the television program(s) set forth in Section 2(a) to 2(i) inclusive, a licence to exhibit such program(s) publicly by means of television broadcasting (as provided in said Section) in each city and commencing on the dates specified in the Section. Distributor agrees that during the term of this exclusive agreement, it will not license exhibition of the program(s) set forth in the said Section to any other TV Station other than as set forth in said Section. Lessee agrees to exhibit such program(s) only in accordance with the provisions herein contained.

2(a) NAME OF PROGRAM

(b) NUMBER OF EPISODES	NUMBER OF TELECASTS PER EPISODE	TOTAL NUMBER OF TELECASTS
(c) LENGTH OF EACH EPISODE	TO BE SUPPLIED ON	

(d) LICENSED STATION(S)

(e) COVERAGE AREA OF LICENSED STATION(S)

(f) LICENCE FEE PER EPISODE	LICENCE FEE PER TELECAST	TOTAL LICENCE FEE

(g) PAYMENT SCHEDULE

(h) LICENCE PERIOD

(i) SPECIAL PROVISIONS

3.

Distributor warrants that it has the right to grant this licence and, except for performing rights in the music, agrees to indemnify Lessee against liability, loss, damages, or expenses arising out of or caused by any material contained in the program(s) or the use thereof as herein specified. Distributor agrees to indemnify Lessee against liability, loss, damages and expenses arising out of the performance in the program(s) of music, the performing rights of which are not either (a) controlled by BMI Canada Limited or Composers Authors and Publishers Associaton of Canada Limited or Society of European Stage Authors and Composers Incorporated, or (b) in the public domain.

4.

Distributor agrees to deliver to Lessee at its address hereafter set out or other address designated by Lessee one 16MM positive colour print or colour videotape of each program in sufficient time for the scheduled broadcast thereof. Lessee agrees to return each print or videotape to Distributor at the address indicated above, or to such other place as Distributor may designate, prepaid by air or fastest method available after the broadcast thereof by Lessee. Each print or videotape shall be returned in good condition, normal wear and tear expected. All shipping shall be at Lessee's expense.

5.

All of the programs shall at all times be Distributor's property, subject only to Lessee's rights as herein expressly provided. Risk of loss, damage, destruction or disappearance thereof shall be borne by Lessee from the time of actual possession by Lessee until the time of actual re-possession by Distributor or Distributor's designee. In the event of any such loss, damage, destruction or disappearance, or in the event of Lessee's failure to return prints or videotapes as specified in section 5 above, Lessee agrees to indemnify Distributor against any liability, loss, damages or expenses caused thereby. Lessee will not permit any of said programs or any part thereof to be reproduced or to come into or remain in the possession of any one other than the Lessee or personnel connected with the broadcasting of the programs licensed hereby.

6. Neither party shall be responsible to the other for any failure or delay in delivery of prints or videotapes due to labour difficulties, failure of carriers or any causes beyond the control of the party so failing to deliver.

7. Lessee agrees to broadcast each program in its entirety, without any deletions additions or alterations, except for insertion of commercials, except as authorized by Distributor. All commercials attached to a program by Lessee will be removed prior to return of the program to Distributor. Each program will be broadcast to non-paying audiences only. Lessee may have a studio audience present at the time of broadcast, but no admission shall be charged of such audience.

8. In the event that any broadcast of a program in any city specified in the schedule should be cancelled because of unavailability of broadcasting facilities due to Act of God, labour difficulties, government regulation, appropriation of facilities to present a special event, or any other similar or dissimilar reason beyond Lessee's control, the period for broadcasting to such city shall be extended for a reasonable period of time to allow any such cancelled broadcast to be broadcasted.

9. Lessee is hereby given the right to use, prior to the broadcast date of each program, the title of the series and of the programs, and the name of the star performer or performers in such program in advertisements regarding the broadcast thereof, which do no more than state the title of the series, the title of the program, the name of the star performer or performers, the time of broadcast, the station, and the sponsor. In no event shall the Lessee make use of any material in connection with the program which is capable of being interpreted as an implied or direct endorsement of any product or service without the written consent of Distributor or the party whose name is involved.

10. Lessee agrees to pay Distributor the licence fee per exhibition as specified in the said section 2. All such payments shall be net to Distributor without any deduction therefrom whatsoever and without restricting the generality of the foregoing, no advertising agency commission shall be payable therefrom.

11. In the event of any default by Lessee hereunder, Distributor may, at its option, terminate this agreement forthwith or suspend delivery of additional programs hereunder until such default has been remedied. In the event Lessee fails to pay any amounts due to Distributor hereunder, Distributor may at its option declare such failure a breach of this agreement, whereupon Distributor shall have the right to recover from Lessee as liquidated damages therefore the amount payable in respect of all programs to be furnished hereunder but not theretofore paid for by Lessee. The liquidated damages so recovered shall be in addition to any other right or remedy the Distributor may have against Lessee at law or in equity.

12. If Lessee is an advertising agency executing this agreement on behalf of a sponsor, Lessee may assign this agreement to the sponsor or another advertising agency acting for sponsor acceptable to Distributor providing such assignee assumes the obligations of the Lessee hereunder in writing, and upon such assignment being made and communicated in writing to Distributor, all the rights and obligations of Lessee hereunder shall terminate. Distributor may assign this agreement to any corporation controlling, controlled by, or under common control with, Distributor, or to any person, firm or corporation which may hereafter become the distributor of the programs. Except as hereinabove provided, neither party shall assign this agreement without the written consent of the other, which consent will not be unreasonably withheld.

13. This agreement expresses the entire understanding between the parties relating to the subject matter hereof and may not be modified, renewed, extended, or discharged, except by an agreement in writing signed by the party against whom enforcement of the modification, renewal, extension or discharge is sought, or by such party's agent. This agreement shall be construed in accordance with the laws of the province of Ontario. Waiver of any breach of this agreement must be in writing and shall not be deemed a waiver of any preceding or succeeding breach of the same or any other provision.

14. This agreement is to be read with all changes of gender or number required by the context.

15. Any notice given hereunder as well as payments to be made hereunder shall be mailed by registered or certified mail as follows:

IF TO DISTRIBUTOR:

IF TO LESSEE:

The above addresses may be changed upon written notice thereof by the party changing such address to the other party.

IN WITNESS WHEREOF these presents have been executed as of the day and year first written.

PER _____
DISTRIBUTOR

BY _____
LESSEE

CHAPTER SEVEN

The International Market

by Jan Rofekamp

*J*AN ROFEKAMP *is President of Films Transit Inc., a Quebec-based distribution company. Before his appointment as President, Rofekamp served as Vice-President and Secretary/Treasurer. Recent sales by Films Transit include:* Anne Trister, Pouvoir Intime, La Femme de l'hôtel, Samuel Lount, Sonatine, *and* The Dog Who Stopped the War (La Guerre des tuques). *At Films Transit, Rofekamp has developed specialties in foreign sales, most notably features and international political films. Before joining the company, he was President of Fugitive Cinema Holland, a 16 mm distribution company which he founded in 1971.*

Canada's yearly film and television output is comparable to that of much smaller countries such as Finland, Holland, or Greece. Canada does have one advantage: we produce films in two of the three main "film languages" (Spanish is the third) of the western world. But in the international market we must confront the same competition as the other small countries; our theatre chains are subject to the same takeovers; and the mass-releasing of multimillion dollar American films diverts the domestic audience from our own films just as it does in other countries.

To export Canadian films, we need the same government support as the Finns need for the export of their films, unless, of course (as some Canadian producers do) we make films American-style, with the loss of Canadian identity that frequently ensues. I believe, however, that 80 percent of all Canadian film and television productions seek to reflect and illuminate the culture that produced them, as much as they seek financial reward. Because most of our films have a strong cultural identity, and because of the fierce competition in the international market, we have to fight very hard to gain a foothold.

This chapter will not address the exportability of specific Canadian productions, although an example will be given now and then. Rather, I will try to give you an idea of how the international market is structured and how it operates. If you, as producer, want to take on this fight, either on your own or through a sales agent, I hope the following pages will provide you with some useful tips to make this job easier.

The International Market Place for Canadian Film and Television

The "international market place" can be roughly divided into the following sections:

a. theatrical distribution and exhibition (nearly always 35 mm);

b. home video (one-half inch tape cassettes in VHS or Beta formats or, in some countries, the Philips 2000 system, as well as video discs, although the latter have yet to gain a significant share of the market);

c. The educational circuit for schools, universities, and other institutions (mostly 16 mm but also recently on video);

d. television networks and stations, whether public, state-run and state-financed, or private and commercial, as well as cable and satellite transmissions, pay television and, in the near future, pay-per-view television; and

e. the art-house and film society circuit (mostly 16 mm).

The international market place (which is really a number of very different markets) thus presents a complex challenge to the Canadian filmmaker. When you begin planning and producing a film, it is very useful to think well in advance about the interests and needs of your intended audience. If you are not aiming at a specific audience, your chances of selling and successfully promoting your film will be much lower.

Theatrical Distribution

Theatrical distribution and exhibition is a very risky business. Filmgoers aged 14 to 24 make up the biggest share of the audience, and they favour American-style action and comedy films. Further, the costs of advertising are very high, and theatre chains are being bought up by a few companies, so that access to cinemas is more and more limited. In Brussels, for example, there are now only two or three independently owned theatres left. The rest are owned by the major French production companies, who program mainly their own films. Thus independent distributors in Belgium who import the occasional, less commercial Hungarian, Dutch, or Canadian film have difficulty in finding a screen for it. Similar developments can be seen in Holland, in Great Britain, and in Italy.

If you want to sell your independently produced film in foreign theatrical markets you have, basically, two choices. First, you can try to approach an international major with access to theatrical chains in foreign countries. If you take this route, however, you usually have to give away many of your rights (not only theatrical rights but, in many cases, also world home video, cable, satellite, and television rights). For one reasonably high sum (which, however, rarely covers your production costs), you lose all possibility of future income from your film. It is more of a challenge (and, if you are lucky, much more lucrative) to try to sell your film country by country, either personally or through a sales agent, which means lots of work and revenues stretched over a long period. However, you have more control over whether or not your film will be seen.

Generally speaking, the foreign theatrical market is only interested in feature films. Documentaries or short films – unless they win Oscars – rarely get to a foreign screen. If you plan to make a short film and you want to try the foreign theatrical market, bear in mind that audiences come to the theatre for the feature, and that shorts, if they are used at all, are considered fillers. Consequently, distributors are not very interested in shorts and pay very little money for them. In some countries, there are laws obliging cinemas to play short films, but in these cases, they are shorts produced by the country's own filmmakers. Theatrical shorts must be available in the 35 mm format and usually run no longer than 15 minutes.

Home Video

Today there are home video stores on almost every street corner in Canada. In many foreign countries, home video is equally popular. Home video is dominated by productions from the same countries that dominate the theatrical market. Video store shelves are filled with crime, sex and violence, horror, science fiction, and the occasional wacky comedy, and there seems to be little space for the less commercial, more cultural film in this area of distribution. However, a great deal of money can be made in this market. If you have a production that seems to fit among the films already available (in recent years, David Cronenberg's horror flicks and big-budget Quebec films like Louisiana and Le Matou have done well in the international video market), have a try.

Be wary, though: video distribution companies, apart from the largest and best run, can have the life span of Mayflies. The golden promises made to producers are worth nothing if the distribution company goes under. It takes attentive reading of the appropriate trade papers to keep informed about all this.

The one-half inch video formats are also widely used in the educational field. With more and more schools, universities, and other educational institutions equipped with video, special-interest video distribution has sprung up and may become a significant market in the future. Most of the distribution companies active in 16 mm distribution (see the next section) are now in the process of expanding into video distribution.

The Educational Circuit

If you want your film to be seen in schools and universities, by organized groups, or other audiences within the educational market, it would be advisable to make your film no longer than 50 minutes. Since films used by school systems are usually rented or bought to stimulate class discussion, a film must be short enough to allow for post-film discussion in a one-hour class. Educational films must be easily adaptable to foreign markets. If your film has narration, it should be recorded on a separate track before you make your final mix, so that the foreign distributor can easily replace your narration by one in another language.

If you want to produce for the educational market, part of your research should consist of looking at other films on similar subjects. You can learn from these films how to shape your message. This research may also prevent you from making an unnecessary film, if you discover that there are ten very good films on the same subject, already on the market in different countries.

Television

Whereas the international theatrical and home video market are tough nuts to crack for the Canadian producer, international television is a lot more open to less conventional material. Especially in the European countries, Canadian producers and exporters have, in the last few years, done a great job of selling our films and television programs for television. Most of the customers have been (and still are) public, state-run television stations. These stations usually have cultural rather than commercial mandates, and many of them are not dependent on commercials to keep their operation running. They can take more risks in programming, and although there is local competition – for instance, between Sweden 1 and 2, Netherlands 1 and 2, and among the three West German channels – this competition is less fierce than if they were privately owned television networks run with money from commercials, as are the American networks.

Television requires some tailoring of your productions. Feature films shown on television are rarely allowed to run longer than two hours; children's programs are usually a half hour long; documentaries need to fit into either an hour (40-50 minute) or half-hour (24-26 minute) format. Individual shorts are rarely purchased, although there are some television stations that still have a slot for international short and animation films. Swiss-French TV, for example, has a slot called *Ciné-bref*, in which short films are treated with respect, and the title and filmmaker's name are even mentioned in the program guides. If your film is considered to be a "current affairs" documentary, programmers at television stations sometimes cannot use the whole film, but buy the right to edit your film to fit their time slot. (For example, West German TV in Hamburg has a weekly 42-minute current affairs slot, which cannot exceed its length.) In this case, they will pay you for the whole hour of film. Alternatively, programmers may buy the right to use a portion of your film in a "magazine" program, which is an hour-long show treating three to five different subjects. Perhaps 20 minutes of your documentary would be needed, and you would be paid according to the number of minutes actually used.

Under pressure of new technological developments (the coming of cable, satellite, and pay-TV), there is a tendency even among public television stations to compete and become more commercial, with the inevitable result that less commercial productions will have less chance of being bought. Television documentaries have to have commercial appeal and preferably be in series (*The Big Rivers, The Big Ships, The Brain*, etc.). One TV buyer said, for example, that if a documentary on mountain climbing was not shot on the Kilimanjaro, he would not be interested. Information programs are being slashed and transformed into magazine programs, during which attention is given to a specific subject only for a maximum of 20 minutes. Typical examples of this tendency are very close to home: since the creation of *The Journal* and *Le Point*, there have been fewer one-hour special documentaries on international subjects. On the American Cable News Network, the news is often cut up and served in 3-minute portions.

The Art-house Circuit and Film Co-ops

The parts of the international market place that we have been discussing are full of rules that more or less dictate to filmmakers or producers how they should make their films if they want to make some sales. But there are filmmakers of another kind, those who do not compromise, who make their own films regardless of whether there is a sizeable audience for them. It is interesting to note that it is often these people who end up in the history books of cinema and win the prizes at international film festivals. Some of them become famous and some of them contribute to the creation of new cinema audiences.

Throughout the history of cinema, there have been organizations that defy the rules of commercial distribution and exhibition, organizing, for and with filmmakers, outlets for non-commercial, offbeat cinema. In many countries, during the 1960s and the 1970s, these mostly non-profit art-house distribution organizations and film co-ops were very active in marketing "difficult" feature films and political documentaries. Many of these groups, however, were dependent on government subsidies. In the 1980s, many have had to close down or become more commercial, because of cutbacks in government cultural spending. However, there are still many groups around the world that remain faithful to the philosophy of helping independent filmmakers obtain recognition. They market these films to film clubs, art houses, schools, and universities, and organize tours for the filmmakers and their films. They have found new outlets such as art galleries and museums where "cinema and video art" is recognized.

This is the area for the filmmaker-artist or for the militant filmmaker, demanding a lot of hard work here and yielding relatively little money. This distribution method can be extremely gratifying for the filmmaker who is looking for contact with an audience and for recognition rather than financial returns.

Who Is the Seller of Your Film?

Just as distribution and exhibition are considered separate areas of expertise, the distribution of films and television programs into foreign markets is also a specialized job of its own. Before you start thinking about how to sell your own film, it might be worthwhile to ask yourself whether you are the right person for the task. International sales will take up a great deal of your time and if you are about to start a new project, you may realize that you do not have time to market your previous film effectively. It may then be advisable to hand your film over to someone who specializes in international sales. In some cases, however, it may make sense for you, as a producer, to make the sale personally, because the buyer may be someone who can participate in your next project. If you are working through an international sales agent, you can in some cases work with the sales agent to arrange financial participation in your next project after your earlier film has been sold.

Letting yourself be represented by an international sales agent may save you a lot of headaches, because no one will have a better understanding of your film's potential in the international market than this agent. Paying the agent the standard 20 to 30 percent commission pays off in the long run. We will go into more detail about this arrangement later in the chapter.

The Practical Side: How to Prepare for International Sales

Information Materials

Buyers, whether they are television programmers or film distributors, are solicited on a daily basis. There are far more films and television programs produced every year around the world than there are buyers with time slots and money. Buyers are inundated with flyers and brochures either mailed to them or given to them during international markets. Only if your brochure is informative and attractive will the busy buyer notice it and perhaps ask for a preview of your film.

A brochure or a flyer *must* contain a detailed synopsis, credits, format, length in minutes or feet, screen ratio, and the address of the production company or the international sales agent. Furthermore, a short bio-filmography of the director and some stills must accompany the brochure, unless they are incorporated in it. If you have an M/E track (a music and effects track; that is, a soundtrack without the narration or the dialogue), this should also be mentioned. If your film has played at international film festivals or won prizes, you should make sure your brochure highlights these achievements. If you have already made some sales to foreign countries, mention them. All this will help to promote your film.

It is advisable to write your brochure in both English and French and, if you can, include a short synopsis in Spanish. Although the Spanish language market is a difficult one to penetrate, your chances improve if there is some Spanish information in your brochure.

Videocassettes as a Sales Tool

In recent years, videocassettes have begun to play a major role in the promotion and sale of films and television productions. It is much cheaper and easier to send a videocassette to a buyer for preview than expensive and weighty 16 mm or 35 mm prints. Television buyers and distributors all over the world are now used to seeing films on video for selection, and most of them have video equipment for screenings or have easy access to it. Television stations usually have tristandard equipment that allows them to screen the three different video systems used around the world. The differences have nothing to do with the way cassettes are constructed, but relate to the way the film has been transferred onto the cassette. Canada, like the United States, Japan, and Latin and Central America, uses the NTSC system; Europe and parts of Africa and Asia use the PAL system; France, Eastern Europe, and the Soviet Union use the SECAM system.

Before you send a videocassette to a potential buyer, you should check on what system is used in the buyer's country. If you do not have a compatible cassette in this system, you should find out whether your client can screen the cassette you are sending. You can get information on the different systems used around the world by calling a representative of a major video manufacturer or a video distribution organization.

The most commonly used type of cassette for preview in international sales is the three-quarter inch U-matic cassette, which can be either NTSC (in North America) or PAL, or SECAM. But new formats are rapidly conquering the market. Many people now use one-half inch VHS or Beta for preview purposes. The cassettes are smaller and cheaper, and the quality of reproduction has improved enormously over the last few years. For the one-half inch format, though, tristandard video recorders and monitors are still rare, so you will have to check whether your client will be able to play back your tape. U-matic, VHS, and Betamax are not interchangeable. You cannot put a VHS cassette in a Betamax machine, and vice versa. If you are not sure whether your buyer can screen Beta or VHS, send a U-matic three-quarter inch cassette.

The big advantage of a videocassette as a promotion tool is its relatively low cost and ease of shipment: it can be posted anywhere by ordinary airmail. *Never* send someone your original "master" tape, however. If this gets lost you will have to re-transfer your film to video, which is much more expensive than making a simple video copy. Keep your "master" casette in a safe place so that you can make new copies as they are needed. Although this business of NTSC, PAL, and SECAM seems unnecessarily complicated, it does have one advantage: if you send an NTSC cassette for preview to a country where the PAL standard is used, you can worry less that your cassette will be pirated, because transfers from NTSC to PAL and the reverse are very expensive and cause loss of quality. The increasing popularity of one-half inch as the video preview standard also discourages piracy, because copying a one-half inch cassette also causes considerable loss of quality.

English is the international language of the film and television business. Buyers are usually sent an English version of a film or, if the film was made in a language other than English, a version with English subtitles. If your film has no dialogue or narration, you're in luck.

Films made in French need to be versioned or subtitled for international marketing. In Canada, if your French film has been selected for a major international film festival, the Film Festivals Office of Telefilm Canada will buy a print of your film and subtitle it in English. Your sales agent will have to obtain this subtitled print for transfer to video before the print is shipped out of the country. It is often advisable to include in your production budget a sum of money for versioning your film in the other official language if distribution in the other part of Canada seems likely, or if you or your sales agent think international sales are a possibility.

Postproduction Transcript / Music Cue Sheet

As soon as your film is finished, you must start working on what is called the postproduction transcript. This means writing down every line of dialogue and every bit of narration that is spoken in the film. In the case of dialogue, state, at the beginning of each line, the name of the character who says the line. In the case of narration, write "voice-over" or "narration". Foreign buyers need your postproduction transcript for translation into other languages for versioning or subtitling. If you can also "time" your transcript, this will be very much appreciated by foreign buyers.

The music cue sheet is a list of all the pieces of music used in your film, stating their length and who wrote and published them. The music cue sheet is needed for proper notification regarding music performing rights when the film is screened in a foreign country.

Author Rights

When you sign a contract with a buyer, you will find a clause in the contract in which you as a filmmaker or a producer must indemnify the buyer from any sort of trouble concerning ownership and claims on certain rights involved in your film. For example, if you buy archival material from a third party to include in your film and you later sell your film to German television, you must have the right not only to include this piece of material in your film, but *also* the right to sell your film with this footage included. If you use material that you did not shoot or record yourself, you can consider buying selected rights to it: for example, the right to *one* broadcast on Canadian television, or you can buy the right to broadcast all over the world, for a limited number of years or for perpetuity.

Basically, any piece of film or sound used in your production, which was not shot or written specially for the production, is protected somewhere. In Chapter 9 you can read more on this subject.

How International Sales Are Made

Distribution Agreements

Distributors are national or international companies or institutions that agree to buy the rights to rent or sell your film, on your behalf, in their territory, after you and the distributor have agreed upon certain conditions laid down in a contract, valid for a specified period of time. Most distributors take on a film, or a package of films, for five to seven years, although periods of 10 or more years are becoming quite common.

A distributor may buy your film "outright", which means it will pay you or your sales agent a flat fee for the right to exploit your film in the distributor's territory for the number of years agreed upon. Other distributors may offer you a percentage of the income they generate on your film, from which will be deducted: first, any advance they have paid you, and second, the cost of their investment in prints and publicity. Of course, when you sign a percentage deal with a distributor, you must have confidence in its business ethics, because it may be difficult to verify the distributor's reports to you.

After the initial period of the agreement, a contract may be renewed or terminated. In the latter case, there must be an arrangement about what the distributor will do with the prints of your film. They can either be destroyed, in which case you must receive a certificate of destruction issued by a national organization (such as an association of distributors in a given country) or they can be returned to you, usually at your expense. A more creative solution is to add a clause to your contract stating that the prints of your film must be donated to the local national film museum or national film archive for conservation. You can then authorize the film museum to screen the film in its own cinema or to make the print available to film schools for study.

There are different distributors for different market areas, although very often a distribution company will cover several of them. You can sell theatrical, non-theatrical, and even television rights to a distributor. In the latter case, the distributor will control the sale of your film to television stations in its territory, paying you a percentage of the income, if so agreed upon, or a flat fee paid to you when you sign the contract. If you sell non-theatrical rights, you must specify the different formats in which you will allow the distributor to work: 16 mm or video in the form of rentals and/or sales of prints and cassettes. Many distributors offer different percentages to the filmmaker for the different rights they obtain.

| *An Example of a Distribution Deal* | In this example, a distributor buys all media rights to your film for a specified number of years for a certain territory and offers you a percentage deal right from the start, which means that you will receive money from the first sale or rental the distributor makes (this is known as a gross deal). The distributor offers you the following percentages: |

Theatrical: 35 percent (for the producer)
Non-theatrical rentals on 16 mm: 50 percent
Print sales on 16 mm: 25 percent
Non-theatrical rentals on video: 50 percent
Videocassette sales: 25 percent
Standard television: 75 percent
Non-standard broadcasting (cable): 50 percent

The distributor offers you an advance of $5000, which means that the $5000 will be deducted before you are paid your percentages. Sometimes deals are struck in which the distributor is allowed to deduct more than the advance, to cover the cost of prints, publicity, and so on. With a deal like this, it will take longer before you will see additional money. Generally speaking, it is advisable to accept lower percentages but with payment right from the start and based on the gross revenue, rather than granting distributors lots of deductible costs, which are hard to control.

Choosing the Right Distributor

Before you even think about these details, you will have to find a distributor who will do a good job with your particular film. Do not persuade a distributor of action and horror films to take on your 16 mm art-house film. It is important that you contact other producers or filmmakers to inquire about their experiences with a given distributor *before* you sign distribution contracts. Festivals and international markets are the most suitable places to meet colleagues and to exchange information. If you really do not know whether a distributor is telling you the truth about his or her company and what it can do for your film, your last resort is to have a financial detective agency investigate the distributor's financial position.

In the past, distributors normally took a film for just one country. Recently, however, more and more distributors have been asking for rights to several territories. French distributors, for example, like very much to take on Belgium, Switzerland, and sometimes even the French-speaking countries in North Africa. Video companies in Sweden have a tendency to ask you for all Scandinavian rights, and German distributors like to have rights for German-speaking Switzerland and Austria, and sometimes even for East Germany. Ask them to be very clear about their intentions when they propose this kind of deal to you. You might find yourself in a situation where you sign away Switzerland to a French distributor, not specifying the *French-speaking territory* of Switzerland. Your film might never be seen in the German- and Italian-speaking part of that country if your French distributor does not think it profitable to release there. All these stipulations should appear in contracts. And there are a few more stipulations that can be made: a distributor can undertake, for example, to release your film with a minimum of five prints, or to spend a specified amount on publicity, or to release your film before a certain date. Normally a distributor will ask you for exclusive rights to distribute your film during the term of the contract.

Canadian productions made in the French language are immediately faced with a more difficult road in the international market. English-language films have access to an immense audience in the United States, England, and Australia. In addition, statistics show that other European countries, Asia, and parts of Africa import more films in English than in other languages. Our French productions must either be dubbed professionally into English or are "condemned" to the smaller art-house market, where films are shown in their original version with subtitles in Dutch, Swedish, etc., depending on where the film has been sold. French-Canadian films, however, tend to get more international critical acclaim and play more international film festivals than English-Canadian films, sometimes winning prestigious prizes. As a result they tend to get limited but serious distribution, sometimes in many different, smaller countries.

A commercial English-Canadian film with one or two internationally known Canadian-born actors may get a worldwide video deal much more easily than its French-Canadian counterpart. The theatrical and home video market are, however, very commercial ones. Distribution companies try to avoid risks, and producers and their sales agents increasingly content themselves with smaller but outright sums, rather than risking a jump in the dark on a percentage contract. It is, therefore, hardly surprising that Canadian-based international sales agents representing Canadian producers concentrate more on the foreign television market, where deals are relatively simple and money comes in quickly once the film is sold.

International Television Sales

Foreign television has become a major client for Canadian films and television programs in recent years, in large part thanks to the activities of the Canadian exporting companies. These companies, benefiting from the support of the Canadian government and the increase in Canada's production of quality programs, have found their place in the international market.

Television sales look simple to deal with: most of the countries to which you would be selling have state-controlled public television states, so you may have only two or three addresses and a handful of buyers to deal with. However, since new technologies have been developing quickly, this market is becoming more complex. Yet, since it is a market that needs lots of programming, the chances of getting a film sold are higher than in the area of theatrical film distribution or video.

Who Are the Clients?

There are, basically, three kinds of clients in the international television market. First there are the public television stations. Countries such as Belgium, Sweden, Norway, Greece, France, Germany, and many others have state-run television stations which have, apart from their entertainment function, a strong cultural and educational / informative mandate. It is obvious that they are the logical clients for documentaries, shorts, animated films and the more serious feature films. "Canadian content," which sometimes seems to be a handicap in selling our films, is often seen by public television stations as an asset and makes the films more saleable, provided of course that they are of high quality. The buying departments of all stations are divided in sections, such as TV drama, music, entertainment, documentaries, current affairs, and children's programming.

In some countries, private or commercial television exists alongside public television. This provides a second market. However, since they are dependent on income from commercials, their programming must appeal to larger audiences. This makes them a harder market for Canadian filmmakers to sell into. Furthermore, the more commercial television stations tend to pay less attention to informative programming than to entertainment. A documentary must be really spectac-

ular and of international interest to sell to private television.

Television usually will buy the right to a specified
number of transmissions of your film during a limited
number of years. Sometimes, if the film is a documentary, a television station may buy just one transmission, which then must take place within an agreed-
upon period of time. Unless a television station is willing to pay very well indeed, you would never wish to
sell your program for unlimited runs in perpetuity.

Television stations in bigger countries like German,
England, France, Japan, and Brazil will make their
own language version of your film. For this purpose
they will need a music and effects track and a transcript. In smaller countries, where the audience has
become used to reading subtitles, programs will go on
the air with subtitles electronically generated on a
videotape of your film. The bigger countries will
usually buy a print or a videotape from you, as well as
paying you a sum of money for the rights to transmit.
Smaller countries, like Holland, Belgium, Switzerland,
and the countries of Scandinavia, as well as stations in
Spain, the Far East, and Australia, may want a print or
a videotape on loan, so that they can make their own
videocopy for transmission. The video format commonly used for this purpose is the one-inch format.
The smaller tapes – one-quarter and one-half inch –
are rarely used for broadcast, except in some African
and Asian countries.

The Television *Contract*	When a television sale is made, there are a few impor- tant elements that *have* to appear in a contract:

1. The title of the program bought, for how many
   transmissions, and during which period.
2. The territory for which the transmission rights are
   bought: Danish Television, for example, will buy
   for Denmark; a multinational cable and satellite
   operation may buy for a larger number of territo-

ries. Some contracts state that the film in question must not be sold to another station during the period of the contract, because the signal of that other country can be received in the country for which you are making the deal. Because of this across-border reception, for example, a program transmitted in France may attract many viewers in Belgium and Switzerland, where the strong French signals can be received. Therefore, it is wise to sell the program first to Belgium and Switzerland. Although the signals of these countries spill over into some parts of France, the signals are relatively weak, and France will not hesitate to buy a program because of a previous sale to these countries. Similarly, it is wise to sell first to Norway and Denmark, and then sell to Sweden.

3. A statement that the buyer must pay for all shipping of prints and videocassettes to and from his station.

4. The price for which you sell your film, which can be either a price per minute or a fixed price for the whole film. In some cases, a client will buy the right for one transmission and promise to pay an additional 50 percent of this price, when his or her station wants to buy a second transmission. You will be informed about whether the station wants to go ahead with this once the first transmission has taken place.

5. A specification that the price for your film will be paid as "net to the producer." In some countries, rather heavy taxes exist on the export of capital. Australia, for example, withholds 10 percent of your sales price. Germany might withhold more than 20 percent of your sales price and if you do not know about this, you will receive a nasty surprise when you see your cheque. Some taxes are avoidable if there are treaties between Canada and the other country to avoid double imposition (that is, the levying of taxes on the same item by two dif-

ferent countries). Most contracts mention this and provide guidance on how to fill out the forms to avoid these taxes. You may, however, receive these forms in a language that you do not read, and then you are in a difficult situation. If you are able, instead, to negotiate "net to the producer," you will always received the money you negotiated for.

Prices for films and television productions are reasonably standard around the world, but you can from time to time negotiate. However, a sales agent, who knows all his or her buyers, will be in a better position to negotiate than you, unless you have your own personal contacts. Once a buyer tells you that your film has been sold, you will probably not see this buyer again, because the actual negotiations will be done by the television station's contracts department. A buyer will tell you approximately what you will be paid, but you won't know the exact price until you deal with the television station.

It is difficult to obtain exact information about the prices paid for television programs. Base TV prices are arrived at by calculations that involve the size of the potential audience or the territory that the station reaches. For an ambitious program with internationally known stars, you may get considerably more than the base price. The international trade paper *Variety* issues a listing, every few months, of prices for television programs. Although this list is not always accurate, and includes only features and "half-hour shows," it will give you a rough idea of the going rates. Sales agents are reluctant to share such information with you, because they consider this insiders' knowledge to be "classified business information."

Institutional Sales

Although this is normally the task of a distributor, you might be able to sell a print or a videocassette of your film to an institution such as a university for internal educational use. In the agreement you make with this institution, you must describe very precisely the use for which the client is purchasing the film or the cassette. The client must not be allowed to take the film outside its premises for rent or loan, unless agreed upon. In this type of deal, you will sell the print or the cassette for its lifetime and you also specify the number of copies the institution is allowed to make on video. Do not sell a cassette more cheaply just because the manufacturing costs of making a video copy are lower than the costs of making a film print. Usually videocassettes are sold for about 80 percent of the 16 mm or 35 mm print sale price. In the case of both prints and videos, your fee normally includes the print / transfer costs, plus an additional fee for the use of your program.

Locating the Clients for Your Film

Sending Information Materials

You may be able to sell your film simply by mailing out numerous information brochures about it. As stated earlier, the better and more informative your brochure is, the more likely it is to attract attention. You must, however, compile a good mailing list and keep it up to date. If your client does not reply, send him or her a polite reminder, but realize that no answer may already be an answer: not interested.

After sending out your information brochures, you may receive a request for a videocassette preview copy in a language version that the buyer can understand. If your film is in French and you get a request from the United States, there is a fair chance that the buyer will not be able to understand your film. Call and ask if the buyer can wait until the English version is ready. If there will not be an English version, the buyer may be willing to see your film with an English transcript on the side. Send your cassette by regular airmail unless express is requested. Screening may take a long time and delays of 6 to 10 weeks before the potential buyer gets back to you are quite normal.

Festivals

If your film has been selected for an international film festival, you might consider travelling with your film. If the film has been selected for a competition program, the festival usually invites to attend, paying for your accommodation, and sometimes (although rarely) your airfare. You may be able to get a travel grant from Telefilm Canada, or from the Société générale du cinéma du Québec if you are living in Quebec. But festivals should be thought of more as exhibition places rather than actual market places. Distributors normally go to festivals like Berlin and Cannes to buy films. Television buyers, however, have their own markets and gatherings (described in the next section).

Investigate, at Telefilm Canada's festivals office or by talking to other filmmakers and producers, the "market value" of various festivals – are there lots of buyers present? There are more than 2000 film festivals around the world and many of them are relatively unimportant. Nevertheless, a festival can be of vital importance for reasons other than selling. Because festivals are places where new trends in cinema are unveiled and "discovered", influential critics attend these events and might write positively about your film. You can then use these articles for further promotion.

Festivals tend to compete with each other for exclusive screenings. If your film is in competition in Berlin, for example, you can forget competition in Cannes. It is very important, therefore, to try to determine which festival is the best showcase for your film. Telefilm Canada's film festivals office can be of assistance in this matter. Winning a prize at an important film festival is the best thing that can happen to you. You may receive a cash prize and – more importantly – the award will increase the market value of your film.

Markets

Throughout the world, there are markets for film and television productions, at which buyers and sellers get together and trade. Sometimes these markets are connected with important film festivals, like the ones in Berlin and Cannes, which are the most important showcases for theatrical cinema and home video. Having a market during a film festival seems to be a trend these days and markets are springing up like mushrooms. Because visiting markets and festivals is an expensive undertaking, I will try to give you a list of the most important world markets, at the time of writing (1986). If your time and resources are limited, you can safely miss the rest.

PLACE	MONTH	SPECIALIZING IN:
Monte Carlo	February	Television / Cable / Satellite
Berlin	February	Cinema
Cannes MIPTV	April	Television / Cable / Satellite
Cannes Film Festival Market	May	Cinema / Home video
London Market	October / November	Television / Cable / Satellite
MIPCOM Cannes	October	Television / Cable / Satellite
Milan Indian Summer	October	Cinema / Home video

Markets are organized in two different ways. Monte Carlo and London are examples of hotel floor markets. Sellers rent hotel rooms on the market floor of the hotel in which the market is held, and screen in these rooms for their buyers. Other markets are held in exhibition halls, with constructed and decorated stands that have video screening facilities inside. These markets bear a resemblance to "in-crowd" parties. Everybody seems to know everybody else. Buyers go from stand to stand, greeting long-time business associates. Sometimes screening appointments have been made long before the actual markets take place. For the lone filmmaker without international sales experience, this

can be quite a frustrating experience. So many buyers, so many chances, but whom do you approach, and how?

Canadians sometimes visit these markets in large, organized groups. MIPTV in Cannes, the most important television market, has been attended by Quebecers for many years in the so-called Groupe Québec, which rents a large stand for eight to nine Quebec-based export companies. At markets held during the Berlin and Cannes film festivals, Canadians can shelter under the umbrella of stands organized by Telefilm Canada or by the Société générale du cinéma du Québec (for Quebec-based filmmakers, producers, and companies). Telefilm, however, is now questioning whether it is worthwhile for them to continue providing such stands. Entering a market is usually quite expensive: entry fees may sometimes cost more than $250 per person per day. If you rent a stand during a market, you usually can bring in your staff for free. Participation by an individual producer with a stand at MIPTV can easily cost more than $7000, *excluding* costs like hotel, airfare, and so on. If you are in the international sales business, however, you will find these markets highly effective. They are the best place to see the faces of your clients and find new ones.

It is hard to say which market is the best for Canadian films and television programs. During the last few years, Canadians have had a high profile in the most important markets around the world and buyers for Canadian programming can now be found in Eastern and Western Europe, the United States, Australia, and Japan. You have a better chance of making sales to television than you do of making a distribution deal, whether theatrical, non-theatrical, or home video. Clearly, then, it is much more worthwhile to concentrate on European television during an MIPTV or Monte Carlo market, rather than to invest in a trip to a theatrical market held in Hong Kong or Caracas.

International Sales Agents

Because it is virtually impossible for a producer or filmmaker to know about the distribution situation in each country, the trade of the international sales agent becomes an important and necessary intermediary. International sales agents look around for films and television productions that they think they can sell, on behalf of producers and filmmakers, to buyers for television and distribution. Like any other agent, they will deduct a fee (commission) after they have made a sale, which is considered their income. Sometimes they will give you an advance on possible future sales, to be deducted from the first income on your film. Also deducted from this income, provided you and the agent have agreed to this, will be any expenses the agent has incurred for preview videocassettes, publicity materials, advertising, and so on.

Working with international sales agents has many advantages. They know the market, know the buyers, and know which markets are the most promising for your film. It is part of their task to keep themselves informed about all the new technical developments and the new sales possibilities they create. International sales agents travel to all the major markets in the world, and in many cases they have their own stands at them. In between markets, they will travel personally with films to visit buyers in their own offices. Foreign buyers travelling abroad, in turn, will visit sales agents to screen new material in their offices.

There are many agents around. You will have to talk to them to find out if your film fits into their catalogue, and you will have to evaluate the deal the agent offers to you by talking to other filmmakers and producers about their experiences with the agent. A wildlife documentary, obviously, should be given to an agent with experience in this field. Some agents specialize in children's programming, current affairs, or dramatic features. Because shorts are very hard to sell, only agents with a lot of experience in this field will be able to sell for you. Some agents handle only films from the country in which they are established, thus creating a special identity for themselves.

You do not have to give an agent world rights to your film; however, in many cases they would like to have them and may make it a condition for handling your film. Some agents specialize in specific territories; for example, selling into the Middle East, Africa, or the Far East (including Australia and Japan).

As I said earlier, you will need an English version of your film, either subtitled or dubbed, to sell your film in the international market. If you do not have this, an agent may help you to get one after you have concluded an agreement with him or her. Either the agent can invest in a version and deduct the investment from the income on your film, or the agent can approach one of the institutions like Telefilm or (in Quebec) the Société générale du cinéma for financial aid or investment in a version. If foreign television is considered the only market for your film, it may be sufficient simply to electronically subtitle a video-cassette, because the version will only be for preview purposes. If theatrical distribution seems likely, the subtitling of a filmprint may be worthwhile. This print can then be used for festivals, screenings at a market, and even for the sale itself.

Canadian financing institutions make it their policy to ask you to contact an international sales agent very early in your production. Although an agent may find it difficult to judge the marketability of a project when only a film treatment is available, the agent's input on scriptwriting, research, publicity material, and selection of stills may be very valuable . In some cases, the agent may arrange early publicity in the international trade papers even while the film is still shooting, creating interest among buyers. An agent will frequently ask you if your film will be ready for Monte Carlo, MIPTV, or London. A film that misses MIPTV will have to wait until the fall before serious marketing can be started. A feature that may be a candidate for the Cannes competition and misses it will have to wait a whole year before the next Cannes, with the inevitable risk that fresh new films will edge out your film in the competition program selection.

There are other reasons why it makes sense to have an international sales agent for selling your film abroad. Some territories are extremely complicated to sell into. The United States, for instance, has a market of hundreds of smaller and larger TV stations that are possible customers for your film. Station-by-station selling (syndication) is a tough job and can only be done properly by an experienced company. Germany, which is a feasible market for Canadian films on television, is likely to buy faster through international or local sales agents. Latin America, too, is a very challenging market and sales agents specialized in this area are the best bets. Although the trade magazine

Variety publishes a yearly list of prices for films and television productions, the sales agents will know the current prices better than the individual producer and are in a better position to negotiate the highest price.

Sales agents often work with lawyers who supervise the contracting. Legal advice is expensive and sometimes absolutely necessary. If you work with an agent, the legal part of the work becomes his or her responsibility. The percentage the agent would want for his or her work varies from 20 to 45 percent (25 to 30 percent is most common), depending on the territory the agent sells to and of course depending on the agent. When you negotiate a contract with an international sales agent, you must discuss thoroughly the following points:

a. In what territories may the sales agent operate?
b. What methods of exhibition may the sales agent sell? (Can the agent only sell television rights, or theatrical and home video, too?)
c. What payments does the sales agent receive for what deal? (The percentages may differ on sales to television, theatrical, non-theatrical, and home video.)
d. What will be the agent's investment (for cassettes, brochures, subtitles or other versions) and what will be deductible from the income? What are understood to be deductible sale-related costs? (Costs directly related to a sale: telex, telephone, transports, prints, video masters, travelling, etc.)
e. For how long can a sales agent sell your film and what contract-periods can this sales agent conclude with buyers in foreign countries?
f. Does the sales agent have the right to authorise clients to shorten, adapt, or change your film?
g. Does the sales agent have the right to use sub-agents and, if so, against what payment?
h. Does the sales agent have exclusive rights to represent you?

i. When does the sales agent pay you? When will the agent provide you with income and sales reports?

Some agents work with other agents (sub-agents) for certain territories and these sub-agents will also require a commission for their work. See to it that this does not influence the share you are getting back from your agent. If you have agreed on a 70 percent return to you on all sales, you should get 70 percent in all cases. If your agent decides to use a sub-agent, then both agents will have to share the agreed-upon 30 percent commission.

In general, it is advisable to work with a good agent, if you can find the right one for your film. Further, it is my strong feeling that Canadian filmmakers and producers should work with Canadian sales agents whenever possible, to make our industry strong and to keep the money within our borders. You might find the percentages asked by agents to be high, but you should realize that a good agent can generate more revenue for you than you ever can yourself, provided the film is "marketable".

CHAPTER EIGHT

Publicity and Promotion

by David Novek and Kevin Tierney

*D*AVID NOVEK, the "dean" of Canadian television and film publicists, with close to 30 years' experience in the public relations field, began his professional career with the now-defunct Montreal Herald. In 1969, he joined the National Film Board as Director of Public Relations and Publicity, and during his tenure there he was instrumental in bringing attention to the NFB's feature films. He left the NFB to head the entertainment division of Berger and Associates, before forming David Novek and Associates in 1978. As President of this Montreal-based public relations company, he has overseen publicity for close to 100 feature films while serving as corporate public relations consultant to many of Canada's leading production houses.

*K*EVIN TIERNEY, currently Vice-President of David Novek and Associates, began his professional career as a teacher with Service universitaire canadienne outre-mer in Algeria and Chad. Returning to Canada in the mid-1970s, he began teaching Film and English at John Abbot College in Montreal. In 1982, he was invited to teach at Lanzhou University in China, where he wrote extensively on Chinese cinema. He began working as a freelance film publicist in 1984, and since then has done unit publicity on over ten films and mini-series. Previously a regular contributor to Cinema Canada, he has also written for Sight and Sound, China Daily, Variety and Screen International.

Publicity and promotion are sometimes thought to enter the business of filmmaking when a film is released onto the market. In fact, the producer's agreement with the distributor will include a provision for the producer to hand over publicity materials as part of the producer's delivery requirements. In order for a film to be successfully marketed by the distributor, essential information will be required; and, if the producer understands the value of creating anticipation for the film, some publicity will already have been generated before and during the actual shooting.

A forward-thinking producer will have made use of a publicist even before starting a specific film project. The relationship may well date back to the time when the producer was starting out in the film business, long before the cameras turned on his or her first project. Or the association may have begun following completion of the production company's first projects as a way of capitalizing on their recent accomplishments.

The key word in any discussion of public relations and publicity in the film industry is *information*. Because film is a creative process that may take months or even years to go from the typewriter or word processor to the screen, and because the economics of the undertaking demand that large numbers of people actually pay to see the film, it is clear that an enormous amount of information processing must go on. When a particular film finally comes out, both the producer and the distributor expect that at least some awareness of it will already exist, especially among media insiders. This awareness can then be transformed into publicity in the advertising sense of the word, which will have the required effect of getting people into the theatres to see the movie.

Information processing, then, is the publicist's primary function: co-ordinating the information from the producer, passing it along to other members of the industry, and later making it known to the public via the communications media – print, electronic, and so on.

Corporate Public Relations

Let's look first at the situation in which a producer decides to use the expertise of a publicist in order to establish a name, a reputation, and above all, a level of credibility that will make it possible for the producer to launch a film project. The logic behind all this is straightforward: you may have the greatest script ever written, you may have the most incredible pool of talents ever amassed by a producer, but if nobody knows you're out there, it will be hard to take these assets to the bank.

In specific terms, here is how the strategy might work. Two people from Goose Bay, Labrador get together and decide they want to produce a movie based on their own script or a script written by a genius that no one has ever heard of. Their families may not be thrilled at the idea of having to mortgage their homes to float the deal, but the budding producers' friends are sure to be delighted and impressed – after all, Goose Bay hasn't produced that many moguls.

Now what?

First they need money; maybe just a little more than they were able to scrape together themselves, but more likely a mini-fortune. Public relations people don't lend money – usually they don't even invest it. What they can do, however, is make Goose Bay's gift to celluloid look like credible (as in credit) people whose knowledge, experience, and vision will take them a long way toward becoming successful producers.

A publicist with expertise and imagination can take the givens of the situation and shape them into an "image" that the Goose Bay neophytes can not only live with, but live up to. It's just common sense: before Fred and Freda from Goose Bay find themselves in a position to shoot their film, *Gone with the Blizzard*, on location in their hometown (or anywhere else, for that matter), a certain awareness must exist within the industry that will help them get the backing they need.

In fact, few people try to leap into feature film production with *no* track record. A more realistic scenario would be one in which a production company has been toiling away on modest, low-budget projects and now wants to move on to bigger things. Their most recent projects have garnered strong local reviews, the benign approval of government funding agencies, and generally the time seems ripe to bring attention to the company's past achievements, current projects, and future plans. The company may be looking to do more business with a variety of partners, to attract more investors, to interest more distributors and sale agents, or all of the above.

The producer and his or her associates will then seek out a publicist who can assist them in taking their message to the desired audience or target group. A good publicist will also advise them on how much or how little information to divulge at any particular moment, as well as how to pace their announcements.

Take, for instance, a production company that has six or eight possible projects in various stages of development. Such a company might be well advised to concentrate their publicity efforts on just one or two of them – those that are farthest along and have the best chance of reaching fruition. Making premature announcements about projects which don't work out can lead to a loss of credibility that may take years to overcome. Although it is all too easy, in the excitement of the moment, to make rash announcements, serious industry watchers are well versed in reading between the lines of the most creatively written press release.

A canny publicist knows that a producer who completes two of the six projects announced will be given a much more sympathetic hearing by the media and their readers or listeners than the producer who received front page coverage when he or she announced a slate of 12 new features yet didn't manage to get even one off the ground. The latter producer, no matter how inventive his or her publicist, will be all but ignored when attempting to make a big splash with the announcement of another 10 completely new productions.

The same rules apply to Fred and Freda – once they've decided to increase their public profile, they are putting yet more pressure on themselves to deliver. If nobody knows you and you fail, nobody knows you've failed. If, on the other hand, you've gone out of your way to be known as "about to do something" and you don't end up doing it, you've sustained a net loss. This is one of the reasons a new production company might be well advised to keep a relatively low profile until they've accomplished something concrete. Then, once they decide to heighten awareness about themselves, there is something tangible behind them.

Suppose, though, that these factors have been taken into account, and it is time for Fred and Freda to make their mark. In concrete terms, their publicist will do some or all of the following:

a. discuss the aims of Fred and Freda and help them come up with a company name, perhaps a company logo, and most important, a plan of action that will establish them in the public eye;

b. prepare a budget for the various activities that might come under the heading of "corporate public relations," as well as a timeline for the completion of these activities;

c. prepare a company profile, which includes biographies of the principals, stressing relevant experience and education; titles and descriptions of their various projects and whether they are in development, negotiation, preproduction, production, postproduction, and so forth; the company's aims and goals; information concerning the company's financial and legal status, including names and addresses of their banks and legal representatives; and, finally, the name and address of their publicist, to whom all further enquiries should be made;

d. prepare a mailing and phone list of key media contacts to whom a press release will be sent, introducing the new company and the people involved, as well as providing a brief description of *Gone with the Blizzard*;

e. send out the press release to all media representatives and follow up with phone calls (the personal touch).

At this point, the basic goal is to establish the company name and presence. The media involvement will assist the new company in obtaining the sort of moral support that is important in the longer term and may well be used as the basis for the second stage of the company's development: attracting investors, co-producing partners, TV networks, pay and cable TV companies, and theatrical and videocassette distributors.

Taking the Show on the Road

Depending on the available funds, the publicist may decide that following a relatively warm media reception given to the new company from Goose Bay and the title of its forthcoming film, it is time to take the show on the road: bring Fred and Freda to Montreal and Toronto to meet the media and other key industry players. A press conference might be in order, especially if food is served. (A Labrador-style cocktail party could be held outside, even in February!)

The purpose of such events is twofold: to show the other players the new faces and to give Fred and Freda a crash course in an important, even necessary, stage in the business of filmmaking.

Media relations is quite obviously the publicist's forte; each medium's needs and specifications, from deadlines to format, must be understood, just as each journalist's personality or quirks must be accommo-

dated. By knowing these details, the publicist is in a better position to pitch ideas and angles so that his or her clients will receive the right quantity and quality of coverage.

Since the publicist will act as spokesperson for his or her clients, it is essential for the producer to select a publicist whose personality and style – as well as professional credentials – mesh well with the professional image the producer wants to convey. A publicist can, after all, only be effective when he or she has the trust and co-operation of the client. For example, a producer who decides to grant an interview to the local newspaper without contacting or informing his or her publicist, and during the interview decides to "quietly" announce a new project may well be, however inadvertently, undermining what is even more important to the publicist than a prized address and phone book – his or her credibility.

The relationships that develop between publicists and their media contacts demand a level of trust and honesty. Suppose that journalist A asks the publicist for an interview with the producer and is told that none are being given for the time being, yet later opens the newspaper of journalist B and finds an "exclusive" interview with the producer. The publicist's credibility has just suffered a major setback. So has the producer's. Obviously, then, these efforts have to be co-ordinated and even orchestrated *before* the fact, so that whatever information is released fits into the design agreed upon by producer and publicist.

Following the road show, Fred and Freda may well have attended a mind-numbing number of meetings and interviews, exhausted all their "cute Goose Bay stories," and smiled more than they ever thought possible. They catch the next plane back to Labrador and their publicist is at the airport to wave good-bye, before returning to the office to gather Fred and Freda's clippings and send them off to Goose Bay.

"Media Events" – Good and Bad

Back in Goose Bay, Freda has come close to murdering Fred over a line of dialogue in the eighteenth rewrite of *Gone with the Blizzard,* but instead decides that the best revenge might be to let him direct it instead. At the same time, the publicist hears from one of his or her innumerable sources about a new CBC program called *Denture* – a spin-off of their very successful business series *Venture* – focusing on people who will succeed because of good, strong teeth. Fred and Freda have some of the best bicuspids the publicist has ever seen, and minutes later he or she is pitching Fred and Freda to the producer of *Denture* in Toronto. The hot streak continues, because the producer has just finished reading something about these Goose Bay wonders in the "People" section of *Maclean's* magazine, contributed by a freelancer as a result of their recent press conference.

With any luck, the CBC profile of Fred and Freda will air on *Denture* at the same time as the last draft of the script is ready; an Albertan billionaire will catch the show, fall in love with *Gone with the Blizzard*, agree to finance it and ... well, the rest is history, the only appropriate place for this long illustration to be interred.

The unsung hero of the story is, of course, the publicist who, through his or her contacts in the media, knowledge of the industry and its machinations, acute sense of timing (when to push and when to ease off), and belief in the clients, their talents and goals, has managed to take two unknowns and helped them become a pair of muklukked moguls who just might pull off *Gone with the Blizzard.*

This stirring success story almost begs to be filmed, complete with the publicist dressed as a Mountie riding into the Labrador sunset. Before going too far, however, it should be noted that not all media events can be handled by a publicist with equal aplomb or certainty. For example, suppose that the Alberta oilman who is financing *Gone with the Blizzard*, at the behest of the publicist, agrees to do a telephone interview with a national wire service reporter. However, it goes badly, and the reporter thinks the oilman is a self-serving megalomaniac. Three days later, an unfavourable article appears in papers all over the country. The oilman is outraged and who does he blame? Right – the publicist. After all, the publicist arranged the interview and "sicced" that reporter on him. Yes – but the publicist *didn't* do the talking for him. And then there's something all producers should bear in mind when involving themselves in the public relations game: *the publicist didn't write the piece for the journalist.*

For the publicist, representing a firm at the corporate level means working with the producer to establish basic goals and strategies, and then working at maintaining and even enhancing these as the producer's company grows and becomes more successful. Part of the production company's growth may be manifested in a greater international presence – involvement in co-productions, film markets and festivals at home and abroad, and other types of events. At this stage, the advantages of having an experienced, knowledgeable corporate-level publicist are obvious: in order for the producer to work successfully, he or she must know certain things about the international film industry and markets, just as these same groups must be made aware of the producer. Gathering and disseminating information is a full-time undertaking that requires specialized skills. It should certainly not be left until the last moment, to be done in a haphazard manner by someone already carrying out five other jobs in the producer's office.

The proof that working with a good publicist pays off? Just the other day I read that Fred and Freda St. Bernard had signed a three picture co-production deal with England, France, and Germany, based on the strength of their Gemini and Emmy award-winning mini-series *Gone with the Blizzard*!

Unit Publicity

To the average person, the word "publicist" has come to mean "mouthpiece of someone famous, who is either too embarrassed, too sick, too busy, too important or whatever to speak for himself." A Unit Publicist (UP), however, is not the mouthpiece for any individual; instead, he or she is responsible for the co-ordination of publicity materials generated during the shooting of a feature film for theatrical or television release.

While many of the basic activities involved in corporate public relations apply to unit publicity, the latter is a far more focused operation that follows predictable steps. The activities involved in unit publicity generally mirror the stages of production: preproduction, production, and postproduction, and often the early stages of distribution. A unit publicist is engaged by the producer to co-ordinate and disseminate information on a given production, creating awareness of and interest in the making of a film that will carry through to the film's appearance on the market. (Sometimes – very rarely in Canada – it's better if a film is *not* publicized during production. If the director or one of the stars has been overexposed in the media, or if the subject is very controversial, it may be more useful to save all publicity for the film's release. Nevertheless, the unit publicist will still gather and prepare the materials that will be needed later, when the film is distributed.)

The Preproduction Phase

Like the rest of the production team, everything about unit publicity stems from the script. Before principal photography starts, the UP will have read the latest version of the script and written a concise but thorough synopsis of it, to be approved by the producer. At the same time, he or she should take note of any anticipated highlights, such as special effects, scenes requiring large numbers of extras, and other similar incidents that might be used to interest the media.

When casting has been completed, the publicist will do background research and collect articles about the principal actors in order to prepare up-to-date biographies. The publicist *may* be able to obtain such information from the actors' agents – but not always. Once the shooting schedule has been prepared, the publicist and set photographer will go through it together, choosing the most important dates and times for photo coverage. At this point, they will also discuss what types of photos to shoot: colour or black-and-white, and the quantities of each; and the various possible formats. These photos are known as production stills.

Working with the Set Photographer

The set photographer is hired, usually by the producer, to capture in photos the story of the film and its making. The short-term use of this material is to excite media interest in the making of the film. When the shooting is complete, the photos will become part of the press kit, which will be discussed later in this chapter.

It is essential that the publicist and set photographer work together as a team and that they are in agreement before shooting begins. Once shooting starts it will not always be easy for them to meet on the set. Again, preparedness is the key factor. The following list represents some of the typical shots a set photographer would make on an average shoot:

a. one-shot portraits of stars in and out of character and costume – if the picture is a period piece, in which costumes are important, full-length shots should be taken;

b. two-shots and three-shots of the leading performers, particularly if the script calls for romantic involvement;

c. shots of the director and producer together or in discussion with crew members or the actors – these may be a mixture of "candid" and "posed" shots, both of which are difficult to determine beforehand.

At times, the photographer will have special demands placed on him or her by the movie's art department. The photographer might be asked, for example, to create family shots that will be used to decorate a set which is to be the family home, or to provide dated looking pictures that represent the actors when they were younger, as newlyweds, high school graduates, etc.

The set photographer shoots for a variety of publications, from tabloid to high gloss, so the style must vary. The publicist must be kept aware of what the photographer has already shot and processed so that in making his or her pitch to the media, a guaranteed delivery date can be offered to meet the publication's deadlines. Generally, the publicist will be able to keep up with the photographer's work through contact sheets.

Some stars have stills approval. This usually means they have the right to "kill" up to 50 percent of the stills in which they appear. The publicist has to monitor this situation by making sure that the star looks at contact sheets or prints, and also at colour transparencies.

The Production Phase

By the time shooting begins, the publicist should have: a synopsis of the script; a cast and crew list; a shooting schedule that includes arrival and departure dates of the featured performers; biographical information on the principals – actors, director, producer, executive producers, writer, and perhaps the director of photography; and a description of each of the major locations to be used in the film. With these materials, the publicist can then prepare a press release to announce the start of shooting. This release will attempt to provide an overview of the entire production without going into needless detail and will be sent to a variety of media – print and electronic – in a wide variety of places, either by mail, hand delivery, courier, or telex. As with all information emanating from the production, the press release will be approved by the producer before its release and, if necessary, altered to the producer's specifications. This is an extremely important step in the process, because the document is being released in the producer's name and it is the producer who is privy to the legal and contractual arrangements made with the actors, crew, investors (public and private), and perhaps the producer's own associates.

The shooting of the movie is *news*, above and beyond human interest, celebrity hunting, and general entertainment coverage, and a good publicist should take advantage of whatever "newsy" features might be involved in the shoot. As an integral part of the production team, the unit publicist must be prepared for whatever events arise. Some of these might be occurrences that the producer would prefer not to publicize – such as the star's motorcycle accident, or the director's pneumonia which has shut down production for several weeks. Nevertheless, once the publicist has excited media attention, he or she is committed to giving information on such misfortunes and providing answers to journalists' questions.

On the other hand, there are some situations that the publicist might consider ideal from a publicity point of view, while the production crew wants to avoid the added complications. For example, suppose that a musical-fantasy sequence à la Snow White is to be shot on the roof of an old, downtown theatre. Television crews would love to shoot the parade of goats, sheep, and chickens winding their way up six flights of stairs to the roof, but the first assistant director and the production manager say, FORGET IT. Obviously, they want no time delays and not one more particle of animal droppings to clean up than is absolutely necessary. Out goes the great story. Publicity is directly related to the exigencies of time and budget, and during shooting, it must take a back seat to the needs of the film.

The Relationship of Publicist and Producer

As we've said, the publicist relies on the producer to provide much of the information contained in the press release. It is imperative that the producer not lose sight of the movie's short-term and long-term publicity needs, even though other important aspects of the production are clamouring for attention. Ironic as it may seem in a business that appears to revolve around publicity, some inexperienced producers have been known to all but ignore publicity until the shoot is over. Their lack of interest, effort, and co-operation doom their films to poor publicity coverage.

Later, the time will come either to find a distributor or sales agent, or to turn over the picture to one or the other for release. If there are no appropriate still photos of the production and little information available on the principals, storyline, etc., it will become far more expensive – in time and money – to produce these items than it would have been during shooting. For this reason, many distributors specify in their contracts with producers that the latter supply certain materials, sometimes even listing the number of colour slides and black and white stills to be provided. (For more about this requirement, see Chapter 6 by Daniel Weinzweig and Ralph C. Ellis.)

Despite all that we have said, the producer has very little time to deal with anything but the main task at hand: overseeing the production. Therefore, the producer must trust in the publicist's competence. In effect, the relationship between the producer and the publicist should be no different than that between the producer and any other member of the production team. The producer hires a director based on his or her competence and allows the director to do the work the way he or she sees fit. Unless something goes terribly wrong, the producer stays out of that arena. The publicist, for his or her part, must bear in mind that he or she represents the producer to the media and must, therefore, put the best interests of the production ahead of all other considerations.

Unfortunately the nature of the publicist's work can sometimes cause interruptions and/or problems of temperament. Few people are thrilled to bits to be interviewed by journalists during their lunch breaks or while they're preparing for the next scene. A film set is a highly emotionally charged place. The hours are usually long, exterior locations may be difficult, the crowds may be trying, the weather may be unpredictable. On top of this high-pressure situation, a considerable amount of ego has been known to hover over a movie set.

The producer is, of course, aware of all these factors but he or she is equally cognizant of the importance of publicity and has usually told the cast and crew about the anticipated publicity demands that might occur during the shoot. This does *not* mean that the publicist has been given carte blanche to show up on the set at any time, with a print journalist – or worse still, a TV crew – in tow, and expect to be accorded interviews by the stars, director, cinematographer, and members of their families. On the contrary, a good publicist will have checked beforehand will all the people involved about their scheduling preferences.

Atmosphere of the Set

From a publicity point of view, most film sets run very smoothly when the cast and crew understand and respect everyone's value in the overall scheme of things. This simple recognition factor turns the set into a kind of co-operative, as opposed to an ego-ridden hierarchy. As Martin Harbury and Bob Wertheimer pointed out in Chapter 5, the person most responsible for establishing a healthy, co-operative tone on the set is the producer.

This positive atmosphere is even more important when the film location is isolated and everyone is living in close proximity. In this case, the publicist and producer might work out a different publicity strategy. It might be wise, for example, to stage a kind of media blitz. They will choose a particular day when most of the cast is present – shooting a party scene, for example – where the sets, costumes and logistics of the undertaking will be attractive and interesting to the media. Depending on where the location is and how many journalists can be accommodated, they might be transported en masse to the set, leaving the cast and crew free to get on with their work as soon as the media representatives disappear.

No matter what kind of strategy is worked out, the publicist's function remains the same: to provide the journalists with the background information needed; bring them to the set at an agreed-upon time; introduce the interviewer to the interviewee; and then sit in on the interview in order to clarify any details of the production that the interviewee may not be in a position to know. Following the interview, the publicist will ascertain that the journalist has sufficient and correct information on the production; provide a choice of photographs; and make herself or himself available in case the journalist has any additional questions.

The publicist will also take responsibility for following up on the story by contacting the journalist directly or the journalist's editor or producer. Most cast and crew members are interested in seeing, reading, or hearing publicity about the film, and the publicist should inform everyone if and when that information becomes available. One of the fringe benefits of production publicity appearing during shooting is that when the story is good, the cast and crew can share in a collective morale boost. The flip side, unfavourable reportage, can make the publicist feel slightly awkward on the set, at least for as long as it takes to remind everyone that the bearer of bad news is not responsible for its content.

Some international stars have their own press agents, so a publicist may find that he or she has to get an individual actor's press activities approved. Sometimes stars will refuse to do interviews. In this case, the publicist may try tactful persuasion, sometimes with the help of the producer, if there is something the publicist would like the star to do for the film's benefit. Sometimes stars (and directors) are simply not adept at interviews, and the publicist has to find other publicity methods to compensate for this.

The publicist is not on the set all day, every day, because that's simply not possible. When the publicist *is* there, however, it is with eyes and ears open, jotting things down. An amusing or interesting little incident might serve as a "plant" in the gossip columns or on radio shows; furthermore, at the end of shooting the publicist will be expected to have documented the details of the shooting in a form known as production notes (the story of the making of the film). In other words, nothing is wasted.

Other kinds of materials generated during production might include: feature articles on the film as a whole or stories centered on individuals, most likely the director or stars. There might even be by-lined articles written by a member of the cast or crew with a flair for the printed word, focusing on the particular movie being shot or the artist's career in general. The salient point here is that, in some ways, there is no such thing as bad publicity at this stage of the production, though to be sure, some publicity is better than others. As long as the facts are presented and the title of the film is mentioned, the publicist is doing the job: creating awareness and interest that will eventually lead to better box office and/or more projects for the producer and production company.

The Postproduction Phase

The last formal document to be released on behalf of the production is known as a wrap release, which is, as its name would imply, a notice to the media that shooting on the picture has been completed on time and on budget. This particular type of information is geared more towards industry watchers and the media themselves than to the general public. It can lead to any number of inquiries and deals involving sales agents, distributors and so on, both in Canada and abroad.

With the heat off, the publicist will now concentrate on what's known as a little "fishing". This is the term used when the publicist decides to do a small mailing to the international trade press. The mailing usually takes the form of a mini-press kit, complete with synopsis, first and last press releases, and production photos, which is sent to publications that are distributed in major international markets, such as England, Italy, France, Germany, and Asia. Each of these countries has its own trade magazine and these publications sometimes will run photos with captions and even a short news story on the shooting of a Canadian movie. Their readership is made up of other producers, sales agents, distributors, and exhibitors, so such an item might lead to serious interest in the movie, interest that might not come to fruition until months later. But then, one day, at some festival or market somewhere in the world, someone starts making inquiries: fishing has led to planting of seeds, which in turn has borne fruit, to say nothing of a salad of metaphors!

Preparing the Press Kit

As soon as shooting is complete the publicist pulls together all the materials generated during the production phase, and compiles a press kit. Apart from the production notes already been mentioned, a press kit contains the plot synopsis, biographies of the featured players (usually the producer will decide which actors' biographies are to be included); biographies of the executive producer(s), producer, director, and screenwriter; "column notes" (short, succinct items recounting incidents that occurred during production, which might find a place in a reporter's column); and feature stories on the actors, director, or other interesting aspects of the production that are unique and may catch the eye of a newspaper editor on the lookout for a story on the movie or a filler item.

The press kit materials are handed over to the producer of the movie, along with all the contact sheets, slides, and a "key set" of the best production stills developed by the set photographer. Before handing over the photographic materials, the publicist will caption all of them; that is, write a brief description of the scene shown, as well as the names of the faces seen. The producer will then read the material and, after he or she has made whatever changes are required, the press kit will be sent to the distributor.

Although the publicist prepares a complete press kit according to the specifications agreed upon with the producer, often the distributor will regard the information contained in it as raw material to be reshaped and repackaged according to the overall publicity campaign that will accompany the movie's release. Therefore it is the publicist's responsibility to provide as much material as possible, even though, in all likelihood, not all of it will find its way into the final press kit.

The distributor of the film is also responsible for the distribution of the press kits. Generally speaking, the press kit will be made available to whatever media are likely to cover the opening of the film anywhere in the world. The information contained in the press kit will assist the journalist by providing background information to support what appears on the screen.

As they become available, whatever publicity materials (press clippings, video or audio tapes) generated during shooting will be turned over to the producer and to the distributor. These can sometimes be of value in making future publicity decisions regarding the movie, while serving as a record of that particular production. Press clippings recording the excitement of the movie's production are sometimes included in a press kit as a way of impressing upon journalists that this production was a special one.

Recently, some productions have had audiovisual press kits. These can be from five to twenty-five minutes long, and include interviews with the stars and director – in some cases, conducted by the unit publicist – and interesting footage showing everyone at work. The audiovisual press kit can be used for entertainment-oriented TV shows, or news shows with entertainment segments, worldwide. The cost varies considerably, depending on whether the publicist simply hires a two-person crew for a day or so to shoot "B" roll (background material showing shooting underway) or hires a production company to deliver a complete, edited film. The unit publicist would be involved in finding the appropriate crew or company, budgeting for its work, getting its work approved, and, of course, making sure that the team is able to get interesting footage and interviews.

Press Kits for Television

In the case of films made for television, either as pilots or as mini-series, unit publicity services are essentially the same as those described for theatrical features. The basic process is the same, as is the goal: to make people want to see the production. However, a different medium does create slightly different needs, particularly in the contents of the press kit.

A made-for-TV movie designed to serve as a pilot for a proposed TV series carries with it some specific press kit needs. The press kit will need to explain to the media and potential audiences not only what they will see in this particular two-hour show, but at the same time give a sense of how the series will evolve from the premise offered in the pilot. However, it shouldn't be forgotten that the pilot film may find its way into television and even theatrical release in other parts of the world as a one-shot feature, should the television network decide for whatever reasons that the pilot will not be made into a series. As a result, the press kit should be designed in such a way that it can be readily adapted to the needs of both a distributor and a foreign television broadcast outlet.

The most noticeable addition to a made-for-TV movie press kit is a fact sheet. This is a short, to-the-point reference sheet that includes the necessary production information, including the length of the film, the network it was made for, the concept behind the series, the cast, and the main technical credits. The other slight change in such press kits is that full-length biographies are prepared only for the actors who will be the stars of the series if it is made. The other principal actors, known as guest stars, will be handled within the production notes in the form of mini-biographies.

The press kit for a television mini-series needs a more elaborate synopsis than most press kits. Besides the overall synopsis for the mini-series as a whole, most broadcasters expect an episode breakdown, wherein the important events are highlighted in such a way that the flavour of the episode is captured without giving away the plot.

How Much Publicity Can a Publicist Generate?

There is virtually no way of knowing how much media coverage a given film production is going to receive, but the producer should bear in mind some of the variables involved. A low-budget film being shot at a time when three or four larger productions are also being shot will have to work much harder to find a receptive audience among journalists, editors, and TV and radio producers. There's nothing quite like a star to make a publicist's life simultaneously easier and more difficult: on the one hand, the press corps will be calling the publicist instead of the other way around; but, on the other hand, the publicist will have to deal with organizing interviews and/or appearances around the star's schedule, while dealing with the star's own personality quirks. A film based on a story of national interest will quite obviously lead to more attention than one that is described as "a personal vision of growing up," unless the person growing up is famous.

An imaginative and hard-working publicist will, according to the budget he or she is given to work with, do everything possible to get the movie all the attention it should get, but very few publicists are miracle-workers. The project itself, the names and reputations of the principals, along with the co-operation of everyone involved, from the producer to the director and the stars, will go a long way toward assisting the publicist in achieving the ultimate goal: making people aware of the production and whetting the appetite of the widest potential audience for the movie.

Promotion

The terms "publicity and promotion" are often yoked together, yet in the film and television industries, these terms have distinct meanings. Creating publicity is the art of directing media attention to a production, using air time and print space that has not been purchased either directly or indirectly. Promotion usually refers to the launching of a finished film, and this may be a very expensive proposition, indeed, involving the staging of galas, premières, and so forth.

The Release Campaign

A public relations company is sometimes engaged by a distributor to handle the opening of a film in a particular city or territory, or across the country. The assignment may include arranging press screenings before the première; setting up media interviews for the stars, director, producer, and key technical personnel; circulating press kits to critics and other journalists; advertising in the local media; and various other activities designed to bring attention to the movie, including organizing newspaper, radio station, or prestige "avant-premières". Whether the PR consultant is working on a national premiere or simply a local or regional launch, the size and scope of the campaign will be directly dependent on the budget the distributor has earmarked for such an activity.

In any case, the publicist's media contacts, knowledge of the territory, track record and imagination, to say nothing of his or her oganizational skills, will be put to use in drawing attention to the movie. The types of activities will vary from project to project. Sometimes the publicist will simply be asked to put into motion a local campaign that is part of a larger marketing strategy being employed on a national,

North American, or international level. On other occasions, the company will be asked by the distributor to prepare a plan of action or strategy on a national scale or for the particular market they are most familiar with.

The goal of any release campaign is to focus media attention on the film being launched, so that the public is aware of the première and will be receptive to its release. Media screenings in advance of the première are essential. Unless its stars or director are very well known, journalists will seldom agree to interviews without first seeing the film. While it is not always possible, publicists should try to arrange screenings for magazine writers well in advance of the release because of their much earlier deadlines.

Often a publicist will seek free publicity for a movie opening by holding an avant-première in conjunction with a local radio station and/or a newspaper. Then the station and the paper will publicize the film with a content or a straight ticket give-away. Awareness of media demographics and not just ratings are very important when arranging screenings of this nature. (That is, the publicist would deal with a radio station whose listeners are in the same age-group as the potential audience for the film.)

Also, depending on time and budget constraints as well as the marketing strategy, the publicist may organize a series of opinion-maker preview screenings to reach a particular films' target audiences. His or her knowledge of the community will be a tremendous asset, because it is important to select the right people to perpetuate word-of-mouth publicity about the movie.

Promotion for Canadian Productions

On the whole, Canadian films have not been heavily promoted, certainly not by comparison with what goes on south of the border. We are only now beginning to realize the importance of television advertising, for example, something that mass-market distributors in the United States have long exploited. The main reason for this is budgetary. It is not uncommon in the United States to spend huge amounts of money to advertise and market a picture. There are numerous examples of small-budget films on which four or five times the production budget was spent to hype it in various media.

The bottom line is, of course, the bottom line – the limited amounts of money available to promote Canadian films. One Canadian distributor recently attempted to launch a Canadian family film during the Christmas season. The logic for choosing this particular time seemed impeccable – after all, he reasoned, the Christmas holiday is the perfect time to reach vacationing children.

What was not calculated, however, was the enormity of the competition in that season, not in terms of the quality of these films, but in terms of the advertising and promotional budgets these other – all American – productions could rely on. While the Canadian distributor had allocated a very good budget for the national release of a Canadian motion picture, it could not in any way compare with the campaigns for the American movies. The American films all had full-page announcements. Whereas the Canadian film was advertised on local television stations on a spotty basis, the competition carried out saturation campaigns that made the K-Tel approach look subtle! To further complicate matters, when one of the American films received only mediocre box-office response, still more money was put into a secondary advertising and promotion campaign, including video interviews with people coming out of the theatres describing the film they had just seen as wonderful, while the Canadian film could draw no further on the relatively small budget it originally had to work with.

The result, for that particular Christmas season, was that the Canadian film suffered at the box office despite highly favourable reviews, whereas the highly advertised American pictures did much better despite lukewarm critical response. What was learned from this experience by the Canadian distributor was that, rather than going head-to-head with the Americans during their peak season, it is better to release a good Canadian film at another time of year, such as in February, a period traditionally used by the American majors to release the pictures felt to have limited appeal.

If huge advertising and promotional budgets are endemic to the American feature film, so, too, is a sense of salesmanship and self-promotion that Canadians do not take to so easily. This is not to say that we can't, we won't, or we shouldn't – but simply that, so far, we haven't.

Soundtrack tie-ins, novelizations, and (for adaptations) new editions of books featuring the stars' pictures on the cover, as well as other merchandising schemes, have rarely been tried in Canada, although recently we have seen signs of a new awareness. There is much more talk of marketing strategies within the Canadian film industry today than there was ten years ago. More importantly, there is a new determination to devise marking strategies aimed at Canadian audiences rather than simply assuming that what sells elsewhere will sell here.

What is clear is that, just as the Canadian film industry increased its production capabilities over the past two decades, we are now beginning to take on the subsequent challenge of getting our movies into the market place. Promotion until now has usually been restricted to regional or even local events. To expand these activities into national campaigns, there must be advertising budgets capable of supporting them. And in order to organize promotional and advertising campaigns, there must be first-class publicity materials. Only when all the pieces are put together will we be able to give our films the full publicity and promotional support they deserve and require.

CHAPTER NINE

Production and the Law

by Douglas Barrett

*D*OUGLAS BARRETT *is a partner with the Toronto law firm of McMillan, Binch, specializing in the area of media, entertainment, and communications law. In addition to representing clients in the broadcasting, publishing, and computer industries, he acts for a number of large and small film and television producers and, occasionally, Telefilm Canada. He is also counsel to the Canadian Film and Television Association. He has taught a graduate course in media law at Concordia University in Montreal and lectured regularly on communications issues at the University of Toronto Law School. Recently, he led the 15-hour course Advanced Business Affairs Seminar sponsored by the Canadian Film and Television Association.*

Making the Most Effective Use of Lawyers

There is an old story about a lawyer falling overboard into shark-infested waters. Instead of devouring him, the sharks pick him up and help him back into the boat. "Professional courtesy," explains a veteran crew member to his neighbour.

This parable exemplifies the discomfort and reluctance many people feel about dealing with lawyers or making extensive use of their services. The fact of the matter, however, is that most independently produced film and television productions today are extremely complex commercial transactions. The combination of high budgets, multiple sources of financing, and conventional production risks contribute to a situation in which all participating parties wish to ensure that all the "legalities" are correct. The risks are too high to do otherwise.

The Nature of Legal Services

There are four basic types of service that a lawyer can be expected to perform for clients in the film and television industry. The lawyer should:

a. be able to provide advice on the fundamentals of commercial law and on all aspects of financing, producing, and distributing film and television productions;
b. be familiar with industry "standards" and able to negotiate fair and productive deals for clients;
c. be on reasonably good terms with the key decision-makers in the industry and able to ensure that clients will be seen by these individuals; and
d. be capable of producing understandable and thorough legal documentation in an efficient and cost-effective manner.

Most observers would now agree that these services are likely to be performed more effectively by a lawyer specializing in the communications and entertainment field.

In recent years, the number of Canadian lawyers practising largely or exclusively in these areas has increased. However, the group remains extremely small by comparison with other areas of practice – only about two dozen individuals across the country – and heavily concentrated in Toronto and Montreal.

The "Right" Lawyer

Finding the right lawyer and establishing a successful working relationship can be a difficult and intimidating task. Perhaps the best approach is to contact other people active in the industry to find out which lawyer they use and how happy they are with the services provided. Ask about the lawyer's professional qualifications, accessibility and responsiveness, billing practices, and – possibly most important – congeniality and helpfulness.

Create a short list of two or three candidates and take them out to lunch (one at a time, of course!). This should eliminate the need to pay a consultation fee during your search. Tell the lawyer about yourself and your business plans; ask for a sales pitch on what the lawyer can do for you, particularly in relation to the four types of sevices outlined earlier; request specifics on rates, billing practices and payment requirements; and try to make an realistic assessment of how important your business is going to be to the lawyer.

Remember that if you become a successful independent filmmaker or producer in today's industry, you are likely to have frequent need of legal services. You want to establish a relationship with a lawyer that will last for many years. There are several secrets to establishing such a relationship:

a. the client and the lawyer must respect each other, work well together, and communicate fully to one another;
b. the client must give clear instructions to the lawyer;
c. the lawyer's assistance must be put to effective use by the client and produce practical and recognizable results;
d. the client must believe he or she is receiving good value in return for the fees paid to the lawyer; and
e. the lawyer must believe he or she is being fairly compensated.

Controlling Legal Costs

Knowing when and how to use a lawyer is an acquired skill. Because lawyers charge substantial fees, it is very easy to lose control of legal costs. Hourly fees vary from $50 to $75 for those recently "called to the bar" and from $200 to $300 for senior counsel. Quite aside from the question of affordability, most clients feel they receive better value in the advice given by more experienced lawyers. Often, however, documentation may be more efficiently produced by supervised junior lawyers.

In order to control costs, it is important, on the one hand, to carefully consider what you wish your lawyer to do for you and to prepare for the time you spend with him or her. On the other hand, if you treat the lawyer as if you can't wait to get out of the office or hang up the phone, you will lessen his or her willingness to be helpful. Here are some specific do's and don't's:

a. don't ask your lawyer to teach you how to develop and carry on your business – rather, ask somebody else who is less expensive;

b. don't ask or permit your lawyer to make your decisions for you; you – not your professional advisor – are the boss;

c. don't take your lawyer to business meetings at which his or her attendance is unnecessary;

d. do ask for advice on the most advantageous terms and structure of a business deal *before* you begin negotiations or sign anything;

e. do ask for regular reports if your lawyer is undertaking negotiations on your behalf;

f. don't ask your lawyer to prepare documents that you can prepare yourself;

g. do request your lawyer's comments on any documents· drafted by you that could create contractual relations or liabilities;

h. don't negotiate with someone else's lawyer without seeking the advice of your own;

i. do ask your lawyer to keep you fully informed on an ongoing basis of the approximate cost of professional services you have incurred;

j. do request itemized accounts and pay them reasonably promptly;

k. don't hesitate to discuss fees, billing practices, and accounts in order to avoid any misunderstanding.

Following these rules will ensure that you get the most out of your relationship with your legal advisor.

Business Structures

There are several different legal structures in which to carry on the business of film and television production. Each has advantages and disadvantages; each is more or less appropriate for different types of business situations.

Proprietorship

A sole proprietorship is a business that is owned and operated by one person. It is possible to register a name for such a business, and many people mistakenly believe that such registration gives the business the status of a "company". This is not the case.

In a proprietorship, all the contracts and other liabilities entered into or incurred by the business are the personal responsibility of the owner. The profits of the business are taxable income in the hands of the proprietor.

The obvious advantage of a proprietorship is cost: no formalities are needed to establish the business. The primary disadvantage is the personal exposure or liability of the proprietor to all creditors and claimants. Another, more subtle disadvantage is the perception of the business community that a proprietorship is a marginal form of business, not to be taken seriously.

Partnership

A partnership is like a proprietorship, in that the business is operated on a personal basis, but there must be more than one owner. In a partnership, each partner is considered jointly and severally liable for the debts and obligations of *all* the partners. This means that a claimant can seek recourse against any one partner for the obligations of the entire partnership. The affairs of the partnership are governed by an agreement that stipulates the share of profits and costs belonging to each partner and describes the manner in which the partnership shall be operated.

There are certain tax advantages to a partnership, but they are equally available to the more frequently used limited partnership, discussed below. Because of the need for a written agreement, there is little or no cost advantage to a partnership, and there remains the risk of unlimited liability to creditors and claimants. Partnerships are used most frequently by professional firms of lawyers and accountants in jurisdictions where it is illegal for them to incorporate their practices. (For the record, it *is* possible to create a partnership of corporations, but this is a rarely used business form.)

Incorporation

The corporation is the most common form of business structure. The difficult decision for most independent business people is knowing when to incorporate, since it can cost from $400 to $700 in fees plus about $300 for disbursements, or out-of-pocket costs.

There are three possible reasons for incorporating:

a. your accountant tells you to do so for tax reasons;
b. you want to protect your personal assets from claims arising out of your business;
c. you are making a long-term commitment to growth and believe it appropriate to incorporate at the outset.

In the first year of law school, students are taught that a corporation is a separate legal person, able to do everything that an individual can do except vote, marry, or join the army. Sometimes, however, an individual owner of a corporation finds it difficult to grasp the notion that his or her company is another "person". Yet this is the basis for the concept of limited liability.

It is easy to understand that a creditor or claimant should only be paid out of what you personally own, and have no right to the assets of your family or friends. Similarly, a corporation is only responsible for its obligations up to the value of its own assets. Unless its owner or owners have specifically agreed to it in writing, no creditor may claim against the owners' personal assets to fulfill the obligations of the corporation.

The owners of a corporation are its shareholders. Each year, the shareholders elect a board of directors to manage the operations of the company. The directors appoint officers to assume responsibility for day-to-day matters. Officers serve at the pleasure of the board. This means that they can be removed at any time, subject to individual contractual arrangements to the contrary. At the end of the year, the directors report to the shareholders on the operation of the company, and a new election of directors takes place.

This is how it works in theory. But what happens when the company is a business vehicle for only one or two people? Even though it sounds a little silly, the process is exactly the same – even where the shareholders, the directors, and the officers are all the same individuals. If you are the sole shareholder, director, and officer of a corporation, you will have to get used to wearing three hats. Sometimes you will take certain steps as a shareholder, sometimes as a director, and sometimes as the president of your company.

Most corporations active in the film and television industry are "private" corporations: they have relatively few shareholders, and their shares are not available through one of Canada's stock exchanges. For the most part, shareholders in these companies actively participate in the industry, rather than simply being passive investors.

If the corporation has more than one shareholder, it is common for them to enter into a shareholders' agreement that is intended to limit their capacity to deal freely with their shares and to govern the management and operation of the corporation. Some of the specific matters covered by shareholders' agreements are:

a. the number of shares to be issued to each shareholder;

b. the number of directors to be nominated by each shareholder and the names of the first directors;

c. the name of each of the officers;

d. the role of each of the shareholders in the day-to-day operation of the company and the manner and scale of their remuneration;

e. the right of the shareholders to sell their shares to a third party and the other shareholders' right of first refusal to purchase such shares;

f. the right of the shareholders to force the sale of one shareholder's holding, the method of triggering such a forced sale, and the manner of determining the compensation to be paid for the shares;

g. restrictions on how the shares will be voted in certain circumstances;

h. provisions for breaking unresolved disagreements among shareholders;

i. what to do on the death of a shareholder.

There are, of course, many other possible provisions. Shareholders' agreements can be a few pages in length, or hundreds of pages, or anywhere in between. In order for such agreements to have any value to the signing parties, they must be specifically tailored to individual circumstances and fully understood. Never sign the forty-page form that a lawyer says is "standard" for all his or her companies.

Choosing the
Right Name

A word about names. There are three approaches:

a. you can use your own full or last name, provided you use additional differentiating language such as "Brando Television Production Ltd.";
b. you can use a business-related combination name such as "Filmtel Productions Inc." provided somebody else hasn't beaten you to it or a name like it; or,
c. you can use a unique name such as "Bombast Film Corporation" or "Argbarg Productions Incorporated."

Of the three approaches, the latter is preferable. The first approach makes sense only when the corporation has no other purpose than the provision of the services of its principal shareholder; the second approach frequently runs afoul of similar-sounding or similar-looking names already in use. Even if the name you choose is available for use, it might well have a tendency to get lost among all the other business-related names in current use. A unique name stands out and is far easier to protect. Any name you select must include Limited, Limitée, Incorporated, Incorporée, Corporation or Société commerciale canadienne, or the abbreviation Ltd., Ltée, Inc., Corp. or S.C.C. These are the words that signify that your business is incorporated, and they may not be used *unless* it is incorporated.

A final point on the use of corporations in the film and television industry. It is now common practice for separate corporations to be established for each major project. Usually, the shares in these special-purpose corporations are owned by the corporation engaged in the overall promotion and supervision of film and television projects. This practice is advisable for three reasons:

a. it ensures that the general business assets of the parent corporation and its interests in other projects are not exposed to claims made against an individual project owned by the special purpose corporation;

b. it protects the interest of investors in the project from claims made in relation to other projects in which the parent corporation may be involved; and,

c. it gives each project a clean slate, unencumbered by the banking and other commercial arrangements in which the parent corporation might be involved.

Limited Partnership

The last form of business structure that can be used in the film and television production industry is the limited partnership. Each limited partnership has a general partner, usually a corporation responsible for the operation and management of the partnership, and one or more limited partners, usually individual investors. The primary advantage of a limited partnership is that it has all of the tax advantages of an ordinary partnership, but the liability of the investors is limited to the amount invested by each of them in the partnership.

Unlike a conventional partnership, a written agreement among the partners is a legal necessity. In the case of a limited partnership, the agreement tends to be longer and more sophisticated. This level of detail is generally necessary because the limited partners do not know each other and are delegating a great deal of power and authority over the affairs of the partnership to the corporate general partner. As always, the lower the capacity of the parties to trust one another, the greater the need for complex contractual provisions.

Limited partnerships have been gaining favour recently as a mechanism for private investor financing of large budget film and television productions. Since they are relatively complex to establish and administer, they are not likely to be relied upon for small projects.

Legal Implications in the Acquisition of Literary Property

Copyright

Copyright has always been considered a tricky and subtle area of the law in Canada. At the time of writing, the Government of Canada is in the midst of developing major revisions to the *Copyright Act*, to modernize what is widely thought of as an antiquated approach to the protection of intellectual property.

The current law describes the types of works that are protected by copyright, including literary and dramatic works. The owner of the copyright in a work is its author, unless the author wrote the work as part of his or her duties as an employee, in which case the owner is the employer.

Canada has a copyright registration system, but unlike that of the United States, it does not require registration in order to obtain copyright protection. Such protection is obtained by the act of creation, and does not demand any further formality. Indeed, since the Canadian registration system does not permit the physical deposit of the document in which copyright is claimed, it only represents evidence of an assertion that copyright is held in an unspecified work. Since this system does not provide the registrant with much protection, many writers send their scripts to themselves by registered mail or give them to another person to hold. These are more effective methods for establishing evidence of creation than that offered by our formal registration system.

Copyright itself is the right to reproduce, publish, perform, or broadcast all or a substantial part of the protected work, and, more importantly, to prevent others from appropriating your work in any of these ways. The *Copyright Act* provides for an array of civil and summary remedies against those who have infringed a person's copyright.

The period during which copyright exists in Canada is the life of the author of the particular work, plus fifty years. It is axiomatic that no right may be granted for a longer period than it is held by the grantor. Therefore, contract provisions that grant various rights "in perpetuity" are, in fact, ineffective beyond the applicable period of copyright. At the end of this period, the work falls into the public domain and may be used by anyone, without compensation to the author or his or her estate.

The aspect of copyright that many people find difficult to understand is its capacity to be divided and to be sold or licensed on a piece-by-piece basis. For example, the writer of a screenplay or teleplay may assign the entire copyright to a producer, or may license the right to make one film or a television series, or may assign all film and television rights including sequel rights. The right to publish a book based on the screenplay or to produce a stage play or a radio play are all separate rights capable of being sold or licensed on an individual basis, as are merchandising rights, adaptation rights, translation rights, and so forth.

When a producer wishes to make a film based, for example, on a popular book, he or she must first acquire the necessary rights from the owner of the copyright in the book. With these rights in hand, the producer engages a writer to write a screenplay. The writer of the screenplay is the owner of the quite separate and distinct copyright in the screenplay, and the producer must again negotiate the acquisition of the necessary rights from the screenwriter. As you might expect, the higher the price paid by the producer, the more rights he or she would expect to obtain in return.

In the course of producing the film, the producer may engage a composer to create an original sound track. Since there is a separate copyright in the music, the producer must also negotiate for the relevant rights with the composer.

Once the film is completed, it will have its *own* copyright, owned by the producer. Based on this right, the producer may then assign or license the commercial exploitation of the film around the world on a market-by-market basis. At one extreme, the film could simply be sold outright to a distributor; at the other, a distributor may only be given the right to arrange exhibition of the film on television stations in, say, British Columbia, after the film has been shown in theatres and on pay television in a specified order and for specified periods of time.

For any producer, the acquisition of all the relevant rights is of necessity a complex process, heavily influenced by a series of business conventions and guild agreements.

Optioning a Literary Property

As is the case with any other type of real or personal property, it is possible to acquire an option to purchase or license the various rights inherent in copyright. An option permits the payment of a relatively small amount of money, often 10 percent or less of the ultimate purchase price, in return for the exclusive right to acquire the relevant rights at a future date. This allows a producer to determine at relatively low risk and cost whether a film or television property can become a viable project. During the period of the option, the producer is able to work on developing the property without fear that someone else might take advantage of this work by acquiring the rights. (Chapter 2 describes various factors – in addition to legal requirements – that a producer would consider when deciding whether to option or buy a property.)

To protect the interests of both parties, a written agreement is a necessity for optioning a literary property. The agreement will specify the nature of the property being optioned, the time period of the option, and the manner in which it is to be exercised. The agreement will also include the amount and manner of payment of both the option price and the acquisition price. Occasionally, the agreement will provide for the option price to be deducted from the acquisition price at the time the option is exercised. There may also be provision for the renewal of the option upon payment of a further amount of money.

It is obviously important for a producer to ensure that the option period is long enough to develop and finance a film or television program based on the optioned property. Because of the vagaries of the Canadian production industry, it is suggested that an option period of at least two full years is necessary.

A producer actually acquires the optioned rights when the option is "exercised". A key element of the option agreement is the manner in which the exercise event occurs. If the option expires without the occurrence of the exercise event, no rights pass and the rights holder is free to negotiate with another party. If the exercise event occurs during the term of the option, the relevant rights are transferred to the optioning party under the terms of the option agreement. Because of its importance, the exercise event must be described quite precisely in the option agreement. Once the project is ready to go ahead, there must be no doubt about the producer's ability to obtain the necessary rights. Often the exercise event is the payment of the full purchase price of the rights; sometimes it is the occurrence of a particular stage in the production process, such as the first day of principal photography.

Adaptations

Frequently, film or television projects begin life with a producer's discovery of a marketable idea in a book or magazine. The producer decides to adapt the story and characters in the work into a format suitable for a film or television production. If the producer wishes to acquire or option the film and television rights in the work, he or she must first ascertain who holds those rights. Often this is not as easy as it sounds. If the work is a book, the rights holder might be the author or the publisher of the book, depending on the provisions of the publishing agreement. If the work is a magazine article, the rights holder could be the author of the article or, if the author is an employee, the magazine itself.

Once the rights holder has been identified, negotiations can begin. Generally, the producer wants as many of the marketable rights in the literary property as possible, while the rights holder wishes to concede as few as possible. As in most bargaining situations, the price the producer is prepared to pay for the rights is usually the critical determining factor. In addition to a fixed acquisition price for the rights, the deal may include a royalty for the rights holder, in the form of a small percentage of the profits (often called "points"), to be earned from the production.

At the very least, the producer should control the exclusive right to make the proposed film or television production and to distribute it in all types of media and throughout the world for the period of copyright in the film. This would include theatrical exhibition, all types of television, videocassettes, and discs. Beyond this minimum requirement, the producer could acquire the right to make other film and television productions based on the property, to make sequels to the initial film, to make productions in other languages, to adapt the property for the stage, to merchandise the characters, and so on.

What producers are generally interested in, however, is the right to make and distribute a feature film and sequels, and the right to make an episodic television series. American agreements often use several pages of small print just to describe these rights. Fortunately this is not yet necessary in Canada. Some American agreements also grant the right to distribute the production in all media "now known or hereafter introduced, throughout the universe." Canadian producers are not usually this ambitious!

**Engaging a
Screenwriter**

Once a producer has acquired, or possibly created, what are known as the underlying rights in a literary property, it is necessary to engage a writer to prepare the screenplay that is to be based on this work. In Canada, most successful film and television writers working in English, and virtually all working performers, belong to the Alliance of Cinema, Television and Radio Artists (ACTRA). The Quebec-based French writers' guild is Société des auteurs, recherchistes, documentalistes et compositeurs (SARDEC), and the French performers' guild is Union des artistes (UDA).

ACTRA is not a legal union in the true sense of the word, because it has not been certified by a labour relations board. Yet it negotiates collective agreements with most of the broadcasting organizations in Canada and with the various associations of independent producers. These negotiations occur more as an industry convention than a legal requirement. However, once the terms of these agreements are settled, ACTRA uses its influence to ensure that the signatories and its own members adhere to them.

For independent film producers, the relevant writers' agreement is commonly known as the "ACTRA/ IPA Agreement for Freelance Writers." "IPA" stands for independent producers' association, but there are in fact several such associations which join in the negotiations.

The agreement for writers is not well understood by many producers, because it is based on a concept newly developed in 1982. A copy can be obtained from ACTRA in Toronto by calling 416-489-1311. The essence of the new concept is that instead of receiving residual payments depending on when and where a program is aired or exhibited, a writer is paid a royalty of 4 percent of all revenues received by a producer from its worldwide exploitation in every medium. The writer receives two types of payments, which are advanced against royalties (that is, paid in advance of revenues being earned, but deducted later from the royalty owing):

    a. the writer must receive a specified minimum payment for writing and submitting the script; and,

    b. on the first day of principal photography, the writer must receive a "production fee", equal to the difference between the minimum writing fee and 4 percent of 70 percent of the gross budget of the production.

The reason that the production fee is 4 percent of 70 percent of the budget is that the producers' negotiators were unwilling to agree to pay the 4 percent royalty on the "soft" costs of a production, such as finance charges, interest, and professional fees. These were estimated at the time to average 30 percent of production budgets, a figure that would be considered excessive today.

Because both the minimum fee and production fee are credited to the 4 percent royalty requirement, a writer would not be entitled to share in revenues until most or all of the production budget has been recouped. In return for these minimum payments and royalty, a producer will acquire the right to make a single film or television program from the screenplay and to exploit it in all media of communication throughout the world for the period of copyright in the screenplay. Under the provisions of the ACTRA agreement, a writer is required *not* to assign his or her copyright in the screenplay to the producer.

It almost goes without saying that a written agreement between the producer and the screenwriter is a necessity. It need not be long or complex, but it must ensure that the producer acquires adequate rights for the production and effective commercial distribution of the proposed film or television program.

Warranties

When a producer enters into an investment, distribution, or exhibition agreement relating to a film or television production, a warranty will be required that the necessary production and distribution rights are held by the producer free and clear of any charge or encumbrance of any kind; and that the film, and hence the screenplay from which it is produced, will not infringe anyone's copyright, contain libellous statements about anyone, or invade anyone's right to privacy.

The effect of a warranty in any legal agreement is that the maker of the warranty is fully responsible for the consequences of the warranty's inaccuracy. For example, a producer warrants to a distributor that all necessary production and distribution rights have been acquired. This turns out to be incorrect, and the distributor is successfully sued for infringement of copyright. As a result of the warranty, the distributor could require the producer to pay for its entire loss, plus all its legal costs. In order to gain a measure of protection when making a warranty, a producer should ensure that the agreements with both the vendor of the underlying rights and with the screenwriter contain a similar warranty to the one the producer will be required to give other parties.

A little-known provision of the ACTRA Agreement stipulates that until the production fee, due on the first day of principal photography, is paid, no rights in the screenplay actually pass to the producer. What the producer has until that point is a sort of irrevocable and exclusive option to acquire the rights, but not the rights themselves. Because of the contractual warranties (described above) that the producer is required to make, a failure to pay the applicable production fee on the specified date can have very serious consequences indeed.

Chain of Title The various documents under which a producer acquires the rights to produce and distribute a film or television production are the fundamental base upon which the producer's own rights finally rest. If the documents are flawed, the copyright to the production is compromised. The documentation of every change in the assignment of these rights, from the author of the underlying work through the work's publisher to the screenwriter, is called the "chain of title." Quite often, tracing the chain of title is an extremely complex task. Consider a situation in which a producer has purchased the rights to a number of books to be blended into a single story, has engaged a team of writers for the initial drafts of the screenplay, and has commissioned a number of rewrites. If the production is to be a musical, there is an additional lineage of rights belonging to the composer and lyricist and subsequently to those responsible for arranging and orchestrating the score.

When a well-informed investor, such as Telefilm Canada, is considering a particular investment, the first thing it requires is evidence that the chain of title safely delivers the relevant rights into the production entity which is seeking the investment.

A final comment about rights. Many producers arrange to have the relevant rights conveyed to their production corporations during the development stages of a project before the commencement of production. If this production company is an active business entity, it is likely to have a line of credit with a bank, and is almost certain to have executed a general security agreement in favour of the bank. Under the provisions of this type of agreement, the bank generally acquires a security interest over all program rights held by the company. A security interest is a form of encumbrance that qualifies the title of the company to the program rights and hence its capacity to convey those rights to investors or distributors.

In order to avoid unnecessary complications in financing a production, it is therefore suggested that a separate corporation be established for each project designed to attract investor participation. The applicable rights for the project should be conveyed to this entity as soon as it is created, adding another step to the chain of title. Once this is done, the corporation must not make any banking arrangements unrelated to the specific project, including the giving of any form of guarantee to the active production company.

Legal documentation

The Importance of Good Documentation

It is an intensely frustrating experience for many beginning producers to find out how much work is required to complete the documentation for an average film or television production. Just when they feel that all the pieces are in place and the real creative work can begin, the lawyers appear on the scene with all sorts of seemingly unreasonable demands.

These demands are often perceived as being excessive, an unnecessary reliance on technicalities and legalese. It must be understood, however, that when an investor such as Telefilm Canada, or a major broadcaster or distributor contributes hundreds of thousands of dollars to the budget of a production, it has an extremely strong interest in ensuring that it gets its money's worth in as risk free a manner as possible.

One of the unique qualities of a film or television production is that as a commercial transaction, it is merely an interlocking web of contractual arrangements dealing with property acquisition, financial packaging, and production and distribution, each layer built upon a previous contractual foundation. If the legal documentation for any layer is incomplete or improperly prepared, it creates a risk that threads its way right through the production.

Consider the implications of not controlling the relevant underlying property rights, or of not receiving borrowed or invested funds on the day upon which they are required, or of losing the lead performer in mid-production, or of not being able to deliver a tape to the broadcaster in time for the scheduled air date. Any of these events would have disastrous consequences, not only for the investors and distributors, but perhaps more importantly for the producer's own organization and reputation. While the best legal agreements cannot ensure that these problems will never arise, they can substantially reduce the attendant risks by making absolutely clear who gets what, and who does what, at what times.

The Role of the Producer	Given the importance of contractual materials, the producer has a critical role in preparing the documents that will frame the production and ultimately bind it together. In the first instance, the producer must ensure that the documentation accurately reflects the arrangements negotiated for the production with all of the participating organizations and individuals. It is a terrible mistake for a producer to

view the critical contracts as inconsequential technical forms. Any careful and professional producer will
read, understand, and actively shape all of these materials.

Another critical matter requiring close attention is
consistency among all of the contracts and agreements. It is amazing how often distribution agreements grant the same right to two different parties, or
grant a right that the producer does not actually have.
High-quality legal documentation is the lawyer's first
responsibility; supervising and working with the lawyer is one of the producer's most important and least
understood functions.

Deal Memoranda

Because of the complexity of many legal agreements,
producers often enter into deal memoranda or letter
agreements which briefly set out the matters that have
been negotiated and agreed upon, and specify that a
"full and formal" agreement will be prepared and executed at a later date. These documents are usually
prepared and signed by the negotiating parties. Deal
memoranda are very helpful in permitting business-
like arrangements to be made quickly, effectively, and
directly between the parties. They are also very dangerous and must be used with great care.

Many producers believe that deal memoranda or
letter agreements are not contractually binding. This
is *not* the case; deal memoranda are no less enforce-
able than a hundred page agreement. More often than
not, they are never replaced by a "full and formal"
agreement, despite the customary provision to the
contrary. This is particularly likely if they contain a
complete description of the transaction contemplated
by the parties. For this reason, deal memoranda
should never be entered into lightly. All contractually
binding documents, no matter how simple or apparently inconsequential, should therefore be carefully
reviewed with a producer's legal advisor *before* their
execution.

Financing Arrangements

In Chapter 4, there is a full discussion of the various mechanisms available in Canada for financing film and television productions. As a result, the comments here will be limited to a review of the legal concepts inherent in such arrangements.

Equity Investment

The term "equity" is a synonym for ownership. In the context of a business corporation, equity is represented by the share capital of the company. In a film or television production, equity is described as a direct, proportional interest in the copyright of the production.

The rights and obligations attached to the equity interest are found entirely in the legal agreement under the provisions of which the equity is acquired. When an investor signs the agreement and pays the purchase price of the equity interest, the relevant proportion of the copyright in the production is actually assigned and sold to the investor. Generally, an equity interest entitles an investor to receive a negotiated share of the revenues derived from the worldwide commercial exploitation of the production, both before and after the recoupment of its cost of production.

If the investor is an individual, he or she is unlikely to have any creative role in the production or in monitoring production activities. However, if the investor is a broadcaster or Telefilm Canada, there is certain to be some form of continuing production monitoring, although the intensity of this activity will vary with the circumstances.

In order to protect the investor from any obligation for production cost overruns, the investment agreement should also protect the investor from any responsibility or requirement for contributing any more than his or her original investment. To ensure that funds are available to cover budget overruns, a producer will arrange for completion insurance from a completion guarantor. Once satisfied that the budget of a production is accurate and adequate and that all the required financing is in place, a guarantor will utilize its own funds to complete the production if the agreed upon budget is exceeded. In order to protect itself, the guarantor closely supervises the production process to ensure that there is no drift away from an "on budget" status. The guarantor reserves the right to step in and take over the production at any time if things are getting out of hand. If the guarantor is required to complete a production, it is entitled to recoup any costs it has incurred from the proceeds of distribution, once the production has returned its budgeted cost to the investors. The cost of a completion guarantee is usually about 6 percent of the cost of production.

As has been indicated previously, the investment agreement will invariably contain an unqualified warranty by the producer that the investor is acquiring the interest in the copyright free and clear of all claims and encumbrances. Once the copyright has been sold to the investors, they assume legal responsibility for infringement of copyright, libellous statements, and invasion of privacy (unless the investment vehicle is a limited partnership, in which case the investors are protected by their limited partnership status). In the event of a successful claim, of course, the investors would in turn claim reimbursement from the producer under the provisions of the warranty. However, this does not provide an adequate measure of protection.

To insure against the burden of copyright infringement, defamation, and invasion of privacy claims, a producer may obtain, along with the usual production coverage, an insurance policy covering what are known as errors and omissions. In order to obtain this coverage, however, a producer must satisfy the insurer that every possible prudent step has been taken to ensure that there will be no claims. Usually, the insurer requires that the producer answer a highly detailed questionnaire relating to the content of the proposed film or television production. If the insurer believes there is any appreciable risk, the coverage will not be offered.

The Tax Shelter

In Canada, investment in a film or television production is made more attractive by provisions of the *Income Tax Act* that create what is known as a tax shelter. When an individual acquires an undivided interest in the copyright of the "master negative" of a certified Canadian production, he or she is entitled to depreciate the cost of the investment by claiming capital cost allowance. The allowable capital cost allowance rate is 100 percent of the value of the equity interest, half of which may be taken in the first year the investment is held.

The Act provides that an investor may purchase his or her investment "unit" by paying 5 percent immediately and by giving the producer a full recourse promissory note, payable within four years, for the balance. Usually the purchaser is also required to give the producer an irrevocable letter of credit for the value of the promissory note. The producer then assigns all the letters of credit to a bank as security for a loan equal to the value of all the promissory notes.

Over the years, the tax shelter provisions for film and television production have become progressively more complex and technical. While it is not appropriate to review these provisions in detail here, they are dealt with in Interpretation Bulletin No. IT-441 issued by Revenue Canada. The tax treatment of film and television investments made by broadcasters and distributors is primarily determined by their active participation in the production industry. As a result, the full advantage of the tax shelter is only available to private individuals. The responsible agency for certifying Canadian productions for the purpose of the tax shelter is the Department of Communications. This and other certification systems will be discussed below.

Securities Laws

The sale of investment units in film and television productions raises another very important legal consideration. Under the various pieces of securities legislation of the provinces of Canada, an investment unit in a film or television property is considered a "security". The sale of securities is governed by extremely complex regulations designed to protect the public from fraudulent statements and misrepresentations made in securities sales literature. Anyone wishing to sell securities must file with the applicable securities commission a prospectus containing a "full, true and plain disclosure of all material facts" relating to the sale. The preparation of prospectuses is time consuming and very costly.

Fortunately, there are a number of exemptions from the general requirement to prepare and file a prospectus. For instance, where film and television investment units are sold in Ontario, an exemption is available if the number of potential purchasers is not more than 75, and the number of units sold is not more than 50. Even if one of the exemptions is available, however, an offering memorandum containing "prospectus-like" information must be prepared and provided to each individual approached. In addition, there are a number of specific provisions that these documents are required by law to contain. Canadian securities laws provide for severe civil and statutory penalties, including jail terms in certain circumstances, for any failure to adhere to the applicable regulations.

Presales

Another frequently used technique for funding film and television productions is known as presales financing. A presales arrangement is one in which a broadcaster or distributor makes a commitment before production begins to pay a licence fee or distribution advance either during the course of production or upon delivery of the final product.

The licence fee would be paid in return for the right to air the production a specific number of times over a

set period in a described territory. The distribution
advance would be paid for the right to distribute the
production in a described territory for a set period
under specific terms and conditions covering the
sharing of distribution revenues.

If the presales commitment is payable on delivery,
the producer might borrow against the broadcaster's
or distributor's promise to pay. Alternatively, a producer might raise private investment for the entire
cost of production and use the presales undertaking
as a form of committed return to make the investment
more attractive.

Most productions that rely on presales commitments as a financing technique arrange several of
them for any given production. For example, a producer might obtain a licence fee from a Canadian
broadcaster, an advance against distribution revenues
from syndication (the licencing of programs to individual stations) in the United States, a licence fee from
a Canadian or American pay television operation, and
so on.

From a legal perspective, the most important aspect
of any presales commitment, aside from ensuring that
it is a genuine commitment, is what is known as the
grant of rights. Quite often, keeping the various grants
separate and distinct can be tricky indeed. For
instance, let us say that a Canadian broadcast network
has purchased the right to air the production four
times over three years; a Canadian regional broadcaster has the right to air it five times over a five-year
period commencing after the network has had three
runs; an American pay-TV service has the exclusive
right to air the production a number of times; and an
American syndicator has the right to distribute the
production once the pay television "window" has
elapsed. In this example, each of the exhibitors or distributors has acquired and paid for a specific right
relating to a particular niche in the market place. The
nature of the right is both inclusive and exclusive. That

is to say, the right is not only defined by what the exhibitor or distributor can do, but also by what he or she cannot do. Each exhibitor or distributor, therefore, has as significant an interest in the clear definition of rights granted to all other exhibitors and distributors as in the definition of the rights he or she has been granted.

Because of the risks and complexities inherent in making a commitment to purchase a film or television production before production commences, presales financing agreements have a tendency to be long and detailed, and to curtail the producer's control, both creative and financial. Those making the commitments usually wish to ensure that they have a sufficient number of contractual rights "in reserve" to take over the production if they believe it to be necessary.

Negotiating with exhibitors and distributors can be difficult and frustrating. More often than not, they insist that the producer sign a standard form agreement, which is heavily weighted against the producer. The only bright note is that when a producer signs such an agreement, he or she is in powerful company: all the best and most experienced Hollywood producers sign equally onerous agreements without flinching.

Interim Financing

Once a project's equity or presales financing has been arranged, a producer may realize that the flow of funds resulting from these deals will not match the cash flow requirements of the production. Usually, revenue from an equity investment or a major presale will not be received until the latter stages of production or even until the production has been completed.

In these circumstances, the producer must obtain a short-term loan to fund production activities. Such loans are very difficult to obtain, primarily because there is little accepted value in the collateral offered to the lender as security for the loan. Film and television productions do not have much in common with hard assets such as land or inventory, for which there is a readily ascertainable market.

In seeking interim financing, a producer may offer a lender one of the following types of security:

a. the right to be repaid out of the sale of equity units purchased by investors; or
b. the right to be repaid out of revenues from the exploitation of the production.

Neither source of funds has sufficient certainty to satisfy most traditional financial institutions. In addition, many such institutions stay away from film and television production because of heavy losses suffered during Canada's boom and bust years in the early 1980s.

So much for the bad news. The good news is that some private and institutional lenders are beginning to show renewed interest in the industry. At the moment, this interest is limited to projects undertaken by the most successful and financially sound producers. If these transactions prove to be profitable for lenders, however, financial institutions will likely become more receptive to producers' blandishments.

Some private organizations will still lend against an assignment of the revenues to be received from a sale of units to investors. However, most financial institutions will only "bank" a specific presales agreement which, for example, makes a commitment to pay a licence fee upon delivery of the completed production. The "bankability" of such presales agreements depends very much upon the individual circumstances of each case. If the presales agreement contains an excessive number of vague conditions concerning payment, the financial institution will either decline to accept it as security or heavily discount its value.

With the resurgent interest in the industry, there is also the possibility that certain institutions will lend against an assignment of revenues which have not yet been contracted for. However, this type of financial assistance will only be made available to producers with very strong track records, and only where the amount of the loan is quite small in comparison with the level of revenue that is virtually certain to be received.

No matter how enthusiastic financial institutions may become about participating in film and television projects, they will always seek as much security as possible for their loans. For this reason, producers dealing with them should expect a routine requirement that they provide corporate and possibly personal guarantees of the production's obligations to the financial institution.

Canadian Content Certification

As every Canadian producer knows, almost no market exists in Canada for his or her productions unless they have been certified as "Canadian" by a government agency. In addition to the predictable complexities and controversies surrounding the attempt to define a Canadian production, there is the added twist of having two (and some would say, three) separate certification systems. The two formal systems are operated by the Department of Communications of the Government of Canada (DOC) and the Canadian Radio-Television and Telecommunications Commission (CRTC).

The DOC System

The certification system operated by the DOC is used primarily by those producers wishing to offer private investors units in a film or television production. This form of certification is necessary in order to take advantage of the tax shelter described earlier in this chapter.

Essentially, certification is available to a production which:

a. has a Canadian producer;
b. achieves 6 out of a possible 10 "points" for key personnel;
c. spends on Canadians 75 percent of the remuneration paid to individuals other than the key personnel; and
d. spends 75 percent of all laboratory and processing costs in Canada.

The 10 possible points for Canadian personnel are allotted as follows:

Director	2 points
Screenwriter	2 points
Highest paid actor	1 point
Second highest paid actor	1 point
Head of art department	1 point
Director of photography	1 point
Composer	1 point
Editor	1 point

In addition to these requirements, *either* the director or screenwriter *must* be Canadian; and *either* the highest or second highest paid actor *must* also be Canadian.

The DOC will also certify productions that are recognized under formal co-production treaties entered into between Canada and a number of other countries (excluding the United States). Unfortunately, it is Telefilm Canada, rather than the DOC, that administers compliance with these treaties. A producer wishing certification of a co-production must first apply to Telefilm Canada for approval of the co-production, and then apply to the DOC for final certification.

For more information regarding the Department of Communications certification system, you should write to:

Canadian Film and Videotape Certification Office
Department of Communications
365 Laurier Avenue West
Room 1634
Ottawa, Ontario
K1A 0C8

The CRTC System

The certification system operated by the CRTC is used for productions that will appear on licensed Canadian television services. The CRTC recognizes for its own purposes the certification issued by the DOC under the rules described above. However, because of certain differences between the two systems, the DOC does not recognize CRTC certification. Therefore, any television production that is made using private investment must be certified by the DOC as well as the CRTC.

The basic CRTC system is the same as the DOC's system, relying on the identical calculation of points and expenditure requirements. The difference between the two systems lies in the CRTC's willingness to certify where:

a. a program is produced under a "co-venture" arrangement satisfactory to the CRTC; or
b. a television series complies *as a whole* with the requirements, even where some episodes do not; or
c. a program package produced by a co-venture meets the overall requirements *on average.*

A co-venture can be certified where the Canadian and foreign production companies have equal approval over all elements of the production, where both have an equity interest in and financial responsibility for the production, and where both have co-signing authority over the production bank account. Co-ventures must attain 5 Canadian points and expend 50 percent of total remuneration and processing costs on

Canadians if the co-venture is made with a producer from a Commonwealth or French language country. Other co-ventures are required to meet the same points and expenditure requirements as domestic productions.

The CRTC allows licensed television services a 150 percent program credit for a drama that achieves 10 out of 10 Canadian points and is carried in prime time. (This means, for example, that a one-hour program scoring 10 out of 10 could be credited to the network in question as one-and-a-half hours of Canadian programming. When the network's license is to be renewed by the CRTC, it must report how many hours of Canadian programming it provides.) In addition, the CRTC has special rules for local station productions, sports programming, music videos, and dubbed programs.

The CRTC certification system is described in Public Notice 1984-94. For a copy, you should write to the Secretary General of the CRTC, Ottawa, Ontario, K1A 0N2.

The so called "third" certification system is that operated by Telefilm Canada. While Telefilm accepts the certification requirements of both the DOC and the CRTC, it sees itself as having a mandate to ensure that the productions it invests in are as Canadian as possible. For this reason, Telefilm often uses its considerable clout to ensure that the minimum Canadian content requirements are exceeded. A few producers feel that this amounts to a separate, and largely unspecified, certification system. The fact is, however, that Telefilm is merely exercising its discretion to give its greatest support to predominantly Canadian projects.

Summary

If there are any points worth re-emphasizing concerning the business of filmmaking and the law, they are these:

First, independent production in Canada is now a

sophisticated and complex commercial enterprise. As one step in addressing this reality, producers should establish a good working relationship with a capable lawyer.

Second, producers must be knowledgeable about all the matters discussed in this chapter and, indeed, in this book.

Third, producers should understand the details of all the agreements they enter into for the financing and production of a film or television project.

Fourth, producers should insist on thorough and professional documentation for all major agreements and should personally supervise the preparation of this material.

CHAPTER TEN

Closing Sequence

by Louis Applebaum

LOUIS APPLEBAUM's contribution to the arts has been tremendous – he has composed hundreds of music scores for theatre (including 33 seasons for the Stratford Festival), radio (including several hundred CBC dramas), television (including The National Dream *and* The Masseys, *for which he won the Canadian Music Council Award), and film (including* Homage to Chagall *and a large number of Hollywood films in the 1940s and 1950s). He has also composed symphonic, chamber, choral, and ballet music. He was the Executive Director of the Ontario Arts Council in the 1970s, and Chairman of the Federal Cultural Policy Review Committee (Applebaum / Hébert Report) from 1979 to 1982. He is also the Chairman of the Academy of Canadian Cinema & Television committee that oversaw the production of this book.*

Without guaranteeing anything to anybody, this single volume will assuredly be helpful to many readers, perhaps most to those who dream, albeit wistfully, of a brilliant career as a film producer. Even they, alongside their more pragmatic colleagues, will have realized by now that – though there is no expressway to glamour, fame, success, and fortune – the road is smoother for those who work diligently, have know-how, can call on the people who are in a position to provide the right answers, can build solid business structures and good budgets, and can raise money.

Nevertheless, we all know there is no one correct way to do things, no single sage who can provide all the right road signs and directions. For every rule and pearl of wisdom, the exceptions will abound. Besides, the business is extremely changeable. Last year's technology is out of date or out of fashion before you can say "cut and print." Only a few years ago, films were shot on highly flammable nitrate stock. Microphones hidden behind potted palms would transmit the dialogue to the hapless sound recordist, who couldn't be sure of what had been recorded until the optical stock on which the sound had been imprinted was developed and a print made for playback.

Some readers will recall the hype that accompanied the introduction of Cinerama or the blue-and-red polaroid glasses through which we could see the wonders of 3-D. (The latter still pops up from time to time in some new guise.) Why not expect that Lucasfilm's latest THX Sound System will soon give way to some newer, even more fantastic innovation? Is computer animation an answer and if so, to what questions? When will Kodak colour film stock be replaced once and for all, and what new device for recording visuals will take its place?

That sort of instability would shake the foundations of any "solid" industry, yet this one seems to thrive on it, decade after decade. But rather than give in to anarchy, this book, with good reason, vigorously advocates sound business practices such as advance planning and basing judgements on the reliable foundations of wide knowledge and substantial craftsmanship. It presents the distilled experience of many leaders of Canada's film business, and not even a maverick genius would want to turn his back on that.

When it comes down to the nub of the issue, it matters little that some miraculous new digital process will have to be mastered; that satellite transmissions will almost inevitably replace Gaumont projectors in movie houses; or that 1200-line high-definition TV sets will be found in every home. The basic truth is that *no magical innovation will alter the fundamental role of the producer.*

The role of the producer is a constant, no matter what the jargon or the complexity of the machinery at hand. Whether he or she functioned in the 1930s, was a contributor to this book in the 1980s, or comes into the business only after 2030, the producer will have to face similar issues. Films have always been, and will always be, made by imaginative, talented, able people, and not by robots or "studios". This business will always flourish on the imagination, ambition, and resolve of those individuals who simply *must* make the films that consume all their thoughts and energy. The successful producer of the future, as of the past, will be the one who can sniff out a great story (or write it) and who, like a brilliant chemist, can concoct the right mixture of talent to work behind the cameras and to perform excitingly before their lenses.

Audiences will always yearn for (and be willing to pay for) good stories told in a fascinating way. Whether the film is long or short; whether it was intended for the big cinema screen or the TV set; whether it involves big stars, casts of thousands, and complex special effects, or was made with unknowns on a shoestring budget; it must intrigue the viewer, and it must be made with honesty and conviction. Film writers tend to be ignored while we put spotlights on performers, yet of all contributors to successful films, they are surely the most vital. Writers with talent and flair should be cherished, nurtured, and protected by everyone in the film industry, since every film job, from star to gofer, could be said to depend on the creative effort of the writer.

Having unearthed and shaped the story (with the help of the writer) and having accumulated enough funds to get going (with the help of providence, relatives, and trusting bank managers) it is up to the producer to assemble his or her team. It is the producer's judgement that defines, first, the "right" director; then directs the selection of designers, composer, cameramen, actors, and the rest of the creative team; and finally oversees the hiring of the hordes of technical people to back them up. In the meantime, the administrative office has been peopled by the producer's personal back-up team – the lawyers, accountants, secretaries, plotters, and protectors who hover around all such complex creative ventures. It is up to the producer to inspire, push, cajole, implore, threaten, and guide these minions, hoping thereby to extract the very best efforts from each of them. How this is done, precisely, is one of those mysteries that this book could never unravel. Some producers are born with the gift, some manage to acquire it, and others, no matter how it is thrust upon them, or by whom, will never master it.

What *is* inevitably thrust upon the novice producer is lots of free advice and alleged "tricks of the trade." "Stars," it will be said, "are the best way to ensure a healthy box office." Yet each of us can make a fairly lengthy list of star-studded, expensive films that have bombed, and an equally lengthy list of films devoid of recognizable "names" that have nevertheless cleaned up at the ticket wicket. The streetwise will urge that distribution deals be made only with the "major" companies, yet we know that even the most solid and reputable of these are as capable of bad judgements as small companies; that their decisions can relegate good and potentially profitable films to dust-gathering shelves while attention and money is lavished on eventual box-office disasters.

"Never go into production until all the money is in the bank," the cautious advisers will insist. Yet we can point to projects so seriously underfinanced that shooting proceeded in spurts, often months apart, reactivated whenever a few more dollars could be deposited in the film's bank account. It has sometimes happened that even such hard-luck film ventures turned out to be artistic and / or box-office winners.

It is a fact that, in Canada, the axioms of Hollywood and New York are rarely applicable. For some time into the future, we must expect to carry on without big studios and affluent distributors, without huge promotion budgets and big-time agents, without the throngs of hangers-on and wheeler-dealers that populate the world's larger production centres. Only a little while ago, the pool of artistic and technical talent in Canada was very small. Yet in a relatively short time, we have been able to generate large numbers of people who are outstanding in all aspects of the filmmaking business. The National Film Board and the Canadian Broadcasting Corporation have played major roles, invigorating our film industry by training and encouraging many of those who are now leading figures.

It is, in fact, the pioneering film activity of both these federal government agencies that led the Canadian government to reconcile itself to a prominent role in film development. Convinced that a robust film industry is an essential contributor to the evolution of our national character, the federal government, and subsequently some of the provincial governments, increasingly involved themselves in ensuring its health. Aside from the actual production programs of the CBC and the NFB, which operate primarily on tax dollars, governments have seen fit to provide grants and other forms of support to independent filmmakers. The federal government even created a new agency for that purpose: Telefilm, which used to be called the Canadian Film Development Corporation. Telefilm is now rather substantially funded, and has therefore figured prominently in the preceding pages.

The federal government has been involved in other, perhaps equally significant, ways. Through use of the tax system, a veritable flood of projects were produced in the late 1970s, all of which called themselves "films" but only a few of which deserved the status. A tax shelter had been created, a 100 percent Capital Cost Allowance that drew an inordinate amount of investment dollars into the film business, dollars that had no concern for the quality of the productions in which the investments were made, but only in the fact that a full tax write-off was possible in one year. When the tax regulations were changed, the well of dollars abruptly dried up. The quasi-filmmakers returned to their regular lines of work and the investors concentrated once more on the gaping mouths of the patients in their dental chairs. However, the serious, able, determined filmmakers stuck with it.

The government tried again when it acquiesced in the introduction of pay-TV. However, the CRTC managed to botch the arrangement when it granted too many licences in the first round. It was expected that the pay-TV companies would invest large parts of their revenues in film production (actually a condition of their licences) but this became impossible, since none of them was financially healthy as things stood. The several movie channels soon had to merge, the "culture" channel went out of business, and the anticipated blossoming of new production never occurred.

Undaunted, governments still try to deal positively with a stream of proposals to improve the lot of the filmmaker. They are concerned, as they should be, that our means of communication remain in Canadian hands, the better to reflect the Canadian reality, however that may be perceived by our artists. Since enormous sums of money can be spent to make a film, it is natural for governments to turn to less costly devices whenever possible. New laws, regulations, licensing, advice, studies, investigative commissions, and such don't eat up a lot of money, at least at first. Even less affluent provinces can be found considering low-cost support in areas like marketing, distribution, training, and promotion, even if they can't afford to get into major granting and investment schemes. Cities are

now vying with each other to entice film companies into their precincts, because a little help from town council can mean an infusion of big bucks into the local economy. Schools of film study and filmmaking are proliferating at all levels of the educational system. Because governments can be helpful to you as a novice filmmaker, and might even become your partner, it may well be worthwhile for you to study and master the latest batch of regulations and to wade through the mounds of red tape that government bureaucracies use as protective wrapping.

When it comes to TV, the CBC is still a sort of lifeline for the independent producer, being by far the biggest buyer of Canadian productions, and it has indicated its intention of purchasing more programs from independents in the future. CTV, which to date has not been a bountiful user of Canadian film production, is being pressed on all sides to do more. Like the independent broadcasters, the network can turn to the Telefilm fund for help. The CRTC, which through its regulation, licensing, and monitoring is supposedly a watchdog over our cultural and national broadcasting interests, has been rather permissive in the past, showing concern first for broadcasters' financial viability and then almost shrugging away failures to live up to the promises made in licence applications. But even here, the tune seems to be about to change, and producers can only hope that the new melody will be sweet to their ears.

All in all, as I write in 1986, the prospects for future Canadian filmmakers look bright. It seems clear that in future more films will be made by more producers in more places for acceptance by more people in Canada and elsewhere. Even statistics justify the optimism. In 1961, no features were made, although some 67 production companies were producing a few shorts and a lot of TV commercials. In 1983, 45 feature films, 104 shorts under 60 minutes, and 1023 shorts under 30 minutes flowed out of 322 production companies. Apparently the desire to get into the crap-game called the film business draws both high-rollers and eager but penurious novices, in numbers sufficiently large to make a rather steep line on a graph. If the line is extended to cover the next decade or two, it should be no less sharply angled.

Though new technological tools do not change the basic role of the film producer, they do offer some fascinating challenges. Perhaps the huge IMAX screen can be an unexpectedly creative tool, even lending itself to films with fictional story lines. At the opposite end of the scale, has the small TV screen really been understood; have its limitations of scale been properly exploited as a story-telling medium? In other words, have we taken enough pains to tune our approaches to production to the means of delivery? And to what degree should audience size affect production techniques?

Some are predicting the imminent demise of the cinema as we know it now. They point out that the number of "theatre establishments" in Canada has been reduced by half in the last 35 years. Income has been maintained only because ticket prices have risen in that period from 35 cents to over five dollars. But we have to remember that talkies were supposed to spell doom to live theatre and that long-playing records were to empty all concert halls. The videocassette and the compact disc are the current hitmen: supposedly, they're about to eradicate, with one mighty blow, all film houses, live theatre, *and* the concert hall, as well as all other forms of communal recreation and enlightenment. The proverbial grain of salt (as well as a pinch of history) will help us to realize that though the TV blockbuster will continue to attract audiences in astronomical numbers (the billion mark has already been passed for special broadcasts like the U.S. Academy Awards program) the cinema, live theatre, and concerts will also continue to draw their specialized audiences. Movie house operators may have to solve some deep-rooted problem – like how to deal with gum on the floor and the pervasive stench of popcorn oil – but, given the right film to show, the exhibitor will also have to deal with long line-ups waiting on the street to get in.

Yes, the future for Canadian filmmakers seems rosy, indeed. Our filmmakers and film companies are constantly getting better at what they do. They not only serve as models for the steady stream of graduates pouring out of our training institutions but also hold up hope of employment for at least the best of these. Outstanding acting talents are being nurtured in theatre companies and schools in all regions, and many of them will find their way onto film and TV screens. For those lucky enough to slip through the narrow cracks in their formidable walls, the CBC and the NFB still offer irreplaceable experience to aspiring producers and directors. Governments show no sign of pulling back; rather they are stepping up their support. Modest projects, such as the recently approved apprenticeship scheme being mobilized by the Academy of Canadian Cinema & Television, take their place beside the federal government's recent allocation of an additional $33 million to aid theatrical film production, supplementing last year's approximately $65 million made available to encourage production for TV. The tyro should find it increasingly easy to gain entree, experience, and a solid career in the Canadian film and TV business.

Disappointments cannot be avoided, whether caused by Telefilm's rejection of a funding application for your hard-won project, the expiry of the option on your favourite book, or even the recent bankruptcy of your first cousin's film company. But someone with a strong will should be able to make it as a film producer (or director, camera operator, set designer, or whatever other job appeals). The film business is undoubtedly a strange one, hard to live with and next to impossible to understand fully. As we have seen, it must make headway against fierce competition for the time and money of its audience. However, the response is likely to be enthusiastic for a fresh and entertaining show, irrespective of the format or the delivery system. The successful producer will continue to be the one with an especially keen eye for a good story, with the ability to assemble the talent to realize it, with an instinct for audience response, with a sensitivity to our distinctive cultural milieu, and, of course, with a flair for business.

That could be you, couldn't it?

Glossary

Above-the-line costs In a production budget, the amounts to be spent on "the principal creative elements," such as story and script, producer, director, and lead performers.

Adaptation A screenplay based on another work, most commonly a novel, short story, or stage play.

ADR *See* **Automatic dialogue replacement.**

Answer print The colour-corrected print made from the master negative with the final mix soundtrack, used for checking the technical quality of the film before the release prints are made.

Art director The person responsible for creating the "look" of the production, which can include supervision of the visual elements such as locations, sets, props, wardrobe, makeup, and hair. If there is no production designer, the art director is head of the Art Department. *See also* **Production designer.**

Assistant director *See* **First assistant director.**

Audiovisual press kit A video to publicize (usually) a theatrical feature film, featuring interviews with stars and director, and location footage showing the making of the film, to be made available to television news and entertainment programs.

Automatic dialogue replacement (ADR) A simpler, more modern version of looping. *See also* **Looping.**

Barter deal A three-way financing arrangement, whereby a corporate sponsor may invest in a production in return for free commerical time from the broadcaster who will be airing the production.

Below-the-line costs In a production budget, all the amounts to be spent on the production of the film that are not included in above-the-line costs, including cast (other than leading performers), crew, travel / living expenses, laboratory, legal and accounting fees, insurance, financing expenses, and postproduction expenses.

Best boy The assistant to the gaffer.

Blackout period Time during which a film or program will not be shown. For example, a purchaser of pay-TV rights may have the right to exhibit the production for a 12-month period plus a 3-month blackout before it can be shown on network TV.

Board *See* **Production board.**

Breakdown A scene-by-scene analysis of the script, identifying and listing locations, studio sets, characters, character/days, etc. Every department within the production will create its own breakdown to suit its own responsibilities.

Budget The detailed financial plan for the production, which dictates all details of how the production will be achieved.

Buyout Prepayment to performers for the right to exhibit or broadcast the production in which they appeared, in specified markets and for specified lengths of time.

Call sheet A form, distributed at the end of each day, listing all the scenes to be shot, all the cast, crew, extras, props, and extraordinary equipment required, and all the basic logistical needs for the following shooting day.

Caps Payment schedules that put a cap, or limit, on the amount of money to be paid to cast or crew.

Capital Cost Allowance This is a tax deferral program administered by the Canadian Film and Videotape Certification office of the Department of Communications, designed to encourage private investment in Canadian productions. A private investor financing a production that is certified Canadian is entitled to deduct 100% of his or her investment from personal income tax, over a period of two years. *See also* **Certified Canadian production.**

Cash-flow projection A timetable derived from the budget and production schedule that indicates the points at which income will be needed to cover anticipated cash outflow.

Casting director A person who advises on the selection of actors for roles in a production.

Certified Canadian production A production approved by the Canadian Film and Videotape Certification office of the Department of Communications to qualify as a Canadian production under the terms of the definition in the Income Tax Regulations, for purposes of the Capital Cost Allowance program. *See also* **Capital Cost Allowance.**

Chain of title A series of documents attesting to every change in ownership of the property.

Cinematographer *See* **Director of photography.**

Colour reversal intermediate (CRI) A negative printed from the original cut negative (after approval of the answer print), from which release prints will be made. This is an alternative to making an interpositive and internegative.

Completion guarantor The person or company who contracts to deliver a finished production at no additional cost to its investors, should it go over budget. The guarantor's fee is 6% of the budget excluding contingency.

Contingency (fund) An extra allowance added to the production budget to cover unexpected expenses. The contingency has to be at least 10% of the above-the-line and below-the-line expenses to satisfy the completion guarantor.

Continuity The matching of actions, costumes, and other details from take to take, which to some degree is the responsibility of everyone on the set, but is the special responsibility of the script supervisor. *See also* **Script supervisor.**

Contra deal A financing arrangement whereby suppliers provide services, props etc. to the production, in return for the prominent placement of their products in the production or a promotional listing in the credits of the production.

Copyright The right to reproduce, publish, perform, or broadcast all or a substantial portion of a protected work. The owner of the copyright in the work is the author, unless the work was produced as part of the duties of an employee, in which case the owner is the employer. In Canada, the period of copyright is the life of the author plus 50 years *See also* **Public domain.**

Cost report A document prepared weekly during production and monthly during postproduction (usually by the production manager and the accountant), showing how much has been spent, how much remains, and the predicted final outlay in each budget category.

Co-production The term commonly used for any production that qualifies as an official co-production under the terms of treaty agreements signed between Canada and several foreign countries. Official co-production status provides the production with all the benefits of an indigenous production in both co-producing countries. *See also* **Joint venture.**

Craft services Members of crew who make sure that coffee, snacks, etc. are continuously available on the set.

CRI *See* **Colour reversal intermediate.**

Cross-collateralization In a distribution deal, an arrangement whereby losses or unrecouped advances from the theatrical distribution of a film will be recouped by the distributor from revenue received from other media such as TV and home video. *See also* **Non-cross-collateralization.**

Dailies *See* **Rushes.**

Daily production report A detailed report on each day's shooting, including number of hours worked, number of scenes and pages shot, footage used, footage printed, and the personnel and equipment involved.

Day-out-of-days A calendar cross-plot that groups scenes and actors for the most efficient expenditure of time and money.

Deal memorandum Contractually binding document, setting out in summary form the terms that the negotiating parties have agreed upon. Usually followed by a "full and formal" agreement at a later date. Also called *letter of agreement.*

Deferral An arrangement by which director, cast, crew, suppliers, etc. may agree to wait for all or part of their money until a later, defined time – usually after the production begins to generate revenues.

Development The work necessary – which may include acquiring the property, writing script drafts, budgeting, packaging of stars, director, and other creative personnel – to get a project to the point where it receives production financing. This is the stage in the production process when money is hardest to raise and most at risk.

Development financing The financing needed at the first stage of a film or television project, when the property is acquired, the screenplay completed, preliminary budget prepared, and some key creative personnel obtained. *See also* **Development, Production financing,** *and* **Direct sales expense financing.**

Direct sales expense financing The financing needed to secure commercial release of the production and to report on and disburse revenue to financial backers.

Director The person with overall creative control of the production, which includes having input into casting and script, and translating the script into film or video form by choosing the images and moulding the performances.

Director of photography (DOP) The camera and lighting supervisor on a production, overseeing the work of the camera crew. Also known as the *cinematographer.*

Distributor A person or company holding the right to market and distribute films or videos to such markets as theatrical, non-theatrical, network television, home video, etc.

Editor The person responsible for piecing together the various elements that have been filmed and recorded, to form a coherent whole.

Equity investment An investment arrangement by which the investor gains an ownership interest in an asset. (For the purposes of this book, the asset would be a film or television program.)

Exhibitor The owner or operator of a movie theatre.

Fact sheet A short reference sheet in a television press kit, listing length of program, network for which it was made, concept for the program or series, cast, and technical credits.

Financing *See* **Development financing, Production financing,** *and* **Direct sales expense financing.**

Fine cut The final edited picture cut of a film.

First assistant director (1st AD) The director's right hand. During preproduction, the 1st AD will plan the shooting of each scene with the director, do the breakdown of the script, and prepare the board and day-out-of-days. On the set, the 1st AD transmits the director's orders to the crew and cast to the point when the director says, "Action."

Flats Payment arrangements that provide cast or crew with a flat daily rate, no matter how many hours they work.

Foley A system for creating synchronized sound effects during postproduction.

"French day" provision An arrangement by which cast and crew agree to work a seven-hour day with no provisions for overtime or meal breaks, but with an all-day buffet to which they can help themselves.

Gaffer The head of the lighting and electrical departments on the set.

Grip *See* **Key grip.**

Gross deal A type of distribution deal in which the gross receipts are shared between the distributor and the producer from first dollar, with no deductions other than the producer's advance, if there has been one. *See also* **Net deal.**

Interim financing Short-term funding arranged by the producer to bridge periods when cash flowing in will not cover predicted cash outflow.

International track *See* **M / E track.**

Internegative A duplicate negative derived from the interpositive and from which release prints are struck.

Interpositive An intermediate step between the cut negative (after the answer print is approved) and the internegative.

Joint venture A production undertaken with a partner in a country that does not have a co-production treaty with Canada. *See also* **Co-production.**

Key art The design concept used to identify a film or television program for packaging and marketing purposes, including such items as script cover design, advertising and promotional material, company logo, and title design.

Key grip The head of the grip department, in charge of moving cameras and lights, laying track for dollying, etc.

Licence Fee A payment made by a broadcaster in return for the right to broadcast a program on a specified number of occasions over a specified length of time.

Limited partnership A partnership in which the liability of each partner is limited to the amount invested in the partnership.

Location Any site where the production may shoot that is not in a studio.

Location manager The person responsible for finding, negotiating for, securing, and administering locations for a production.

Looping The recording of dialogue to replace orignal dialogue that is unusable because of noise, accent, or performance, done to match previously filmed lip movements of the performer. *See also* **ADR.**

"Majors" The key Hollywood-based studios that produce and distribute major motion pictures, including Columbia Tri Star, 20th Century-Fox, MGM / UA, Universal, and Warner Bros.

Music and effects track (M / E track) A film's sound track excluding the dialogue, needed for dubbing the film into a foreign language. Also called an *international track.*

Music cue sheet A list of all pieces of music in a production, stating length, composer, publisher, affiliation (Performing Rights Organization – PRO or Composers, Authors and Publishers Association of Canada – CAPAC), and usage (feature or background).

Mixing The combining of sound tracks – dialogue, music, and sound effects – to produce a single, balanced sound track.

Negative cutter The person who cuts the original negative (the film exposed in the camera) to match the fine cut of the workprint.

Net deal A type of distribution deal in which the gross receipts are shared between distributor and producer *after* deduction of distributor's fee, agreed-upon distribution expenses, and advances to the producer, if any. *See also* **Gross deal.**

Non-cross-collateralization In a distribution deal, an arrangement whereby the distributor is prevented from recouping losses from theatrical release with income from other rights sold, such as home video. *See also* **Cross-collateralization.**

Offering memorandum A legal document regulated by the Securities Act, similar to, but more flexible than, a prospectus. It is commonly used in Ontario to sell shares in a production when there is an exemption from the prospectus requirement. With an offering memorandum, the producer may approach no more than 75 potential investors and sell to no more than 50 of them.

Option (on a literary property) The payment of a (usually) relatively small sum of money in return for the exclusive right to purchase rights to the property within a specified time period.

Pairing *See* **Twinning.**

Partnership A business with at least two owners, who share profits according to an agreement. Each partner is liable for the debts and obligations of all the partners in the business. *See also* **Limited partnership.**

"Pay or play" A "pay or play" obligation is a contractual commitment to use (and pay for) the services of an individual, or to pay for these services *even* in the event that you do not use them.

Pay-TV TV service paid for by viewers, as opposed to "free" (advertiser supported) commercial TV or public (mainly government supported) TV.

Playdates Dates when a film is scheduled to be exhibited in theatres.

Play-off period Period of time in which the purchaser of a TV program or film can exercise the rights purchased.

"Points" Percentage participation in the profits of a production. Points may be defined in many ways, and must therefore be very clearly specified when they are being negotiated.

Postproduction The work done on a film after principal photography is completed; generally the editing, sound, music, mixing, and final lab work leading to the final answer print.

Postproduction transcript A written copy of every line of dialogue and narration in a production, used by foreign buyers to subtitle or version (dub) the production in other languages.

Presale A sale made to a distributor or broadcaster before the project has begun production.

Press kit A package of materials designed for the media, prepared under the supervision of the unit publicist (and often later reworked by the distributor). The kit contains photos, plot synopsis, bios of feature players, producer, director and screenwriter, column notes, and feature stories. A press kit on a television show will also contain a fact sheet.

Principal photography The shooting of all scenes requiring the main body of the crew and any of the leading performers.

Preproduction (prep) All aspects of preparation for production that take place after production financing has been confirmed but before shooting begins. *See also* **Development, Production, Postproduction.**

Producer The person with overall responsibility for the production, who exercises ultimate control over financing, hiring, spending, the selection of key creative personnel, commercial exploitation, and so forth. Producer's duties may be shared or delegated to co-producers, associate producers, line producers, and executive producers.

Production The period of time during which the production is being put on film or videotape. *See also* **Preproduction, Postproduction.**

Production board (the board) A graphic representation of all the scenes and characters in the production, arranged according to the sequence in which they will be filmed, and coded for interior/exterior and day/night. The information is displayed on flexible, removable strips.

Production co-ordinator The production manager's right hand, usually with specific responsibility for communicating changes in script and schedules and for organizing and disseminating logistical information.

Production designer The creative head of the Art Department, responsible, with the director, for the overall look, mood, and style of what will be shot.

Production fee Payment due to the screenwriter on the first day of principal photography, as specified by the "ACTRA/IPA Agreement for Freelance Writers". Rights in the screenplay do not pass to the producer until this payment is made.

Production financing The financing needed for completion and delivery of a project, including the preproduction, production, and postproduction phases. *See also* **Development financing** *and* **Direct sales expense financing.**

Production manager (PM) The person who oversees all business and logistical arrangements for a production.

Production notes Detailed documentation ("the making of …") of the shooting of film, prepared by the unit publicist.

Production stills Photographs taken by the set photographer during the course of shooting a film or television program.

Profit All revenues generated by a production from all sources *after deduction* of all the costs associated with production, distribution, and exhibition.

Property The written description of a specific creative concept, stressing its unique characteristics. A *story property* would include a detailed description of characters, plot, and other distinguishing details.

Proprietorship *See Sole proprietorship.*

Prospectus A very detailed legal document regulated by the Securities Act in force in each province, which provides full financial information about a production as well as details about the business and everyone involved, used to sell shares in a production to the public.

Public domain Works in the public domain are unprotected by copyright. *See also* **Copyright.**

Publicist A specialist in co-ordinating and presenting information about a client in such a way that media attention is directed toward the client. *See also* **Unit publicist.**

Release print The print of a film ready for distribution and exhibition, struck from the CRI or the internegative. *See also* **Colour reversal intermediate** *and* **Internegative.**

Rough cut An arbitrary stage of picture cut that falls somewhere between the first assembly and the fine cut. *See also* **Fine cut.**

Rushes The positive film or video rendering of a particular day's shooting, usually screened the following day; also called *dailies.*

Screenplay The script written for a film.

Screenwriter The person who writes screenplays and treatments for films.

Script The detailed written version of a film or television program, including dialogue and narration, and brief descriptions of characters, settings, action, and sound effects. The final version of a script is called the *shooting script.*

Script supervisor The person on the set who is responsible for checking that details match from one shot to the next, noting any changes in script and dialogue, and noting the director's choice of takes.

Second unit The backup crew on a production, which shoots additional footage that requires no dialogue or closeups.

Set photographer The person who takes photographs on the set (known as production stills) during the time the film is being shot, to be used for publicity and promotion.

Shot list A list of all the shots to be made for a production, on a scene-by-scene, location-by-location basis, prepared by the director with input from other personnel.

Simulcast The simultaneous broadcasting of a program by two or more broadcasters.

Slash print A low-quality contact print from the fine cut of the work print, used by sound editors to prepare the soundtracks for the mix.

Sole proprietorship An unincorporated business owned and operated by one person, who receives all profits from the business and is liable for all of its debts and obligations.

Star Performer who is sufficiently well known that he / she is perceived to bring an economic benefit to any production in which he / she appears in a leading role.

Story property *See* **Property.**

Storyboard A graphic depiction of the sequence of shots and action, as planned before shooting the production.

Syndication sales Sales of TV programs or films made on a station-by-station basis.

Theatre circuit The chain of theatres belonging to a particular exhibition company.

Timing Colour correction of the negative in the laboratory.

Trailer Selected scenes from a coming attraction, usually used to promote a theatrical feature film.

Treatment A narrative synopsis of a screenplay, including descriptions of the characters, the plot in which they are involved, and perhaps some dialogue.

Twinning The contractual linking of two productions, one Canadian and one foreign, so that each is eligible for the support given to indigenous productions in its country of origin, and any financing secured can be cross-collateralized across the two productions. Also called *pairing.*

Unit publicist The person responsible for co-ordinating and disseminating information to the media about a film while it is being shot. *See also* **Publicist.**

Video-assist A small video camera attached to the film camera, which allows the director to see exactly what is being shot.

Weather cover Optional plans for the day's shooting schedule, so that interior scenes can be shot if poor weather makes the originally planned location impossible to use.

"Window" A period of time during which a purchaser of rights (e.g. pay-TV, network, video, theatrical) receives the exclusive right to exhibit the production.

Work print A copy struck from the negative after processing, to be used by the editor to cut the film, and later by the negative cutter to match the original negative to the fine cut of the work print.

Wrap End of shooting, either on a given day, or at a given location, or of the entire production.

Wrap release A press release prepared by the unit publicist, noting that shooting has been completed.

Bibliography

Audley, Paul. *Canada's Cultural Industries*. Toronto: James Lorimer, 1983. Includes a section on key policies affecting the Canadian film industry.

Benzion, Schmuel and Rene S. Ash, eds. *The Producer's Masterguide*. New York: Producer's Masterguide, 611 Broadway. Exhaustive guide to film and video production in U.S., Canada, and Great Britain, updated annually.

Blum, Richard A. *Television Writing: From Concept to Contract*. Boston: Focal Press, 1984. Guide to film and television writing and marketing a script in the U.S. Covers public, cable, and network televison.

Bronfield, Stewart. *How to Produce a Film*. Englewood Cliffs, NJ: Prentice-Hall, 1984. Assumes no previous knowledge – stresses technical aspects of filmmaking.

Burrows, Thomas D. and Donald N. Wood. *Television Production: Disciplines and Techniques*. 2nd edition. Dubuque, Iowa: William C. Brown Publishers, 1982. Introductory textbook on video production.

Carrièrre, Louise. *Femmes et Cinéma Québécois*. Montréal: Boréal Express, 1983. Critical discussion of women filmmakers in Quebec. Includes an index to directors, producers, and films.

Chamness, Danford. *Hollywood Guide to Film Budgeting and Script Breakdown*. 3rd edition. Hollywood, CA: S.J. Brooks, 1981. Includes full shooting script breakdown and advice on budgeting.

Cinema Canada. Monthly trade journal of the Canadian film industry. Includes comprehensive production guide updated for each issue, listing films and television programs in negotiation, preproduction, production, and postproduction.

Collier, Margaret, ed. *ACTRA Writer's Guild Directory*. 2nd edition. Toronto: ACTRA, 1986. Lists members.

Craig, Jane, ed. *Face to Face with Talent: Performers Catalogue*. 9th edition. Toronto: ACTRA, 1986. Lists ACTRA and Equity members, including photographs, credits, and agents.

da Silva, Raul. *Making Money in Film and Video: A Handbook for Freelancers and Independents*. New York: Prentice-Hall, 1986. Emphasis on selling and marketing films and videos in the U.S. Includes bibliography and glossary.

Desjardins, Claude. *Qui Fait Quoi – Répertoire*. Montréal: Qui Fait Quoi Inc. Magazine annual which includes film and industry listings for Quebec. Includes selected Toronto listings. Updated annually.

Drabinsky, Garth H. *Motion Pictures and the Arts in Canada: The Business and the Law*. Toronto: McGraw-Hill Ryerson, 1976. Business and legal aspects of the motion picture industry in Canada as it was in the mid-seventies.

Frame by Frame. Toronto: Frame by Frame Publications. A guidebook to Toronto-based film, television, radio, and recording industries, listing production companies, production facilities, production services, freelance personnel, agencies and consultants, and much more. Updated annually.

Goodell, Gregory. *Independent Feature Film Production: A Complete Guide from Concept to Distribution*. New York: St. Martin's Press, 1982. Guide to independent film production. Includes sample budgets, references, and sources useful to the filmmaker.

Gregory, Mollie. *Making Film Your Business*. New York: Schocken Books, 1979. Covers financial and legal aspects of making independent films in the U.S.

Harcourt, Amanda, Neil Howlett, Sally Davies, and Naomi Moscovic. *The Independent Producer: Film and Televison*. London: Faber and Faber, 1986. Comprehensive guide to independent production, stressing the U.K. situation, including sample business forms and appendix of useful addresses.

Hardin, Herschel. *Closed Circuits: The Sellout of Canadian Television*. Vancouver: Douglas and McIntyre, 1985. A highly critical examination of the CRTC and its role in the development of Canadian television.

Hurst, Walter E. and William Storm Hale, eds. *Motion Picture Distribution: Business or Racket*. Hollywood, CA: Seven Arts Press, 1975. Basic guide for the U.S. Aimed at students and teachers. Part of the "Seven Arts Entertainment Industry" series – other titles include: *Your Introduction to Film / TV Copyright, Contracts and Other Law,* and *The Movie Industry Book*.

Jaffe, Chapelle, ed. *Who's Who in Canadian Film and Television*. Toronto: Academy of Canadian Cinema and Television. A comprehensive directory of Canada's screenwriters, producers, directors, production managers, cinematographers, art directors, editors, and composers; with addresses, biographies, and filmographies. Updated annually.

Kemps International Film and Television Yearbook. London: The Kemps Group. International production listings, stressing the British film industry. Includes a section on Canada. Updated annually.

Kiely, M. Sean and J.D. Szeles, eds. *The Guide to Film, Television and Communications Courses in Canada*. Ottawa: Canadian Film Institute. Lists all undergraduate courses in film and video in Canada, updated annually.

Klein, Walter J. *The Sponsored Film*. New York: Hastings House, 1976. Covers aspects of film production and distribution in the U.S. – stresses dealing with the sponsor.

Lazarus, Paul N. *The Movie Producer: A Handbook for Producing and Picture-Making*. New York: Harper and Row, 1985. General outline of the producer's role from development through to production and marketing.

Lipton, Lenny. *Independent Filmmaking*. New York: Simon and Schuster, 1983. Technical guide to 8 mm and 16 mm filmmaking. Includes a chapter on video for filmmakers.

London, Mel. *Making It in Film: An Insider's Guide to Succeeding in the Film Industry*. New York: Simon and Schuster, 1985. Recommended guide to breaking into the business in the U.S.

– – . *Getting Into Film*. New York: Ballantine Books, 1985. Recommended beginner's guide to all aspects of filmmaking in the U.S.

Lukas, Christopher. *Directing for Film and Television: A Guide to the Craft.* New York: Doubleday, 1985. Guidebook specifically aimed at the novice director, covering all stages of production.

Maltin, Leonard, ed. *The Whole Film Sourcebook.* New York: New American Library, 1983. Useful directory to film schools, film festivals, unions, distributors, and exhibitors, mainly in the U.S., with related industry information.

Mayer, Michael F. *The Film Industries: Practical Business-Legal Problems in Production, Distribution, and Exhibition.* rev. 2nd enlarged edition. New York: Hastings House, 1978. Legal and financial aspects of filmmaking in the U.S. Part of the "Studies in Media Management" series.

McQuillan, Lon. *Video Production Guide.* Indianapolis, IN: Howard W. Sams, 1983. General introduction covering all aspects of video production from preproduction to distribution. Includes glossary.

Miller, Pat P. *Script Supervision and Film Continuity.* Boston: Focal Press, 1986. Detailed guide covering all aspects of film continuity through each stage of production.

Morris, Peter. *The Film Companion.* Toronto: Irwin, 1984. Critical guide to selected Canadian producers, directors, writers, and films.

Naylor Ensign, Lynn and Robyn Eileen Knapton, eds. *The Complete Dictionary of Television and Film.* New York: Stein and Day, 1985. Defines over 3000 words and phrases in use in the film and video industries.

Newcomb, Horace and Robert S. Alley. *The Producer's Medium: Conversations with Creators of American T.V.* Oxford: Oxford University Press, 1983. Interviews with major U.S. television producers.

Oakey, Virginia. *Dictionary of Film and Television Terms.* New York: Harper and Row, 1983. Contains 3000 technical, artistic, and business terms in use in film and video.

Pincus, Edward and Steven Ascher. *Filmmaker's Handbook.* New York: New American Library, 1984. Introductory guide to filmmaking in the U.S. – emphasis on technical aspects.

Playback. Bi-monthly trade journal covering the Canadian broadcasting and film industries.

Qui Fait Quoi / Entertainment Coast to Coast. Montreal: Qui Fait Quoi Inc. Covers the Canadian entertainment industries. Ten monthly magazines, 12 monthly newsletters and an annual directory.

Reed, Maxine K. and Robert M. Reed. *Career Opportunities in Television, Cable and Video.* 2nd edition. New York: Facts on File, 1986. Comprehensive U.S. guide to television careers, including employment prospects and salaries.

Reid, Tom and George Meditskos, eds. *The Toronto Film and Video Guide.* Toronto: Shuter-Springhurst Communications. Hefty directory of film, video, and multi-image facilities, personnel, and current rates; updated annually. Similar guides are available for Montreal (Répertoire Cinéma / Video Montréal) and Western Canada (Northwest Master Guide), from the same publisher.

Reel West Digest. Vancouver: Reel West Productions. A directory of film, video, audiovisual, photography, and graphic production in Western Canada. Updated annually.

Roberts, Kenneth H. and Win Sharples Jr. *A Primer for Filmmaking: A Complete Guide to 16mm and 35mm Film Production.* Indianapolis, IN: Bobbs-Merril Educational Publications, 1984. Guide to all aspects of 16 mm and 35 mm filmmaking, aimed at professionals and serious students.

Robertson, Joseph F. *Motion Picture Distribution Handbook.* Blue Ridge Summit, PA: Tab Books, 1981. Legal and financial aspects of distribution and sales for television and film in the U.S.

Rowlands, Avril. *Script Continuity and the Production Secretary in Film and TV.* London: Focal Press, 1977. Much broader in its coverage than title suggests – many useful charts and forms. This is one of the excellent "Media Manuals" series – other titles in the series include: *Your Film and the Lab, Effective TV Production, Basic Film Techniques*, and *Motion Picture Camera Techniques.*

Sapan, Joshua. *Making It in Cable T.V.: Career Opportunities in Today's Fastest Growing Media Industry.* New York: Putnam Publishing Group, 1984. Vocational guide to cable television in the U.S.

Shanks, Bob. *The Primal Screen: How to Write, Sell and Produce Movies for Television.* New York: W.W. Norton, 1986. The subtitle says it all – designed for the U.S. market.

Silver, Alain and Elizabeth Ward. *The Film Director's Team: A Practical Guide to Organizing and Managing Film and Television Production.* New York: Arco Publishing Inc., 1983. Recommended practical guide, stressing the role of the assistant director and production manager. Glossary.

Singleton, Ralph. *Film Scheduling: Or How Long Will It Take to Shoot Your Movie?* Beverly Hills, CA: Lone Eagle Publishing, 1984. Guide to professional film scheduling. Includes production board and sample breakdown sheets. By the same author: *The Film Scheduling / Film Budgeting Workbook* and *Movie Production and Budget Forms . . . Instantly!*

Squire, Jason E., ed. *The Movie Business Book.* New York: Simon and Schuster, 1983. Each chapter is written by a different U.S. film industry insider, and the stress is on the Hollywood studio system. Several sample forms.

Thompson, Patricia, ed. *Film Canada Yearbook.* Toronto: Cinecommunications. Indispensable guide to production, distribution, and exhibition of films across Canada. Fully indexed, updated annually.

Topalovich, Maria. *A Pictorial History of the Canadian Film Awards.* Toronto: Stoddart / Academy of Canadian Cinema, 1984. Canadian film awards from 1949 to 1984. Includes brief history of Canadian film industry. Illustrated.

Trojan, Judith and Nadine Covert. *16mm Distribution.* New York: Educational Films Library Assoc., 1977. Distribution and exhibition of 16 mm films in U.S. and internationally. Chapter on television distribution.

Tromberg, Sheldon. *Making Money, Making Movies: The Independent Movie Maker's Handbook.* New York: New Viewpoints / Vision Books, 1980. General guide to screenwriting, production, distribution, and exhibition for independent filmmakers in the U.S.

Van Deusen, Richard E. *Practical AV / Video Budgeting.* White Plains, NY: Knowledge Industry Publications, 1985. Discusses effective cost control of production budgets.

Wiese, Michael. *Independent Film and Videomaker's Guide.* Westport, CT: Michael Wiese Productions, 1984. Detailed introductory guide to the production, distribution, and marketing of independent films and videos. By the same author: *Film and Video Budgets,* a comprehensive guide to cost effectiveness in film and video production. Includes sample budgets.

Wolfe, Morris. *Jolts: The T.V. Wasteland and the Canadian Oasis.* Toronto: James Lorimer, 1985. A positive discussion of the state of Canadian television.

Index